RELATIONS OF INDIAN, GREEK, AND CHRISTIAN THOUGHT IN ANTIQUITY

Kenneth Reagan Stunkel

University Press of America™

Library of Congress Catalog Card Number: 79-63750

For

MARY CAROL AND MIRA

PREFACE

The huge subject of this brief study may seem out of proportion to the weight of evidence and argument assembled to cope with
it. A note of caution to the reader may succeed in heading off un-
realistic expectations. The claims surveyed in the first chapter
seem to me inflated, doubtful, simplistic, and misleading; nevertheless, they have been defended on a wide front by internationally
known scholars in a horde of articles and books. Reservations about
the soundness of the claims exist, but only in a form that is un-
systematic, scattered, and allusive. So far, no one has put together an organized, reasonably detailed challenge to what I shall call
the "Indian hypothesis," or the notion that Buddhist and Hindu ideas
diffused to Greece and Rome with significant and lasting effects,
the auxiliary notion that parallels link specific Indian, Greek,
and Christian ideas, and the somewhat vaguer notion that a homogeneous mystical tradition is to be found in the religions and philosophies of all three cultures. This essay is an attempt to clarify
and sharpen the issues by developing a case against the Indian hypothesis. Unfortunately, the nature of the evidence does not favor
a conclusive refutation of the hypothesis in its historical guise.
We must settle for a strategy of largely negative argument. On the
other hand, the claim that certain religious and philosophical parallels exist, and that a mystical tradition exists, turns out to be
vulnerable to direct criticism. All in all, my purpose is to create
in the reader's mind a reasonable doubt that the credentials of the
Indian hypothesis can pass muster.

Conflict of opinion on most questions relating to the Indian
hypothesis makes a critique of it difficult and tangled. In his
Asia in the Making of Europe, Donald Lach sees no lasting Indian
influence on the Greco-Roman world. He surveys an unimpressive exchange of material culture and concludes that "the Orient, whether
India or China, was still too far removed physically and spiritually
to make a deep impression upon the classical world."[1] In a review
of the book, Hajime Nakamura remarks that Lach's inquiries might
have included the ancient and medieval periods of Western history,
for "it has been made clear how influential Indian thought was in
the making of early Christian theology and Neo-platonic philosophy."[2] Supposedly among those who make it clear are Ernest Benz,
in his Indische Einflusse auf die fruhchristliche Theologie (1951),
and Nakamura himself, who has authored a work in Japanese, Indo to
Girisha tono Shishō Koryu, or "Interchange of Ideas Between India
and Greece." Tentative explorations in the direction suggested by
Nakamura have been attempted by V.V. Barthold in his La découverte
de l'Asie: histoire de l'orientalisme en Europe et de Russe (1947),
but the treatment is spotty, weak in the handling of ideas, mostly
concerned with the activity of Western scholars who pioneered the
study of Eastern cultures and their literatures, and adduces no
proofs of enduring Indian impact on Western religion or philosophy.

An abundance of material on the Indian hypothesis is summarized in Richard Garbe's older work, Indien und das Christentum (1914), and in a more recent volume of Henri Lubac, La rencontre du Bouddhism et de l'Occident (1952). Both works cite scholars who see evidence favoring the Indian hypothesis, while others are cited who see none at all. Garbe devotes half of Indien und Christentum to evidences of Christian influence on Indian myth, parable, and religious practice, which turn out to be no more striking than the Indian features he squeezes from the Christian tradition. His cautious analysis of parallels yields only meager returns. In sum, unqualified assent to all the positive suggestions of influence in Garbe would not add up to a viable proof that a mystical tradition passed into Greek philosophy and Christian theology from Brahmanical and Buddhist sources.

To his credit, Lubac is consistently skeptical of those writers who believe that Indian thought is concealed in the religious and philosophical systems of Persia, Greece, and the Roman Empire. After summarizing scholarly opinion that Gnosticism was indebted to Buddhism, he concludes that "les preuves manquent."[3] It is a mistake, he warns, to overwork the eclecticism and cosmopolitanism of the Hellenistic period.

> Certes, on aimerait á songer, avec M. Edmunds, que
> le même souverain "qui patronna la version des Sep-
> tante," et qui apparaît friand des problems religi-
> eux "recut un message du grande empereur bouddhique;"
> mais les rèves ne sont pas l'histoire.[4]

Gauranga Nath Banerjee has produced a more recent book, Hellenism in Ancient India (1961), which discusses religious and philosophical exchanges between India, Persia, and Greece. Apart from a relationship based upon an ancient and common Indo-Persian-Greek center of diffusion somewhere in Asia, Banerjee argues his case against any subsequent mythical or philosophical borrowings of importance.[5] It is too bad that his exposition and analysis are rather cursory, and that his contribution is mostly suggestive. While he is surely correct in saying that "in the matter of details, a profound and searching inquiry is indispensable," his own efforts have failed to provide such an inquiry.[6]

One might infer from the clash of views that the Indian hypothesis is far from substantiated. Nevertheless, the case for an Indianization of western thought in antiquity has received a much wider hearing than any argument against it. A contemporary drive for synthesis in comparative religion and philosophy has tended to obscure the real limitations dogging any program to reconcile diverse cultural traditions. Those who insist on parallels between Indian, Greek, and Christian ideas are lured on to insist that historical exchanges have occurred which explain the parallels.

iii

if true mechanisms of exchange cannot be isolated, the next step is to insist that parallels are the core of a trans-historical mystical tradition. In any case, the slender threads of evidence have been used to hold up massive loads of speculation, such as the inference from the presence of Ashokan Buddhist missionaries in Western Asia to the transformation of Jesus into a quasi-Buddhist.

Most of these excesses derive not from purely historical analysis, but from the careless use of religious and philosophical parallels whose superficial aptness has sent scholars to history in search of an explanation. This fact has shaped the format of my argument. While generous space has been allotted to a critique of historical and textual evidence bearing on the Indian hypothesis, the main body of this discourse has been reserved for discussion of an assortment of parallels often held to be improbably coincidental. If the parallels cannot be vindicated, then the Indian hypothesis is left without most of its foundation.

The other major issue is whether or not a universal mystical tradition bridges East and West, expressing a timeless view of human nature and destiny. Were Greek philosophers, Christian mendicants, Hindu rishis, and Buddhist bonzes speaking with one voice beneath differences of language and cultural milieu? Not a few scholars, not to mention a host of popular writers, have taken the affirmative side of this question. The issue is not minor, for it encompasses the nature of man, his intellectual and spiritual scope, his relations with the physical world, his attitude toward his own potentialities, and the limitations of any kind of ecumenicism in religion. The issue touches also the relationship of humanity to history, by raising the question of whether human fulfillment is to be realized within or outside the historical process.

As to the organization of this book, it is designed to be read as an extended argument. The effect ought to be cumulative, each chapter preparing for the one which follows. The notes ought to be consulted along with the text, for they contain necessary qualifications, supplementary information, and comment on source materials. The reader should not be put off by some inconsistencies in the orthography of words from Indian languages. They come from a variety of sources using different systems of transliteration.*

* I would like to acknowledge financial aid from the Monmouth College Grant-in-Aid-for-Creativity Committee.

1. Asia in the Making of Europe: The Century of Discovery (Chicago: University of Chicago Press, 1965), p. 19.
2. Journal of the History of Ideas, 30 (July-September, 1969), 454.
3. La rencontre du Boudhisme et de l'Occident (Paris, 1952), pp. 22-23.
4. Ibid., p. 12.
5. Hellenism in Ancient India (Delhi: Ram Manohar Lal, 1961), pp. 248, 250, 258-259.
6. Ibid., p. 262. John Steadman, in his elegantly allusive The Myth of Asia (New York: Simon and Schuster, 1969), attacks the dichotomy of East and West and the notion that an "Asia" exists in monolithic unity, spiritual or otherwise. His judgments often coincide with mine, especially in the chapters entitled "Eastern Religions and Western Culture" and "Mysticism in Europe and Asia," where he shows that correspondences and differences are often not what they seem. His discussion of "an exaggerated stress on parallels as evidence of borrowing" is a welcome reinforcement of my own position. He deals with a considerable range of topics, countries, and time-periods. Only a small part of his analysis is given to the topics dealt with in this essay.

TABLE OF CONTENTS

CHAPTER 1

HISTORY, MYSTICAL TRADITIONS, AND A QUESTION
OF INFLUENCE

Historical circumstances appear to favor lasting exchanges between India and the West in the ancient world. Phoenician traders were carriers of Indian commodities for centuries. Persia imposed a long rule on northwestern India, bridging east and west. Alexander the Great's hellenizing crusade as far as a tributary of the Indus brought in its wake artists, philosophers, historians, and naturalists, thus preparing ground for the remarkable Greco-Bactrian kingdoms of the following century. The powerful empire of the Kushans was in touch with the masters of Rome, and the Roman eagle adorned trading posts on the coast of Coromandel. All the while, except for interludes when old rulers vanished and new ones appeared, merchant enterprise kept a stream of goods moving, and emissaries from one government or another sailed across the Arabian Sea or trekked the dangerous Hindu Kush. Persian, Greek, and Roman officials, civilian and military, had direct experience with India for about seven hundred years. Moreover, anonymous individuals of miscellaneous character and motive no doubt crossed the frontiers of India and western Asia, from both sides, and returned home brimming with anecdotes. On the face of it, an exchange of ideas should have been more than casual, particularly in the cosmopolitan era of the Hellenistic dispersion, when during the two centuries flanking the ministry of Jesus, the mystery, miracle, and magic of Persia, Mesopotamia, Asia Minor, and Egypt flooded the crannies of the Roman world. Did these multifarious "oriental" influences encompass India?

Eminent opinion, both implicit and explicit, has inclined to the view that India's role in the formation of Greek and Christian religious experience was considerable. These writers convey an aggressive impression that both religious and philosophical ideas in the Greco-Roman world were profoundly, even decisively, leavened by myths, metaphysical speculation, and mysticism derived from the faiths and philosophies of India. Ostensibly there are dramatic parallels which link Indian, Greek, and Christian thought. The similarities invite an obvious explanation: that Indian ideas diffused to the cultures of the West, especially with respect to concepts evincing a mystical content, for the Indian versions are far older.

What is meant by "mysticism"? As used by authors discussed in this essay, the term is stretched frequently to include nearly all otherworldly trends of thought. These trends embrace belief in the preexistence, immortality, resurrection, or reincarnation of the soul; belief in a non-discursive, intuitive apprehension of a supernal reality; a tendency to devalue the physical world and sense

1

experience in the course advocating the primacy of an order of su-
pra-sensible perfection; and a conviction that mankind's authentic
destiny is realizable solely in a transcendental realm. A second
and more limited meaning has to do with the attainment of cosmic
consciousness, or an experience of total unity with some all-inclusive ground of being. Many of these writers have postulated an
historical dichotomy, which amounts to the assertion of a mystical
tradition originally "natural" to India, where mystical predispositions have flourished, and "unnatural" to the West, where rationalism, humanism, and natural science have been conspicuous
tendencies. The surface plausibility of this opposition has fostered the notion that monistic and mystical inclinations in western thought were fed into the main stream of feeling, belief, and
speculation from the outside.

In his "India in European Literature and Thought," Hugh Rawlinson assumes that the monistic speculations of Milesians and
Eleatics, the otherworldliness of Plato, the Orphic bifurcation of
soul and body, the acceptance of metempsychosis by Pythagoras and
Empedocles, the similarities of parable, miracle, and biographical
detail surrounding the lives of Buddha and Christ - that all are
more or less attributable to Indian sources transmitted through
the medium of the Persian Empire to Greco-Roman culture.[1] B.J.
Urwick has proposed that Plato was a Greek "Brahman." His The Message of Plato is an interpretation of The Republic "based largely
upon the philosophic thought of India,"[2] in the course of which
virtually every important idea in Plato is linked to the Vedas and
the Upanishads.

In Eastern Religions and Western Thought, S. Radhakrishnan
details a host of resemblances between Indian and Greek ideas,
Upanishadic teachings, Buddhism, and Christianity.[3] He is careful
not to embrace unequivocally the position that India was the spiritual mother of Western civilization, but the tone and emphases of
his argument suggest that he accepts it covertly. Thus in a discussion of Orphic theology, doctrines similar to those of the Upanishads are affirmed to be so close that "the suggestion of natural coincidence is somewhat unconvincing."[4] At another place, a
passage is quoted from Rawlinson's previously cited essay, in
which the Pythagorean theorem of the quadrature of the hypothenuse
is assigned rather loosely to India, where it may have been known
in Vedic times (ca. 1000-500 B.C.). Radhakrishnan chides the subject of the quote, A. Barriedale Keith, for being "needlessly critical of this view,"[5] but fails to explain why the criticism is
indeed needless.[6]

In spite of cautions to his readers not to assume borrowing
whenever Indian and Western ideas converge, or appear to do so,
Radhakrishnan just as often advances propositions which violate
his own admonitions. Ambivalence shows up in the chapters on

Greece and Christianity, and particularly in the notes, where authors are quoted and cited who are much less circumspect about attributions of Indian influence than he.[7] Thus in one passage he espouses a standard of evidence far above the modest level of probability acceptable to most scholars, saying that

> the affiliation of ideas is a useless pursuit. So long as it is not possible for us to establish with certainty the exact manner in which ideas travelled between India and the West, so long as we do not know who the intermediaries, what the opportunities and times were, it will be unwarrantable optimism to maintain the theory of direct borrowing.[8]

So far, so good. What could be more rigorous than "to establish with certainty the exact manner" in which India transmitted ideas to the West? But in his discussion of the Jesus movement, he says that

> faith in the high destiny of the human soul is not to be found in the religions of Palestine, Greece, and Rome except in the unofficial and un-Greek mystic cults. The mind of Jesus and His immediate followers on this question must have been shaped in the atmosphere where East and West, mystical experience and intellectual speculation, acted and reacted on each other.[9]

In line with this shift of stance, he remarks later that Judaism can be understood properly only if one takes into account, among other things in the "total environment," the fact that Buddhism "closed in" on Palestine two centuries before the Christian era.[10] With regard to Greek thought, Christianity, and the philosophies of India, Radhakrishnan shows confidence in the significance of parallels by observing that "the importance of Indian influence on Greek thought is not to be judged by the amount of information about it which has survived,"[11] a comment apparently at odds with the earlier demand for certainty and exactitude in the matter of historical fact. He is impressed also by the "un-Greek" character of Orphic, Eleusinian, Pythagorean, and Platonic mysticism, which are represented as a "decisive break with the Greek tradition of rationalism and humanism."[12] Whence came this un-Greek mysticism to a people so rational and humanistic? The point is nailed down clearly enough in a vignette (also used by Rawlinson) quoted from Gomperz.

> It is not too much to assume that the curious Greek, who was a contemporary of Buddha, and it may be of Zoroaster too, would have acquired a more or less exact knowledge of the East in that age of intellectual fermentation (i.e. the 6th century B.C.), through the medium of Persia.[13]

3

What Gomperz may have intended by "a more or less exact knowledge of the East" is not clear. Another Indian scholar, P.T. Raju, believes "the oriental influence, however subtle, on Plato and Neo-Platonism...was not unimportant," the influence alluded to being the transmission of mystical doctrines and practices.[14]

In a short, provocative article, A.N. Marlow claims merely to be setting forth a handful of notable parallels between Hinduism, Buddhism, and Greek philosophy; his purpose is "to indicate their affinity of type more than their identity of origin." Yet, in noting the resemblance of Heraclitus' doctrine of the flux to the views of early Buddhist schools on impermanence, he says that "it seems almost too great a coincidence to imagine that two such striking and radical doctrines should have arisen independently in two places at about the same time."[15] Like Radhakrishnan, Marlow thinks mysticism is alien to the intrinsic character of the Greek intellectual tradition, appearing here and there as a clearly distinguishable foreign intrusion: "a distinct tradition of mysticism runs through Orphism, Pythagoras, and Plato which is unlike anything in Greek thought as it is like the Hindu mysticism of the Upanishads."[16]

Writing on the relationship of Greek with Indian medicine before Alexander the Great, J. Filliozat, in a chapter entitled "Communications Between Greece and India," tries to establish a case for intellectual exchange to support his conviction of Indian influence on the medical lore of the Hippocratic Corpus and Plato's _Timaeus_. He informs us that "sure paths and intermediaries... were there for assuring scientific communication between India and Greece before Alexander." Although neither Greek nor Indian publics were affected,

> they were easily able to carry across the notions on
> which minds on both sides, whether by conscientious
> emulation or not, marked (sic). This is the explana-
> tion why there are, between Indian and Greek medicines,
> so very particular and precise similarities which are
> not easy to ascribe to chance. This is again why we
> come across, both in Greece and India, so many similar
> speculations during the same moments.[17]

What this argument amounts to is the postulation of a mechanism of intellectual and spiritual transmission beyond historical verification, but which one must adopt and respect if parallels "not easy to ascribe to chance" are to be explained. The diffusion of religious attitudes and ideas is construed as tenuous, piecemeal, unconscious, fragmented in time, and unspectacular in the act of transmission and reception. One might say that neither the Greeks nor the Indians knew what hit them when exchanges occurred. As Filliozat puts the matter, "it was not in the least necessary that the corpus of entire doctrines had to be carried and taught with a popular repercussion so that the memory of the same could not have failed to reach us."[18]

The indebtedness of western thought to Indian ideas is largely taken for granted by several writers who have been a force in the popularization of Hindu mysticism in Europe and America. Perhaps the best known of these authors is Aldous Huxley. His The Perennial Philosophy (1944) is an encyclopedic array of parallels belonging to the mystical genre; it reflects a long Platonic tradition of belief in a universal ground of truth and being. Huxley believed not only in the identity of mystical experiences and utterances in all times and places, but also in the specific debt of western religious experience to India, for "during the fourth and fifth centuries, neo-platonism and along with it, at several removes, the most valuable elements of Hindu religion, entered Christianity."[19] Thus Christian belief and experience fattened on Platonism and Neo-Platonism, which, in turn, fattened on the mystical tradition of India, establishing an organic connection between seemingly unrelated bodies of thought.

It is sometimes imagined that serious academic students of comparative religion and philosophy are more cautious than "merely popular" writers like Huxley, and that older proponents of the Indian hypothesis, like Radhakrishnan, are no longer taken seriously by a wiser and better informed generation of scholars. Unfortunately, the evidence supports a contrary view. The example set by Martin Larson's widely used text, Religion of the Occident (1959), ought to put one on guard, for he derives virtually the entire fabric of Christianity from oriental sources. This book supplies an antidote to that kind of thinking, but attempts to do so on a level more general and comprehensive than can be found in esoteric journal articles and occasional monographs. The need is to bring all key issues to the bar under one cover. How, then, are we to proceed?

We shall be concerned with two separate premises often held simultaneously by the same person, Radhakrishnan being a cogent example. The first premise holds that mysticism, in its broader definition, is essentially alien to the Occidental temperament, and that a spiritual vacuum in western Asia and Greece attracted the ripe, highly systematized mystical ethos of neighboring India. In the course of the past 2500 years, east and west have come to share nearly identical outlooks on spiritual reality, whether that reality is called Brahman, Nirvāṇa, the Form of the Good, the One, or the Godhead. But when the mutual contributions of India and the West to spiritual insight are drawn into perspective, the two cultural traditions are seen to have had different talents. India's genius was for spiritual experience and practice, while in the West the flair was for rationality. From India, mankind is the

5

recipient of spiritual heroes, writings, and disciplines richly expressive of a human need for communion with ultimate reality. From the West came a rational quest for understanding and control of nature, a vision of the good life structured by intellect. Although western thinkers eventually united these opposites in a species of synthesis, the West began its own deeper spiritual adventure with the mature mysticism of India in ancient times, while India waited some 2500 years before plucking the choicest fruits of western thought and science.

The second premise, often held in conjunction with the first, but also defended alone, is that mysticism lies at the core of a philosophia perennis.[20] No matter, then, if Hinduism and Buddhism are unrelated historically to Orphism, Pythagoreanism, Platonism, and Christian otherworldliness, for these religions and philosophies, insofar as they contain a mystical element, are speaking with one voice about truths inaccessible to reason. Whatever their cultural backgrounds, Indian sages, Greek transcendentalists, and Christian contemplatives are walking, in Ananda Coomaraswamy's phrase, "many paths that lead to the summit of one and the same mountain."[21] This perennial philosophy found its strongest western advocate in René Guénon, a French traditionalist and Vedantist who expounded tirelessly the "Primordial Tradition which, in reality, is the same everywhere, regardless of the different shapes it takes in order to be fit for every race and for every historical period."[22]

Plausible grounds have been adduced to support these premises and to flesh them out: long centuries of Indo-Occidental contact through trade and conquest; references to India in classical and patristic literature; copious parallels between Indian and Greco-Roman cosmological, religious, and philosophical ideas. Our task is to examine critically the proposition that Greek and Christian thought were beholden to Indian religion and philosophy.[23] We must also scrutinize the view that, in the absence of historical exchanges, the "mystical" features of both cultural traditions answer to an identical outlook on the meaning and purpose of human life. Accordingly, several lines of argument are developed: (1) relations of Indian, Greek, and Christian ideas have been exaggerated, especially where the element of mysticism is involved; (2) these exaggerations are founded on historical, philosophical, and religious materials open to more than one interpretation; (3) it is doubtful that Persian, Greek, Roman, or Christian intermediaries came to understand the substance of Brahmanical, Hindu, or Buddhist thought, or that missionaries from the latter religions proselytized effectively in western Asia; (4) the parallels so often cited and appealed to, whether philosophical and religious in the conventional sense, or "mystical," can be explained independently of the hypothesis that Indian thought diffused westward; (5) the Indian, Greek, and Christian mystical traditions do not,

when seen in cultural and textual context, express what Radhakrishnan has called "the same view of life."

As it turns out, the Indian hypothesis is not subject to direct historical verification. Consequently much depends on the integrity of the parallels so commonly invoked as a body of circum-
stantial evidence. Precisely what kind of "influence" is supposed
to account for the parallels, assuming they have any foundation?
What seems to be meant is a process of diffusion of the sort described by Filliozat: vague, amorphous, inarticulate, indistinct,
and unconscious.

Now, whenever a process of diffusion is relied upon to explain apparent or demonstrable similarities between civilizations
and cultures, the burden of proof is on the one who uses that mode
of explanation. Defenders of the Indian hypothesis have been less
than scrupulous about facing up to the kind of evidence necessary
to establish an instance of cultural diffusion as a high probability. They assume too readily on the basis of alleged parallels
that diffusion was the mechanism that linked India to the Greco-
Roman world wherever ideas are the issue. It is undeniable that
all cultures have borrowed more than they have created, at least
this seems to be true of the ones we know about. [24] Difficulties
arise when we ask in a specific instance what and how much has
been borrowed from whom. Both Greeks and Christians owed a good
deal to the Near East, and their debt has been well documented.
Whether or not they were indebted also to India depends on how
well available evidence can sustain a case for the diffusion of
particular traits. The mechanisms of cultural diffusion have been
studied intensively by anthropologists, who have tried to con-
struct viable generalizations about the transmission of material
and non-material cultural traits. With the Indian hypothesis in
mind, we shall appeal to anthropological theory for criteria by
which an authentic case of diffusion may be identified.

Proponents of the Indian hypothesis frequently argue in a way
reminiscent of Wissler's old "law of diffusion": that "anthropological traits tend to diffuse in all directions from their center
of origin."[25] Thus, in way of an example, Buddhism and Hinduism
originated in India, thereafter to diffuse eastward to China, Japan, and Southeast Asia, and also westward to Greece, Palestine,
and Rome. Wissler's law was the basis of the "age-area principle,"
by which the age of traits are gauged by their distance and distribution around the center of diffusion. Perhaps it is sufficient
for immediate purposes to remind the reader that recent anthropological field work and theory have neutralized the force of Wissler's argument. Indeed, "the 'law of diffusion' is a highly unreliable guide to actual historical events and can be applied only
with the greatest caution."[26] Until recently, for example, it
was believed that certain megalithic monuments found in western

Europe had diffused westward from the Near East. The hypothesis was worked out by Gordon Childe, who set forth a believable pattern of transmission in The Dawn of European Civilization (1925). The carbon-14 dating technique later revealed some anomalies in this famous piece of diffusionist analysis, but left Childe's work substantially intact. He was later discredited by a tree-ring dating technique, for it turns out that artifacts in the western sites, notably the megaliths, are older than their counterparts in the Near East.[27] The point is that diffusion should never be taken for granted as an adequate explanation of similarities between two cultures.

Sometimes the Indian hypothesis is clothed in the conceptual garb of the "cultural-historical" school of Germany and Austria, developed by Fritz Graebner and Wilhelm Schmidt.[28] Their theory holds that basic cultural elements are organized into a limited number of "culture-circles" (Kulturkreis). Each circle is viewed as a complex of traits subject to analysis by the application of certain principles of form and quantity, thus permitting generalizations about historical relationships.[29] Let us suppose that India was a culture circle harboring the complex of traits known as the "mystical tradition," and that Greece was another circle within which the complex appeared in modified form. By applying the criteria of form (how the traits fit into the culture) and quantity (how many similarities there are), one should be able to establish that diffusion has or has not occurred. Moreover, it would not be necessary to identify historical mechanisms of transmission to prove that borrowing had taken place.[30] An important corollary of this theory is that "whenever a phenomenon appears as an inorganic element in its ethnic surroundings, its presence is due to transmission."[31] Obviously this last point coheres neatly with the judgment that mystical ideas in Greek thought are suspiciously peripheral to a dominant humanism and rationalism. Unfortunately for those writers who deliberately or unconsciously rely on the culture-circle theory, the entire matter is highly controversial, has been subjected to much damaging criticism, and has failed to produce the fruitful results promised in its influential beginnings.[32]

Despite thorny problems besetting diffusionist theory, it can yield some analytical criteria bearing on the immediate question of India's philosophical relations with the Greco-Roman world.[33] In the first place, the distance between two cultures is less important than their differential receptivity to specific novelties. The mere fact of contact between India and Greece signifies very little. Banerjee suggests that "the Greeks...seem to have been little alive to or little interested in religious ideas specifically different from their own."[34] He notes further that "when the Persians were brought into contact with the Indians on the one hand, and with the Greeks on the other, they regarded the religion

of either as foreign and hostile worships."[35] As a later chapter
of this study will try to show, there is little reason to believe
that Christians were avid about features of Indian belief and worship they may have known.

There would be difficulties with geographical and historical
relationships even if Persia and Afghanistan did not stand between
India and the peoples she may have influenced, for "under no circumstances can geographical-historical propinquity constitute a
valid explanation of cultural differences and similarities."[36] If
a mystical tradition diffused from India to the eastern Mediterranean, then an intervening trail of ideas associated with that tradition ought to be visible. Buddhism did not appear suddenly in
Japan without first making its way through China and Korea. Brahmanism percolated down from the Gangetic Plain to the extreme
south of India by way of intervening territories.[37] Few interme-
diate clues are discernable in the overland connections of India
with Greece and Palestine. The existence of a sea route raises
other problems of a different nature, to which we shall turn in
due time.

In the second place, cultural traits can pass from one society to another only if they are communicable. Without an effective presentation they cannot be accepted, even if the donors are
respected and honored.[38] Material items and certain skills are
easier to present and accept than ideas, for the latter require
verbalization. Without the aid of language, it is possible to ob-
serve a sculptor or painter and learn something from him. Philosophical or theological notions can be displayed only in spoken or
written form, so the obstacle posed by language differences must
be surmounted.[39] Even an active, intelligent exertion to absorb
the ideas of another culture not uncommonly ends with a level of
comprehension both garbled and distorted.[40] An impressive example
is China's experience with Buddhism from the second to the eighth
centuries A.D.

The stage was set for the intrusion of Buddhism with the dis-
integration of the Han dynasty (206 B.C.-220 A.D.) amidst civil
war, famine, foreign invasion, and intense suffering, all of which
"transformed China from a powerful empire into a vast cemetery."[41]
These disasters brought into disrepute the prevailing Confucian i-
deology, with its emphasis on social and political virtues, and
stimulated a Neo-Taoist counter-culture devoted to reclusiveness,
quietism, philosophical subjectivism, and pursuit of individual
gratification. These escapist tendencies served as a bridge for
the entrance of Buddhism into a spiritually exhausted and an-
guished land, but there were, nevertheless, formidable linguistic,
social, and philosophical barriers.[42] The barriers were penetra-
ted because the Chinese wished it. They were drawn to Buddhist
mythology, metaphysics, ethics, and art. Most attractive was the

9

spiritual solace afforded by myriad compassionate bodhisattvas (it was Mahayana Buddhism that made the deepest impact). Magic also played a role, for Buddhist priests were credited with powers of sorcery exceeding those of taoist adepts.[43] All in all, Buddhist culture satisfied felt needs and introduced fresh, stirring possibilities of experience in an age of turmoil and insecurity.

As Linton has observed, a "new trait of idea must be better than what is already available; it must be worth the trouble."[44] This condition was fulfilled in China. Furthermore, the exceptional efforts made to adopt new ideas and practices are satisfyingly in the open. We know who many of the translators were, how they went about rendering Sanskrit and Pali into Chinese, and how traditional Chinese ideas were reconciled with flatly antithetical Buddhist ideas.[45] We know also of Chinese pilgrims who journeyed to India, men like Fa Hsien (resident in India from 405 to 411), whose purpose was to study Buddhism at its source.[46] Some of these travelers left detailed accounts of their experiences, and there are Chinese historical records which give an account of Chinese pilgrimages.[47] Even with these well documented advantages, the Chinese had trouble grasping and assimilating major Buddhist ideas like karma and reincarnation, thus supporting Linton's point that "a society can apprehend only those parts of a total complex wgich can be commnicated to it plainly and directly."[48] The Chinese were most receptive to what they could understand and identify with easily: art forms, relic worship, iconography, the bodhisattva ideal, and magic, rather than metaphysics, cosmology, or logic.

In the case of India's religious and philosophical relations with the Greco-Roman world, a markedly different situation prevails, namely, diffusion beneath the surface of the historical record. The presence of Indian embassies at Hellenistic and Roman courts, the fact of reciprocal commercial activity, the existence of suggestive artifacts, whether Gandhara art or the images of Indian deities found in western sites, prove nothing whatever about the presentation and acceptance of ideas. Evidence is lacking that relevant Indian languages were mastered by Greeks or Christians, or that significant Indian works were readily available in other accessible languages. The approximate meaning of prestige and influence supposedly accrued by Indians resident at Alexandria and elsewhere in western Asia remains obscure. There are no Greek or Christian equivalents of Fa Hsien, nor are there eastern texts mentioned in which one finds either interest or comprehension. With Buddhism in China, and with the transmission of Chinese culture to Japan between the sixth and ninth centuries A.D.,[49] specific agencies of transmission are clear: embassies, pilgrimages, the names and even biographies of translators and scholars, a record of schools and monastic communities, and so forth. No like array of historical mechanisms sustain the Indian hypothesis. As a

10

result, the structure of argument tends to rely heavily on the alleged existence of numerous, significant parallels, from which concealed mechanisms of transmission are inferred.

The anthropologists provide some additional guidelines for coping with this question of parallels. We find that "diffused innovations tend to show greater cross-cultural resemblances in finer detail than independently invented innovations."[50] Moreover, "several similarities prove more than a single one."[51] A central purpose of this study is to show that the "finer detail" is absent from parallels commonly adduced to verify the Indian hypothesis, and that where real similarities can be established, they are, on close examination, isolated and generally unimportant. It was noted earlier that part of Graebner's "method of proving cultural relations" is to assume transmission when an element is not organically related to its cultural matrix, an assumption which appears to support Radhakrishnan's argument that Jesus' teaching was a radical break from Judaism, and that mystical notions are alien to native Greek thought. This diffusionist principle can be challenged with the observation of Franz Boas that even primitive societies are not homogeneous, and that conflicting cultural elements are often found side by side.[52] But rather than depend wholly on this authoritative admission that cultural inconsistencies do not require an inference of transmission, I shall attempt to argue, through detailed analysis, that many key Greek and Cristian ideas which are said to be foreign to their environments are organically related to them. Banerjee has put the issue succinctly where Greek mythology and philosophy are concerned: "the old shift of attributing to Oriental influences everything in Hellenic religion that clashed with the purer idea of Hellenism was naively unscientific."[53]

Even though it was formulated to explain material traits of culture, Alexander Goldenweiser's principle of "limited possibilities" is of some use in working with ideas. [54] Is it not reasonable to expect that basic conditions of human existence, need, and experience have given rise to similar ideas separately arrived at? The universal facts of birth, death, suffering, the round of the seasons, the appearance of the heavens, the behavior of physical substances - with these and similar matters, the range of interpretation and explanation seems definitely limited. That is to say, man can attain some kind of sentient existence apart from his body or he cannot; the physical world is made of one kind of thing or more than one kind; the world was created or it was not; there is a divine, spiritual reality or there is not, and so on. In the words of Franz Boas, "the metaphysical notions of man may be reduced to a few types which are of universal distribution."[55] One must hasten to add, however, that within limited categories of thought there can be, and normally is, considerable diversity. The cosmologies of Jainism and Greek atomism are both pluralistic, but

11

they by no means are reducible to the same purposes and values. Both Shankara and Plato fixed ultimate reality beyond the realm of normal sensuous experience, and were, in a loose sense, "idealists" in common, but the detailed content of their philosophies is quite different. In what follows, there is ready acknowledgment of resemblances deriving from limited possibilities; what is denied is resemblance in detail, and the necessity of diffusion to explain even the cruder similarities.[57]

It is impossible to prove that no diffusion of ideas whatever linked the more ancient Indian culture to western Asia and Greece. Fortunately, there is no rational obligation even to try.[58] The only meaningful issue at stake is the credibility of assertions that such influences have a substantive basis. One task of this inquiry is to distinguish clearly where the Indian hypothesis is grounded in knowledge and where it is simply generating plausible speculation. If the parallels do not survive examination, and they are the bulwark of the Indian hypothesis as well as the philosophia perennis, then only the thinnest justification remains for saying that India supplied the ingredients of a mystical tradition to Greeks and Christians. Moreover, the notion that Buddha, Plato, and Jesus were viewing the world and human destiny through the same pair of spectacles will be exposed as largely untenable.

1. In Geoffrey Garratt, ed., The Legacy of India (Oxford: Oxford University Press, 1937), pp. 3-5.
2. B.J. Urwick, The Message of Plato (London: Methuen and Co., 1920), p. vii.
3. Sarvepalli Radhakrishnan, Eastern Religions and Western Thought (2nd ed.; Oxford: Oxford University Press, 1940), Sections iii and iv of Chapter IV, Chapter V, and Section i of Chapter VI.
4. Ibid., p. 138.
5. Ibid., p. 143 n. For what it is worth, James Legge, in his article on Confucius in the Encyclopedia Britannica 6 (1942), p. 238, notes a remarkable similarity between Pythagorean number mysticism and the divinatory system of the I Ching. In Joseph Needham et al., Science and Civilization in China (Cambridge: Cambridge University Press, 1954 -), the second of the projected seven volumes contains a wealth of parallels with, and anticipations of, western ideas. See, for example, pages 18-23, 40, 42, 67, 75, 161-163, 170, 188, 190, 199-200, 270, 299, 368, 390, 451, 475-476, 502, 508-509, 531, 579. Few scholars have ventured to interpret the meaning of such parallels as evidence that Chinese tributaries have poured into the mainstream of western thought. Chinese inventions, however, did reach the West. See Joseph Needham, The Grand Titration (Toronto: University of Toronto Press, 1969), Chapter 2.
6. A. Barriedale Keith, "Pythagoras and the Doctrine of Transmigration," Journal of the Royal Asiatic Society (1909), 569 ff. Keith concludes that no justification can be found for the view that Pythagoras's religious and philosophical doctrines were borrowed wholly or in part from Indian sources.
7. Radhakrishnan, Eastern Religions and Western Thought, pp. 133 n, 149 n, 161 n, 185 n.
8. Ibid., p. 186.
9. Ibid., pp. 174-175. For more ambivalence, see page 149.
10. Ibid., p. 158.
11. Ibid., p. 151.
12. Ibid., p. 153.
13. Theodor Gomperz, Greek Thinkers: A History of Ancient Philosophy, trans. Laurie Magnus (New York: Charles Scribner's Sons, 1901, I, p. 127. Gomperz is suitably cautious, however, about the "non-Greek origin of metempsychosis." Ibid., p. 546.
14. In Charles A. Moore, ed., Essays in East-West Philosophy: An Attempt at World Philosophical Synthesis (Honolulu: University of Hawaii Press, 1951), p. 232.
15. A.N. Marlow, Hinduism and Buddhism in Greek Philosophy," Philosophy East and West 4 (April, 1954), 37-58.
16. Ibid., 39.
17. Jean Filliozat, The Classical Doctrine of Indian Medicine: Its Origins and Its Greek Parallels, trans. Dev Raj Chanana (New

Delhi: Munshi Ram Monohar Lal, 1964), p. 257.

18. Ibid., p. 248.

19. Aldous Huxley, Grey Eminence (New York: Meridean Books, 1959), p. 62.

20. Bhagavan Das maintains that "differences between religions are differences only of words, names, langauges, or of nonessential superficial forms, and sometimes of emphasis, on this aspect of Truth, or Virtue, or of Duty, rather than another; never, of Essential Ideas." The Essential Unity of All Religions (Wheaton, Illinois: The Theosophical Press, 1939), p. 66. G.R.S. Mead takes much the same position in his useful book, Apollonius of Tyana: The Philosopher-Reformer of the First Century A.D. (New York: University Books, 1966). He aims "to sense the facts of universal religion under the ever-changing names which men bestow upon them." Ibid., pp. 62-63 (my italics).

21. Ananda K. Coomaraswamy, Am I My Brother's Keeper? (New York: The John Day Company, 1947), p. 50. Coomaraswamy also says "a philosophy identical with Plato's is still a living force in the East." Ibid., p. 11.

22. Quoted by Marco Baistrocchi, "The Last Pillars of Wisdom," in S. Durai Raja Singam, ed., Ananda Coomaraswamy (n.p., 1974), p. 351. This essay is informative about intellectual relations between Coomaraswamy and Guénon, as well as about Guénon's views and writings. The latter's best known work is L'Homme et son devenir selon le Vedanta (1925). Aldous Huxley admired both the men and their work. For a more detailed look at these two champions of the perennial philosophy, see Gai Eaton, The Richest Vein (London: Faber and Faber, 1949), pp. 183-209.

23. Filliozat believes that few scholars have taken seriously the question of relations and exchanges between India and the Occident: "The vogue of theories on the Greek miracle is in opposition to a deep study of relations with the Orient. Everything in Hellenic civilization must be explained through internal evolution." "Les échanges de l'Inde et de l'Empire romain aux premiers siècles de l'ère chrétienne," Revue historique (1949), 2.

24. Franz Boas, Race, Language and Culture (New York: The Free Press, 1940), p. 286.

25. Clark Wissler, The Relation of Man to Nature in Aboriginal America (Oxford: Oxford University Press, 1926), p. 183.

26. Marvin Harris, The Rise of Anthropological Theory: A History of Theories of Culture (New York: Thomas Y. Crowell Co., 1968), p. 376.

27. Colin Renfrew, "Carbon 14 and the Prehistory of Europe," Scientific American (October, 1971), 63-72.

28. See Graebner's Methode der Ethnologie (Heidelberg, 1911), and Father Schmidt's The Culture-Historical Method of Ethnology, trans. S.A. Sieber (New York: Fortuny's, 1939).

29. "Form" refers to the manner in which a trait is integrated

14

into its cultural matrix, while "quantity" refers to the number of similarities shared by two traits subjected to comparative analysis. See Robert Lowie, <u>The History of Ethnological Theory</u> (New York: Holt, Rinehart, and Winston, 1937), pp. 158, 180-181.

30. Ibid., pp. 178-179.

31. Boas, p. 301.

32. Ibid. Also, see Harris, p. 388.

33. See the exchange between G. Eliot Smith (an extreme diffusionist who minimizes human inventiveness and traces all major cultural developments to Egypt), B. Malinowski, H. Spinden, and A. Goldenweiser, in <u>Culture: The Diffusion Controversy</u> (New York: W.W. Norton and Co., 1927). Malinowski warns that "the comparative method is beset with many pitfalls," and spells some of them out. Ibid., pp. 35 ff. Harris's critique of diffusionist theory is withering, if not always convincing, and he ends by asserting "the fundamental sterility of the attempt to explain cultural differences and similarities by appealing to the non-principle of diffusion." <u>The Rise of Anthropological Theory</u>, p. 258.

34. <u>Hellenism in Ancient India</u>, p. 258.

35. Ibid., p. 241.

36. Harris, p. 378.

37. Nilakanta Sastri, <u>The Development of Religion in Southern India</u> (Bombay, 1963), pp. 26-34.

38. "Since it is only through the observation of these overt expressions that culture elemts can be transmitted from one individual to another or from one society to another, it follows that those culture elements which can be most readily and completely expressed will be those which are most readily available for acceptance." Ralph Linton, <u>The Study of Man</u> (New York: Appleton-Century Crofts, 1936), p. 338.

39. Thus, "even when language difference has ceased to be a serious barrier to the conveyance of such patterns (i.e., patterns of ideas), it is extremely difficult to put them across." Ibid., p. 339. In the same vein, Banerjee is quite right that "in general, the communication of philosophy is exceedingly difficult." <u>Hellenism in Ancient India</u>, p. 258.

40. A clear exception is Gandhara art, where sculptural style and certain ideas interacted with one another. Gilbert Highet, <u>The Migration of Ideas</u> (New York, 1954), pp. 33 ff. There is, however, no need to speculate about this interesting case of cultural transmission. The figure of the Buddha was fashioned by a man who was "artiste par son père grec et bouddhiste par sa mère indienne." Alfred Foucher, <u>L'Art greco-bouddhique du Gandhara</u> (Paris, 1951), II, p. 467. It is also well known that the resemblance of early Christian art to Gandhara styles was due to the representation of both Buddha and Christ as incarnations of the <u>logos</u>, an orator type being chosen as the model

in each case. See Benjamin Rowland, "Gandhara and Early Christian Art," Journal of Archeology 49 (1945), 445-448. This instance of diffusion stands on its own merits. There is no justification for leaping beyond it to other instances which tantalize, but for which there is far less evidence.

41. Etienne Balazs, Chinese Civilization and Bureaucracy, trans. H.M. Wright and ed. A.F. Wright (New Haven: Yale University Press, 1964), p. 194.

42. For example, the concreteness of relatively uninflected, monosyllabic Chinese versus the abstractness of highly inflected, polysyllabic Sanskrit and Pali; the Chinese family system versus the Buddhist monastic ideal; the closed, finite cosmology of the Chinese versus the infinite cosmic cycles of the Buddhists. Arthur Wright, Buddhism in Chinese History (Stanford: Stanford University Press, 1959), pp. 33-34.

43. C.K. Yang, Religion in Chinese Society (Berkeley: University of California Press, 1967), pp. 117-119.

44. Linton, pp. 341-343.

45. Wright, pp. 34-40.

46. See James Legge, trans., The Travels of Fa-Hien (Oxford: Oxford University Press, 1886).

47. For example, Luciano Petach, Northern India According to the Shui-Ching-Chu (1950), which is a Chinese geographer's epitome of accounts of Buddhist pilgrimages to India in the third century A.D.

48. Linton, p. 340. The technique known as ko-i, or "matching concepts," was natural enough but certain to produce grievous distortions, for dharma is not tao, nor does Nirvana easily convert to wu-wei (action through non-action). Wright, pp. 36-37.

49. See George Sansom, A History of Japan, 3 vols. (London: Cresset Press, 1959), I, 68-98.

50. Harris, p. 378.

51. Schmidt, p. 150.

52. Boas, p. 301. Linton is in agreement: "The elements which compose the core of any culture need not necessarily be consistent in all respects. In fact, there are plenty of instances in which a particular society holds values which seem to be quite incompatible." The Study of Man, p. 358.

53. Hellenism in Ancient India, pp. 250, 257. In the area of mythology, a recent work of G.S. Kirk concludes: "Comparisons with Egyptian and Indian mysths have been largely unfruitful in revealing profound influences on Greek myths. Certain isolated themes confirm what history and geography suggest, that there must have been the occasional idea that passed from one culture to the other - or, in the case of Indic myth, passed into both cultures from a common ancestor. The underlying principles and tone of the myths are distinct and suggest that cross-cultural influences were otherwise slight." Myth: Its Meaning and Functions in Ancient and Other Cultures (Cambridge:

Cambridge University Press, 1971), pp. 213-214.

54. Caution is in order here, for one can say of ideas as well as oars and their shapes (Goldenweiser's example of a limited possibility), that "the limited possibilities of nature are none other than the forms which evolution has produced. The task of science is to explain why they were produced." Harris, p. 627.

55. Boas, p. 271.

56. "There are, admittedly, few genuine uniformities in culture content unless one states the content in extremely general form - e.g., clothing, shelter, incest taboos, and the like." Clyde Kluckhohn, "Universal Categories of Culture," in A.L. Kroeber, ed., Anthropology Today (Chicago: University of Chicago Press, 1953), p. 341.

57. Alfred Kroeber has suggested that an idea may be taken up and be given a different content. He calls this process "stimulus diffusion" or "idea diffusion," and cites a number of examples, among them the possible transmission of the idea of writing from Mesopotamia to Egypt, or even to China, the development of a porcelain industry in Europe, stimulated by the Chinese example, and the appearance of drama in China shortly after the creation of Noh drama in Japan. Could not Indian ideas have provided formal possibilities into which Greeks and Christians poured a distinctive content? The trouble with this approach to the Indian hypothesis is that it emphasizes content as well as form, and, as Kroeber admits, that proofs of such stimulus diffusion are "difficult to secure long after the act or whenever the historical record is not full." The Nature of Culture (Chicago: University of Chicago Press, 1952), p. 344.

58. It seems a pointless exercise to imagine contacts and mechanisms which may have been operative. A remark of Lowie reminds us of many Indian hypothesizers: "As easygoing investigators of faunal distribution invent landbridges to suit their purposes, so the diffusionists decree at their convenience a former continuity no longer visible." The History of Ethnological Theory, p. 158.

CHAPTER II

HISTORIC CONTACTS BETWEEN INDIA AND MEDITERRANEAN
CIVILIZATION TO THE FALL OF ROME

The purpose of this chapter is to set forth briefly the main
lines of contact between India and civilizations of the eastern
Mediterranean, the peoples involved, the time and intensity of
contact, and the more obvious, commonly agreed upon exchanges,
commercial or otherwise, which took place. Needless to say, a summary narrative cannot do justice, even on a descriptive level, to
scholarly controversies over many ethnographic, linguistic, religious, artistic, and historical questions. Such controversies will
be mentioned from time to time as a reminder that our knowledge of
east-west relations in the ancient world lacks fullness and precision, but the temptation to shower the reader with myriad references to specialized quarrels will be resisted.

India's commercial ties with western Asia are traceable to
the second millennium B.C., when the civilization of Mohenjo-Daro
and Harappa in the Indus River Valley traded with Mesopotamian
city states near the Persian Gulf. The chief evidence is some 500
seals, bearing engraved animals and cryptic writing, which resemble closely in form the well-known cylinder seals used throughout
the Ancient Near East.[1] Written evidence of commerce survives in
cuneiform inscriptions of the Hittite kings (ca. 1500-1400 B.C.),
when Vedic Aryans were living in the Punjab and beginning to shape
the traditional society and religion of ancient India.[2] In the
early decades of the first millennium B.C., and possibly earlier,
Phoenician galleys of the Levant linked up with intermediaries
through the Red Sea route to India. The Tyrian merchants carried
spices, ivory, apes, and peacocks for the delectation and amuse-
ment of the great.[3] The Phoenicians may be regarded as the earliest nexus between the civilized cultures of India and the Mediterranean, one which remained intact until the Romans obliterated
Carthage in 146 B.C. and rose to uncontested naval and commercial
supremacy, abruptly ending nearly a thousand years of Phoenician
contact with northwestern India. This seems ample time for a people of enterprise and intelligence to learn much about the language and ideas of a foreign culture, yet there is no warrant for
supposing that an exchange of material goods was accompanied by
the transmission of religious and philosophical values.

Soldiers and merchants seldom display the interest and receptivity necessary for an appreciative grasp of an unfamiliar culture. This hindrance would have been compounded if the Phoenician
merchant simply faced the Indian merchant in business deals, assuming that Indians were among the agents and carriers of Indian
trade. That is, the opportunity to learn is no assurance that it
will be seized upon upon. Even had opportunity sparked curiosity,

India's literature and philosophy were complex enough in the first
millennium to deter and confound an astute scholar, much less a
type of mind steeped in the pragmatic broth of commerce and gain.
A similar state of affairs prevailed when Europeans turned to exploration and discovery during the Renaissance. Proselytizing missionaries, rude military adventurers, and ambitious merchants became fixtures in distant lands, but learned precious little about
the cultural achievements of their exotic peoples. The latter genre of discovery, always more subtle and elusive, because it means
lowering one's own ethnocentric shield, had to await the coming
of men schooled in literature, philosophy, art, and science, who
might be willing to trouble themselves with native languages, religions, and ideas. The Phoenicians never reached that stage. They
remained traders to the end, carriers and middlemen to a hundred
ports, sketched by Polybius as a people for whom, at least at Carthage, "no crime that leads to profit is considered disgraceful."[4]
Apart from the alphabet, which had distinct advantages in business
transactions, and a few contributions to the science of navigation
and the craft of shipbuilding, the Phoenicians left no body of
original art or literature, no philosophical speculation, no memo-
rable relgious ideas. With such a record, it would come as a surprise if they had learned anything from India transcending the intellectual currency of the marketplace. If they did so, no record
of the event has survived.

India was approachable by land through several passes on the
northwest frontier. Two great powers of the ancient world, Assyria
and Babylonia, traded with their not too distant neighbor across
the Hindu Kush, importing the usual assortment of luxury items:
gold, silver, ivory, apes, peacocks, almug trees, ebony, spices,
and precious stones.[5] While it seems likely that a bit of Chalde-
an astronomy astronomy and Babylonian mythology passed to India,
there was no reciprocal effect that can be detected. The Assyri-
ans, with their passion for conquest and slaughter, ruthless empire and hunting, borrowed the substance of their culture from the
Akkadians and Sumerians to the south.[6]

With the rise of Persian influence in the sixth century B.C.,
the potential for intellectual cross-fertilization was magnified
enormously, for Cyrus the Great and Darius actually succeeded in
mastering a substantial area in northwest India, which almost certainly included Gandhara, Sind, and a fragment of the Punjab. Indeed, the region west of the Indus became a Persian satrapy, and
as Persian hegemony wore on, some Indian court customs and archi-
tectural styles acquired a Persian flavor. The great lion columns
of Ashoka (269-232 B.C.) owe much to the eastward dispersion of
Persian artists when Persepolis fell to Alexander the Great.[7] Ara-
maic, "the lingua franca of the Achaemenid empire," gave birth to
the Kharosthi alphabet so widely used in northwestern India.[8] As
readers of Herodotus know, he describes vividly the Indian mili-

tary contingents serving in the army of the King of Kings. There is some justification for crediting an historical relationship between Indians and Iranians immediately prior to the founding of the Achaemenid dynasty, but the extent of mutual influence, if any, is virtually unknown.[9] In any event, the authority of Persian administration did not at a subsequent time reach beyond the Indus to the valley of the Ganges.[10] Although Indians were used in the Persian military and administrative framework, there is slight evidence of lasting, important changes in the body of Persian civilization, which was a continuation and fulfillment of patterns bequeathed by Sumer, Akkad, Assyria, and Babylonia, with the addition of some creative novelties. Even if one grants without argument the movement of Aryans, Iranians, and Greeks to their final homelands from a primordial center of "Indo-European" dispersion in the remote past, it is clear enough that sixth century Persians and Indians confronted one another without recognition of common historical ground.[11]

The last point is well illustrated in the doctrines of the prophet and religious reformer Zoroaster (ca. 7th century B.C.), whom Frye describes as "probably a priest of the old Aryan religion," meaning the religion which affirmed the divinity of celestial and other natural phenomena, identifying specific deities with a particular name, or noun.[12] Suppose one concedes that Zoroaster's religious background derived from an antecedent Indo-European source, thus establishing a vague religious kinship with the Aryan faith of India. What, then, does Zoroaster, as a religious reformer, have in common with Brahmanical belief? Very little of religious significance is implied by the evidence.

The Vedic emphasis was on prayer and sacrifice, on the maintenance of cosmic order and harmony by menas of ritual precisely executed and faithfully transmitted.[13] The most impressive theological tendency in the Vedas is toward monotheism; the highest philosophical flight is toward monism and a conception of all-pervading order (rita).[14] Vedic ethical injunctions stress duty to the gods (or God) and to men; sin means disobeying the gods and violating cosmic law.[15] There is some mention of reward in the world of Vishnu and punishment in the world of Yama, but the latter is not characterized as a malevolent being whose evil must be vanquished as a condition for the attainment of virtue. In one instance Yama provides a benign realm of peace for the dead, while in another he is simply to be avoided.[16] He is one of many gods in the Vedic pantheon, all of whom were objects of worship even if one, such as Prajapati or Vishvakarman, might be praised as the supreme being.[17]

On the other hand, speculations of the Upanishadic sages center on the nature of Brahman, Brahman's relationship to the world, and the identification of Atman with Brahman. Evil is associated

21

with attachment to the phenomenal world, sense experience, and the finite.[18] The sage does not struggle against some objectified evil in order to make a purer or better world, but seeks rather to diminish his own ego-striving so as to put the world at a distance and draw closer to God, or to achieve unitary consciousness. As Radhakrishnan puts the case, "it is obvious that the Upaniṣads have for their ideal the becoming one with God...Whatever ethics we have in the Upaniṣads is subsidiary to this goal. Duty is a means to the end of the highest perfection. Nothing can be satisfying short of this highest condition. Morality is valuable only as leading to it."[19] In the Upanishads, morality and ethics are not the preponderant issue. They are a means to the end of transcendence, and have meaning only in relation to an imperfect world in which one cannot attain the "highest perfection."[20] Moreover, realization of perfection requires that the individual actively diminish conflict, distinctions, and "class hatreds and antipathies."[21] In general, the Upanishads settle for two major alternatives with respect to man's relationship to the world. The first is that he accept his place in it without complaint, resistance, ambition for profit, or fear of loss. The second is that he disengage from it by an act of renunciation.

It is clear that ethics and morality are largely of secondary importance in the Vedas and the Upanishads, and that one does not find a sharp distinction between good and evil embodied in warring deities. On the other hand, these distinctions were fundamental for Zoroaster, for "the first novelty of this radically new teaching lay in its treatment in purely ethical terms of the ultimate nature and destiny of both man and the world."[22] For Zoroaster, the cosmic order is corrupt and degenerate, but subject to reform and transformation by the deliberate effort of ethically committed individuals. Zoroaster taught a progressive, optimistic philosophy of history, in which evil vanishes with the establishment of Ahura Mazda's Kingdom of Righteousness, a triumph of Light over Darkness expected to occur in an earthly setting. The means by which this radical purification of the world is to effected is the sentient, self-conscious individual, who will choose good or evil and then act on his choice.

> Hear ye then with your ears; see ye the bright flames
> with the eyes of the Better Mind. It is for a decision
> as to religions, man and man, each individually for
> himself. Before the great effort of the cause, awake
> ye to our teaching.[23]

The ultimate goal of humanity is not conformity to tradition, sacrifice to the gods, or quiescent union with some larger, ineffable spiritual reality, but active, aggressive participation in the mighty struggle against palpable evil. Herzfeld sees the "true Zoroastrian creed" as the inevitable triumph of Ahura Mazda and

22

the force of light over Angra Mainyu and the force of darkness. In Zoroastrian language, "Right shall be strengthened, Evil shall be destroyed."[24] In line with this radical dualism, Zoroaster's vision of the last judgment is a settling of accounts as though in a court of law, where the innocent are separated from the guilty.[25]

This is not to say that similarities between Brahmanism and Zoroastrian are wholly absent. Jackson notes parallels with regard to "purity of body, the care of useful animals, especially the cow, the observance of a strictly defined ritual (in which the preparation of the sacred plant haoma, Indic soma, plays an important part)."[26] Zaehner observes that Zoroaster's notion of cosmic order matches in both etymology and function the Vedic concept of rita: "this, at least, can safely be said to form part of a common Indo-Iranian heritage."[27] There are also parallels between the Avesta and the Rig-Veda, but Zaehner cautions that "in the Gathas we are in a totally different religious world," for they probably contain the authentic religious ideas of Zoroaster, and they have little to do with the Vedas; "the Prophet's originality may be disconcerting, but it is none the less real for that."[28]

It seems reasonable to conclude that India's spiritual effect on the glory of Persian civilization - Zoroaster's lofty ideal of ethical choice and struggle - was minimal, and that very little of his "Aryan" religious background survived in the new doctrine, which signaled a new direction for religious ideas in the ancient world.

After toppling the Achaemenid empire at Arbela in 330 B.C., it was the satrapy of India that Alexander invaded next, ending more than two centuries of Persian rule. He struck across northwest India to the Indus River and crossed over to do battle with King Porus. After defeating him, Alexander was compelled by an exhausted, reluctant army to turn around and go home.[29] There is no question that Alexander had serious intentions of hellenizing his Indian conquests. After the engagement with Porus, he founded the cities of Nicaea and Bucephala to celebrate his victory. The route of his march through India was marked by strategically located garrisons and nascent towns, all calculated to enrich the fabric of a universal state. As the pupil of Aristotle he included in his entourage professionals of the mind as well as those of the sword, scholars and historians to record his deeds, garner knowledge, and sow the seeds of Greek culture. With Alexander's premature death at Babylon in 323 B.C., his empire was partitioned in a fraction of the time that had been taken to assemble it. By 321, Chandragupta Maurya (321-297 B.C.), founder of the Mauryan dynasty, had led a successful movement to end Greek rule in India, which also cut off the prospect of hellenization so effectively realized in Asia Minor and Egypt. The charismatic Macedonian had sped through his age like a meteor. The impact of his ephemeral passage through northwestern India may be summarized in a few sentences.

First, the political balance of power was thrown into disar-
ray as confederations of small tribes disintegrated, thus loosen-
ing the political texture of the region and preparing the ground
for the advent of the Mauryan Empire. Second, paths of communication were opened to the succession kingdoms of the Hellenistic age.
Third, Gandharan art and Greek astronomy passed into India, but
without stimulating any extraordinary cultural transformations.
Bevan has written that "India indeed and the Greek world only
touched each other on their fringes, and there was never a chance
for elements of the Hellenistic tradition to strike root in India."[30] In a similar vein, J.H. Marshall says that "in spite of
its wide diffusion, Hellenistic art never took real and lasting
hold upon India, for the reason that the temperaments of the two
peoples were radically dissimilar."[31] Alexander's spectacular invasion seems to have been a ripple on the sea of Indian tradition
and history.

The foremost personage in Indo-Occidental relations of the
third century B.C. was the famed Mauryan ruler Ashoka, whose conversion to Buddhism inspired one of the spectacular missionary
movements of the ancient world.[32] The spread of Buddhist institutions, doctrines, and monks to most parts of India and to Ceylon
is thoroughly attested.[33] The impact of Ashokan missionaries on
the Near East and eastern Mediterranean is more problematic. The
evangelist Maharakshita may have gone "to the Yavana or Greek
country," possibly Bactria.[34] Rock Edict XIII, which dates from
about 258 B.C., mentions Hellenistic kings of Syria, Egypt, Macedonia, Cyrene, and Epirus who surrendered themselves to the Dharma.[35] A Buddhist chronicle of Ceylon (second century B.C.?) refers to Buddhist monks coming to the island from Alexandria, but
evidence is inconclusive that Ashokan missionaries were at the
Alexandria of Egypt, for other cities throughout Alexander's empire were named after him.[36] The chief evidence for a Buddhist
thrust into western Asia at this time is Rock Edict XIII. Romila
Thapar infers from the date that one must distinguish between the
missions of Ashoka and those of the Third Buddhist Council held at
Pataliputra. The religious missions of the Council, which carried
Buddhist ideas deep into northern and southern India, came some
five years after the missions announced in Edict XIII.

> The Buddhist missions were purely religious in charac-
> ter and were sent out under the direction of the Bud-
> dhist Council and not under the direction of Asoka. His
> own embassies were quite distinct from the Buddhist mis-
> sions, although they may have assisted the latter in
> some way...it is noticeable that the Buddhist missions
> concentrated on areas either within the kingdom or on
> the borders of it.[37]

Even if Ashoka's embassies were intrusted with religious missions, it is difficult to know the connection between their religious teachings and traditional sectarian Buddhism. Judging from the content of the Ashokan edicts, the doctrines were those of neither the Theravada nor the Mahāyāna schools.[38] Ashoka's version of the Dharma omits any reference to the central tenets of Buddhism: the Four Noble Truths (suffering, the cause of suffering, the cessation of suffering, the Eight-fold Path), the Three Signs of Being (suffering, impermanence, no-soul), Reincarnation, the Wheel of Rebirth.[39] Rather, what one finds is a good deal of straightforward moralizing such as is found in most higher religions, and a stress on non-violence (ahimsā), deriving ostensibly from the king's radical change of heart after an initial career of bloody conquest. Ashoka appears to mean by Dharma "few sins and many good deeds," with the latter supported by "kindness, liberality, truthfulness, and purity."[40] Furthermore, "it is by meditation that people have progressed in Dharma most," a more recognizably Buddhistic injunction.[41]

If it was the preceding message that reached the ears of potential converts in the Hellenistic world, it is not possible from existing evidence to determine how much of it took root. It is reasonable to assume that Ashoka's missions were intended at least to convey his fervent moral convictions, and the grandiose claim of "conquest" in Rock Edict XIII need not be taken seriously. In Thapar's analysis,

> The use of the term conquest implies the adoption of the principles of Dharma by the country in question. Thus he includes the Greek kingdoms of Syria, Egypt, Cyrene, Mecedonia, and Epirus as having been conquered by Dharma, whereas in fact all that may have happened was a cordial exchange of embassies or missions or merely the sending of one of these by Aśoka to the Greek kings mentioned.[42]

Ashoka's Dharma gives a strong impression of being a highly personal matter with more than casual political overtones, and one cannot but wonder about its tenuous relationship with historical Buddhism.[43] It is probable "that Dharma was Aśoka's own invention. It may have borrowed from Buddhist and Hindu thought, but it was in essence an attempt on the part of the king to suggest a way of life which was both practical and convenient, as well as highly moral."[44] The king was faced with the hard political task of binding the parts of empire together. The appeal of Buddhism to the lower classes, its promise as a countervailing force against entrenched Brahmans and other privileged groups, and the universality of its ethic would appeal understandably to a king bent on forging a strong, centralized monarchy, even if he did no more than cull from Buddhism a few moral maxims to build a philosophy of life suitable for promulgation as Dharma.[45]

If Ashoka's religious philosophy had the kind of influence implied by his edicts, one might expect to find some hint of it in the historical record. Although the record is silent, the vague, hortatory character of Ashoka's Buddhism may have touched non-Indians simply because such moral principles were conventionally honored on other grounds than being Buddhist, or were acceptable within the legitimate context of another tradition. After a polite and mutually satisfying exchange of convergent views on morality, Ashokan emissaries might have left their "converts," returned to the court at Pataliputra, and announced wonderful triumphs for the Dharma. In the absence of better knowledge of specific Buddhist influence on Hellenistic relgion and thought, it is probably wise to follow Lubac's circumspect example and err in the direction of understatement when speculating on Greco-Roman acquaintance with Buddhism. [46]

After the tripartite division of Alexander's empire, the Seleucid kings ruling in western Asia maintained diplomatic and commercial contact with the Mauryan court at Pataliputra after an abortive attempt to repossess Indian territories by force. Shortly before 250 B.C., the Bactrian Greeks, living in what is now eastern Iran and Afghanistan, threw off the authority of Seleucus Nicator, and asserted their independence.[47] Led by Demetrius, they marched into India and subdued more territory than had fallen to the Persians or Alexander.[48] It appears that Demetrius viewed himself as Alexander's successor; his coins, among the finest of the ancient world, bear a likeness remarkably similar to that attributed to the Macedonian.[49] Yet the Bactrian kings were not the true heirs of the precocious conqueror and hellenizer. Unlike the Seleucids, Ptolemies, Antigonids, and Attalids, their general outlook and cultural loyalties were decidedly un-Greek, which can be seen most dramatically in the themes and legends decorating their coinage. The Indo-Greeks drew freely on Indian motifs and languages, whereas the Seleucids seldom borrowed from Iranians or Babylonians, nor did the Ptolemies dip avidly into rich Egyptian traditions. Bactria was so clearly an apprentice to Indian forms and ideas that it probably should be classified as a Hellenistic kingdom.[50]

Menander (155-130 B.C.), successor to Demetrius, was converted, reputedly, to Buddhism as the outcome of a famous interview with the Buddhist philosopher Nagasena, known in Indian tradition through the popular dialogue The Questions of King Milinda (Milindapañha).[51] This rapport with Indian ways persisted among the Indo-Greeks until they were routed in the first century B.C., first by Scythian (or Saka) tribesmen, and then by Kushan (Yueh-chih) invaders. During the heyday of the Bactrian Greeks, an east-west commerce flourished, with the Bactrian kingdoms serving as intermediaries. Was this potentially convenient access to Indian religious and philosophical ideas exploited by Hellenistic sages?

This is an important question which will be examined presently.

The Scythian invaders who displaced the Indo-Greeks in Bactria and the Punjab may have been feudatories of the Parthian king Mithradates (123-188 B.C.). Whatever their origin, they turned out to be willing links between Greek and Indian cultures, and there may have been a Christian apostle at the court of Gondopharnes, an Indo-Parthian prince known to the Greeks, whose capital was in the vicinity of Taxila in the northwest corner of India.[52] About the middle of the first century A.D., the rule of the Sythians was ended by nomadic Kushans pressing hard from the north. The succeeding Kushan monarchs created an opulent empire which sprawled to the west within 600 miles of Roman frontiers.[53] Physical proximity, mutually cordial attitudes, and improved lines of communication between the two empires fostered commercial ties and occasional diplomatic gestures, notably the presence of Kushan envoys at the coronation ceremonies of Trajan.[54] Rome's appetite for Asian trade was immoderate enough to cause Pliny the Elder worry over the solvency of the state. In his estimate, some hundred million sesterces (converted by Mommsen to a bit more than a million pounds sterling) flowed into the coffers of Asia, about half of it going to India, chiefly for expensive spices used by the Romans in their prodigal funerals.[55]

Unlike the pragmatic and somewhat pedestrian Roman elite, the Kushans were philosophically and aesthetically inclined. Their prosperous, lovely capital at Peshawar opened its gates to artistic, intellectual, and material riches alike, and from all quarters. A mature, subtle Buddhism encountered a nascent, groping Christianity in the cities of Egypt and Asia Minor. Greek artists in large numbers were imported from the Roman west to beautify temples and palaces of sophisticated Kushan royalty. The Gandhara school of architecture, sculpture, and painting thrived in the extreme northwest of India during some two hundred years of Kushan rule; more precisely, "the art of Gandhara is the official art of the Kushan Emperor Kanishka (ca. 144 A.D.) and his successors," characterized by a striking fusion of Greek aesthetic styles and Indian religious motifs.[56] It was in this Hellenistic style that Buddha was first represented as a human figure. The external forms of Greek humanism were transformed insensibly by Indian spirituality into a type of art closer to the taste of a people uneasy with Greek enthusiasm for a rationally idealized nature. In the first century of the Christian era, the sight of Indians walking the streets of Alexandria became commonplace enough to prompt comment on their presence by the philosopher and orator Dio Chrysostomus (ca. 40-112 A.D.), who may also have known about the Indian epics.[57] If ever a favorable period existed in the ancient world for the interpenetration of Western and Indian ideas, it was during this age of Roman and Kushan contiguity, when geographical obstacles in the way of inquiry and discourse were at a minimum.[58]

With the gradual decline of Kushan power, once active channels of contact grew sluggish and eventually were closed off. After the principate of Septimius Severus (193-211 A.D.), fewer Roman coins are found in India, and none at all turn up, at least
for the western emperors, in the years following Arcadius and
Honorius (from 390 A.D.). Indirect relations were maintained between Roman Asia and the East at Alexandria when the Guptas held
sway in India (320-530 A.D.), more intimate contact being dis-
couraged by the emergence of a fresh, aggressive Persian state
(the Sassanian) in 224 A.D., which displaced the Parthian Arsa-
cids. This renaissance of Persian civilization lasted into the
seventh century and was not, when at full strength, notably cordial to the crumbling Roman Empire. A sporadic, feeble trade with
India was continued by the eastern emperors until the reign of
Justinian (527-565 A.D.), when the presence of telltale coins in
the archeological record ceases altogether.

As if to symbolize the decay of intercourse between India and
the West, the last well-known visitor to India before the onset of
the Dark Ages (ca. 500-1000 A.D.) was Cosmas Indicopleustes, an
Egyptian monk of the sixth century, whose Christian Topography is
a crude apology for the faith cast in the form of a geographical
treatise. To give Cosmas his due, the Christian Topography has
some usable material on Ceylon (known then as Taprobana), the Mala-
bar Coast towns, and trade in the eastern seas of the sixth century.[59] Otherwise, Cosmas's purpose and outlook, as well as his
general reliability, are best revealed in the title of Book II of
treatise: "The Christian theories regarding the form and position
of the whole world, the proofs of which are taken from Divine
Scripture."[60] The return of Cosmas to the Mediterranean world
signifies the nearly total eclipse of India by a shadow of fable,
distortion, and preposterous surmise. Donald Lach puts the demise
even earlier, in the second century A.D.

> From the time of Ptolemy until the return of Marco
> Polo to Venice more than one thousand years later,
> very little factual information about India, the East
> Indies, and China was added to Europe's store of know-
> ledge. The pioneering efforts of Megasthenes were either
> forgotten altogether or so lost in a maze of fables
> that separating fact from fiction became next to impos-
> sible.[61]

Even in the perspective of this cursory narrative, it is understandable that some students of comparative thought, already
intrigued by seeming parallels between Indian, Greek and Christian ideas, would tend to draw positive inferences from the long
succession of encounters between India and the Mediterranean world,
encounters about which Warmington and Filliozat have been able to

research entire books. But these indisputable facts of contiguity, the evidence of commercial, diplomatic, and some cultural inter- course, cannot be used to establish the transmission of a mystical tradition from east to west on a grand scale. We must turn from the facts of contact between civilizations to the meaning of the facts for Greco-Roman and Christian thought, which requires an assessment of what the ancients knew about India, as preserved in the extant writings of Greek, Latin, and Patristic authors. Who in the ancient world wrote about India? To what degree can their re- ports be trusted? What was the attitude, the intellectual posture of classical writers who sought to describe and evaluate India? What is the substantive content of their reports where religious and philosophical ideas are concerned? Do the reports of classi- cal authors read like those of converts or onlookers?

Apart from written sources, it is not unlikely that much in- · formation circulated through oral discourse. Without written docu- ments, however, there is no satisfactory means of judging the value or impact of such informal contacts, most of which must have been between traders, soldiers, and government officials, men not usually schooled to appreciate the fine points of philosophical or theological discourse, even if they were fortunate enough to meet an Indian who knew what he was talking about. Speculation on these points is next to useless. Specific texts are needed which clear- ly indicate the transmission and adoption of ideas unequivocally identifiable as Brahmanical, Jain, or Buddhist in origin. In the absence of such texts, the only recourse is to postulate intellec- tual exchanges as a necessary effect of commercial exchanges, an arbitrary procedure at best, or to hold conjectures of seductive but shaky persuasion based on supposed parallels between Indian, Greek, and Christian thought.

But this appeal to analogical method is powerless to come up with much beyond attractive speculations. Noting a resemblance be- tween ideas, even when the resemblance verges on identity, does not amount to a sound probability of influence. In due time, the parallels shall be taken up in earnest. The next logical task is to evaluate sources which may have carried Indian thought to the Greeks and the Christians.

1. R.C. Majumdar et al., <u>An</u> <u>Advanced</u> <u>History</u> <u>of</u> <u>India</u> (3rd ed.; New York: St. Martin's Press, 1967), p. 19.
2. Hugh Rawlinson, <u>Intercourse</u> <u>Between</u> <u>India</u> <u>and</u> <u>the</u> <u>Western</u> <u>World</u> <u>From</u> <u>the</u> <u>Earliest</u> <u>Times</u> <u>to</u> <u>the</u> <u>Fall</u> <u>of</u> <u>Rome</u> (Cambridge: Cambridge University Press, 1916), p. 2. In this earlier work, Rawlinson is critical of the view that important exchanges were made between India and the cultures of the eastern Mediterranean. I cannot explain the change of heart, or mind, in the brief essay cited above, but this earlier work is more cogently argued than the later essay.
3. I Kings 10: 22.
4. Polybius <u>Histories</u> vi. 56. Unless otherwise noted, all classical references are taken from the Loeb Classical Library.
5. For a detailed account of imports and exports, trade routes, and middlemen which is applicable to all commercial contacts between India and the West in the ancient world, see William Tarn, <u>The</u> <u>Greeks</u> <u>in</u> <u>Bactria</u> <u>and</u> <u>India</u> (Cambridge: Cambridge University Press, 1951), pp. 366-375.
6. Rawlinson, <u>Intercourse</u> <u>Between</u> <u>India</u> <u>and</u> <u>the</u> <u>Western</u> <u>World</u>, pp. 14 ff.
7. A.L. Basham, <u>The</u> <u>Wonder</u> <u>That</u> <u>Was</u> <u>India</u> (New York: The Macmillan Co., 1954). pp. 348 f. Garbe believes the familiar agreements between Aesop and a tradition of Indian fables proves the reality of literary exchanges between India, Persia, Asia Minor, and Greece six hundred years before Christ, in spite of the absence of translations contemporary with those cultures. <u>Indien</u> <u>und</u> <u>das</u> <u>Christentum</u>: <u>eine</u> <u>untersuchung</u> <u>der</u> <u>religions-</u> <u>geschichtlichen</u> <u>zusammenhänge</u> (Tübingen, 1914), p. 24. This work has been translated by Lydia G. Robinson as <u>India</u> <u>and</u> <u>Christendom</u>: <u>The</u> <u>Historical</u> <u>Connection</u> <u>Between</u> <u>Their</u> <u>Reli-</u> <u>gions</u> (La Salle, Illinois: Open Court Publishing Co., 1959). She omits Garbe's notes for the most part, but integrates some of them into the text.
8. Richard Frye, <u>The</u> <u>Heritage</u> <u>of</u> <u>Persia</u> (New York: World Publishing Co., 1963), pp. 121, 141.
9. Ibid., p. 38.
10. Various authors, <u>The</u> <u>Cambridge</u> <u>History</u> <u>of</u> <u>India</u>, 6 vols. (Cambridge: Cambridge University Press, 1922-), I, pp. 319-323. Hereafter this work is cited as <u>CHI</u>.
11. In a refresing departure from the German school of philology, whose views dominated the nineteenth century and are still pronounced in writing about "Aryan" origins, Professor Frye observes that one must be cautious about assuming too literally the existence of a single "Indo-European language, religion, and social structure which broke into several parts and diffused to India, Iran, Greece, and Western Europe. The elaborate theories of scholars like Georges Dumézil, who sees a tripartite division of society corresponding to a similar

division of gods among Indians, Iranians, and Greeks, must be swallowed with care, whatever their heuristic value. Dumézil sees a common Aryan "ideology" partially because he assumes the existence at one time of a common language. See his L'Ideologie tripartite des Indo-Européens (Brussels, 1958). See also, Frye, pp. 16, 18-21.

12. Ibid., p. 31. As is true with too many questions of origin and influence discussed in this study, the authority one chooses to invoke is a toss-up. A.V.W. Jackson cites a dozen divergent theories on the origin and component elements of Zoroastrianism. Zoroastrian Studies (New York: Columbia University Press, 1928), pp. 206-211. His own view, which gives little comfort, is that "the origin of the religion ... and the causes which brought it into being remain enveloped in obscurity." Ibid., p. 213.

13. "The sacrifice was believed to have existed from eternity like the Vedas. The creation of the world itself eas even regarded as the fruit of a sacrifice by the Supreme Being ... Sacrifice was regarded as almost the only kind of duty, and it was called karma or kriyā (action)." Surendra Nath Dasgupta, A History of Indian Philosophy, 4 vols. (Cambridge: Cambridge University Press, 1922-1949), I, p. 22. From another perspective, "when ritual grew in importance, R̥ta became a synonym for yajña or sacrificial ceremony." Sarvepalli Radhakrishnan, Indian Philosophy, 2 vols. (2nd ed. rev.; New York: Macmillan Co., 1931), I, p. 110.

14. Rig-Veda 10:82.3; 1:164.46; 4:23.10.

15. Ibid., 5:85.7-8.

16. Ibid., 10:14.9, 13-14; 1:38.5.

17. Dasgupta, I, pp. 18-20.

18. Katha Upanishad 3.3-9.

19. Radhakrishnan, Indian Philosophy, I, pp. 207-208.

20. Ibid., p. 230.

21. Ibid., p. 223.

22. Joseph Campbell, The Masks of God, vol. 3: Occidental Mythology (New York: Viking Press, 1964), p. 190.

23. Joseph Campbell, The Masks of God, vol. 2: Oriental Mythology (New York: Viking Press, 1962), p. 244.

24. Ernst Herzfeld, Zoroaster and His World, 2 vols. (Princeton: Princeton University Press, 1947), II, p. 412.

25. Ibid., I, p. 304. See also Robert Zaehner, The Dawn and Twilight of Zoroastrianism (New York: G.P. Putnam's and Sons, 1961), p. 36. Zaehner says that Zoroaster's ethical dualism is attested in the Rig-Veda, but points out that it is the dominant theme of Zoroaster's religious teaching. Ibid., p. 40.

26. Zoroastrian Studies, p. 7.

27. The Dawn and Twilight of Zoroastrianism, p. 50.

28. Ibid. On differences between the Gathas and the Rig-Veda, see Frye, pp. 31 ff. An excellent translation of the Gathas is in

W. Hinze, _Zarathustra_ (Stuttgart, 1961).

29. This epic event is discussed in William Tarn, _Alexander the
Great_, 2 vols. (Cambridge: Cambridge University Press, 1948),
I, Pt. 2. For relevant ancient sources, see John W. McCrindle,
The Invasion of India by Alexander the Great (2nd ed.; West-
minster: A. Constable, 1893).

30. _CHI_, I, p. 385. For Hugh Rawlinson, Alexander's conquest of
northwest India "passed off like countless other invasions,
leaving the country almost undisturbed." _India: A Short Cul-
tural_ (2nd ed. rev.; London: Cresset Press, 1952), p. 62.

31. _CHI_, I, p. 649. Bevan says, however, that "if a military occupation of eight years or so left no permanent trace upon the
north-west of India, we can hardly infer from that the essential unreceptivity of India for Hellenism." Ibid., p. 384.
One can leave open the question of receptivity while noting
the _de facto_ absence of significant cultural influence.

32. See Romila Thapar, _Aśoka and the Decline of the Mauryas_ (London: Oxford University Press, 1961), pp. 36 ff. Here is a full
and careful assessment of Ashoka's conversion.

33. See Jean Filliozat, "Aśoka et l'expansion bouddhique," in
René de Berval, ed., _Présence du Bouddhisme_ (Saigon: France-
Asie, 1959).

34. _CHI_, I, p. 499.

35. N.A. Nikam and Richard McKeon, _The Edicts of Aśoka_ (Chicago:
University of Chicago Press, 1959), p. 29. Thapar, pp. 40-41.
CHI, I, p. 502.

36. Lubac, _La rencontre du Bouddhisme et de l'Occident_, p. 16.

37. Thapar, p. 49.

38. Ibid., pp. 150 ff., for the content of Ashoka's teaching.

39. _CHI_, I, p. 585.

40. Pillar Edict II: Nikam and McKeon, p. 41.

41. Pillar Edict VII: Ibid., p. 40.

42. Thapar, pp. 167-168. The words _Dharma_ and _Dhamma_ both refer to
Ashoka's teaching.

43. Ibid., pp. 148-149, for various interpretations of Aśoka's relation to Buddhism.

44. Ibid., p. 149.

45. Ibid., pp. 146-147.

46. Lubac, p. 32. Lubac sees no evidence of Buddhist activity west
of India before the third century B.C. Ibid., p. 12.

47. Awadh K. Narain, _The Indo-Greeks_ (Oxford: Oxford University
Press, 1957), pp. 12-13. Narain concerns himself almost wholly with political history. For cultural and intellectual history, one must consult Tarn's _The Greeks in Bactria and India_.

48. Ibid., p. 130.

49. Ibid., pp. 131-132.

50. Narain sees the history of Bactria as "part of the history of
India and not of the Hellenistic states; they came, they saw,
but India conquered." _The Indo-Greeks_, p. 11. It is curious
that the Persian conquerors do not fall into the third part

of that paraphrase of Caesar.

51. Menander did not join a Buddhist order, but there is reason to believe that his sympathies transcended a mere intellectual fascination with the stimulating paradoxes of Nagasena. Ibid., pp. 97-99. See Edward Conze, trans., Buddhist Scriptures (Baltimore: Penguin Books, 1959), pp. 147-162, for the dialogue itself. Also of use is S. Lévi's "Le bouddhisme et les Grecs," Revue de l'histoire des Religions, 23 (1891), pp. 43-44.

52. Jack Finegan, The Archeology of World Religions: The Background of Primitivism, Zoroastrianism, Hinduism, and Jainism (Princeton: Princeton University Press, 1952), pp. 149-150. Finegan concludes that "although much of the legendary has gathered about the story of Thomas, the main facts of his work in north and south India may possibly be historical, and certainly the knowledge of, and contact with, India on the part of early Christianity is attested." Ibid., p. 150.

53. On the extent and contacts of the Kushan Empire, see J. Hackin, Nouvelles recherches archeologiques à Bégram (Paris, 1954). Also worth consulting is R. Ghirshman, Bégram, recherches archeologiques et historiques sur les Kouchans (Cairo, 1946).

54. On this general topic, see Osmand de Beauvoir Prilaux, "On the Indian Embassies to Rome from the Reign of Claudius to the Death of Justinian," Journal of the Royal Asiatic Society, 19 (1862), pp. 274-298, and Ibid., XX (1863), pp. 269-312.

55. Pliny Natural History xii, 18, 41. Most of this trade flowed from the west coast of India. According to M.P. Charlesworth, few Greco-Roman ships reached the eastern side of India before the advent of the second century A.D.. See his "Roman Trade with India: A Resurvey," in P.R. Coleman-North, ed., Studies in Roman Economic and Social History (Princeton: Princeton University Press, 1951).

56. Benjamin Rowland, The Art and Architecture of India (Baltimore: Penguin Books, 1953), pp. 72 ff. For a brief statement of controversies over the origin of the Gandhara style, see Frye, pp. 167-168.

57. Dio may have been aware of resemblances between the Homeric epics and the Mahabharata and the Ramayana, the two classic Indian epics, although a close look shows the similarities to be rather thin. Orations i.3.

58. The long era of Persian rule was equally favorable from the viewpoint of sheer contiguity. Rawlinson observes, however, that one might marvel at Greeks who learned anything from Persians, much less from Indians. Intercourse Between India and the Western World, p. 156. Commercial relations between India and the Roman World are discussed in E.H. Warmington, The Commerce Between the Roman Empire and India (Cambridge: Cambridge University Press, 1928. Warmington asks: "Did this traffic have any influence upon the institutions or habits of the Roman Empire and India? On the whole, the answer must be

33

no." Ibid., p. 319. He goes on to list traces of "Indian influence upon the West," i.e., Jatāka tales and "Indian elements" in Manichean, Gnostic, and Neo-Platonic doctrines, but no further elaboration of these "traces" is attempted.

59. See Anthony D'Costa, "Cosmas Indicopleustes as a Source of Indian History," Journal of Indian History, 132 (December, 1966), 693-698.

60. J.W. McCrindle, trans. and ed., The Christian Topography of Cosmas, An Egyptian Monk (London: Hakluyt Society, 1897), p. 23.

61. Lach, p. 20.

CHAPTER III

CLASSICAL KNOWLEDGE OF INDIA

The literary heritage of the ancient world has reached us in fragments. Very often the classical scholar or ancient historian resemble the paleontologist who must reconstruct a complex organism from an unimposing heap of bones. Actually, the task of the paleontologist is more likely to succeed, for it is less of a problem to spot a herbivore of uncertain species in a single tooth than to deduce from uneven literary remains the presence and influence of foreign ideas in the mental outlook of a civilization.

Those who are convinced of an historical and substantive connection between Indian, Greek, and Christian thought interpret classical and patristic literature in the most favorable light, as though not to do so would be repudiation of a great opportunity, or a mark of perverseness. Every suggestively mystical passage, every "otherworldly" idea, is loaded with its burden of affirmative inference and speculation. The objective of this chapter is to test the strength of the literary evidence bearing on the Indian hypothesis, with a view to showing that classical references to India cannot be used to establish beyond a reasonable doubt the infiltration of Buddhist or Hindu ideas into the minds of Greek philosophers or religious thinkers of the Hellenistic and post-Hellenistic periods. On the other hand, to be fair, neither can one establish definitely from the same evidence that such influences did not occur. At best, the literary evidence is inadquate and inconclusive, and provides only tenuous, gratuitous ammunition for the inflated speculations associated with the Indian hypothesis.

All significant classical references to India were translated and annotated by J.W. McCrindle in the last decades of the nineteenth century, a service which made easily available for study the main body of relevant literary material from Greek and Latin authors. A brief summary of the texts is in order.

First, Ancient India as Described by Megasthenes and Arrian (Calcutta, 1877). A text of major importance.

Second, The Commerce and Navigation of the Erythrean Sea (Calcutta, 1879). A navigator's manual, or Periplus, of the first century A.D. which describes coastal routes to India from Egypt. It constitutes also Part I of Arrian's Indika.

Third, Ancient India as Described by Ktêsias the Knidean (Calcutta, 1882). An influential text, although it is notoriously unreliable. It is Part II of the Indika.

35

Fourth, Ancient India as Described by Ptolemy (Calcutta, 1885). This is the portion of Claudius Ptolemy's Geography (2nd century A.D.) which deals with India, but his interest was limited strictly to cartographic and geographical analysis.

Fifth, The Invasion of India by Alexander the Great (rev. ed.; Westminster, 1893). Various accounts of Alexander in Afghanistan and India by Arrian, Q. Curtius, Diodorus Siculus, Plutarch, and Justinus.

Sixth, Ancient India as Described in Classical Literature (Westminster, 1901). This convenient volume contains material from a number of additional sources, including: Herodotus, The Persian Wars (ca. 468 B.C.); Strabo, Geography (ca. 7 B.C.); Pliny the Elder, Natural History (79 A.D.); Aelian, Peculiarities of Animals (ca. 220 A.D.), which describes some Indian fauna; The Itinerary of Alexander the Great, by an unknown author, written for the Roman emperor Constantine (d. 337 A.D.); Cosmas Indicopleustes, Christian Topography (6th century A.D.); Dionysius Perigêtes, A Description of the Whole World (ca. 300 A.D.), a poem of 1187 lines, 85 of which are on India; Philostratus, Life of Apollonius of Tyana (ca. 200 A.D.), which is about the career of a religious figure of the first century A.D.; Nonnus, Dionysiaka (5th century A.D.), an epic about Bacchus and his "conquest" of India; Diodorus Siculus, Bibliotheca, a "world history" written ca. 60-30 B.C. One also finds in this volume brief notices of India from Polybius, Pausanias, Frontinus, Plutarch, Ammianus Marcellinus, Appian, Dion Cassius, and a few Latin poets. Moreover, there are passages from works which have something to say about Brahmans and Buddhists. These include: Porphyry (d. ca. 305 A.D.), On Abstinence From Animal Food, which contains a valuable fragment from Bardesanes the Edesan (ca. 200 A.D.) on "gymnosophists"; Stobaeus, Physics (5th century A.D.), which contains still another fragment from Bardesanes; Dion Chrysostom (d. 117 A.D.), Orations, which has an enthusiastic description of Indian life and a brief mention of the Brahmans; The Pseudo-Kallisthenes /Romance History of Alexander/, written ca. 350 A.D., contains a brief work of Palladius: About the Nations of India and the Brachmans; this collection is rounded off with notices from Clement of Alexandria, Origin, St. Jerome, Archelaus, Kadrenus, Rufinus, and Hierokles.

One other source must be mentioned which Jean Filliozat believes is of major importance: St. Hippolytus's Refutation of All Heresies , written at Rome about 235 A.D., and containing a description of Brahmanical, or, more precisely, Upanishadic doctrine. Filliozat argues that the exactness of Hippolytus's knowledge justifies a reevaluation of the assumption that Brahmans guarded their secrets effectively and denied outsiders any clear understanding of Vedic or Upanishadic doctrines.[1]

Classical texts relevant to this inquiry are those which have some bearing on the presence of Indian ideas in Greek and Christian thought, especially in suitable time periods, say before the fourth century B.C., if Plato were to know of them, or during the first and second centuries A.D., if the shaping of Christian doctrine were to be affected by them. Furthermore, we are concerned only with those passages in which there is reference to, or discussion of, religious doctrines and philosophical concepts, which eliminates at once those passages about physical geography, climate, flora and fauna, mineral resources, urban life, grotesque and fantastic races, material culture, military affairs, government, secular customs, and so forth. This criterion of selection leaves very few texts for consideration, the most significant being those of Megasthenes, Strabo, Philostratus, and St. Hippolytus. There are some texts, not previously cited, which will be relevant in later chapters - e.g., Diogenes Laertius's Lives of Eminent Philosophers and Porphyry's biography of Plotinus - but for the issues at hand, the four sources just mentioned are the key ones. They place us in the fourth and first centuries B.C. and the first and third centuries A.D.

The most notable references to India in the ancient world, before the Christian era, fall roughly between 510 and 250 B.C. These were works by Greeks of Asia Minor: Scylax of Caryanda, Hecataeus of Miletus, Herodotus, and Ctesias of Cnidus; works by soldiers who accompanied Alexander on the eastern campaigns: Nearchus, Onesicritus, and Aristobulus; and various works by Greek ambassadors sent from Syria and Egypt to the court of Pataliputra in northwestern India during the Hellenistic age, the leading representative of this group being Megasthenes. The greatest part of all other classical allusions to India are third or fourth hand compared to these, which, in several instances, are themselves second hand. Contact with India after the third century B.C. did not result in a correction, refinement, or augmentation of knowledge found in treatises on India down to the time of Megasthenes. The earlier works were repeated mechanically and uncritically, as though cultures, peoples, governments, the earth itself, did not change with time. It is much as though our contemporary knowledge of India were based on information published in Henry Lord's A Discovery of the Sect of the Banians ... (1667) or Francois Bernier's Description des États du Grande Mogol (1669). There was no systematic effort to secure fresh information. When better knowledge became available through extended trade relations of the Roman Empire, it was not used to amplify or modify the older sources. Books written generations before "had become classical and shut out further references to reality. The books themselves perished, but their statements continued to be copied from writer to writer."[2]

Plato had been dead for nearly twenty years when Alexander marched into India, launching the first direct, extensive contact between Hellenic and Indian civilizations. Anyone prior to Aristotle who might have sought out less than firsthand knowledge of India would have been obliged to settle for wildly unreliable sources, if Megasthenes is taken for the standard of what was best among the treatises finally available.[3] For example, Hecataeus, Herodotus, and Ctesias were widely read in their time, but none had ever been to India. A vivid first impression of these early Greek "Indologists" is their propensity for swallowing fanciful tales whole, or for lumping them indiscriminately with relatively sane, credible information, leaving one to wonder if everything seen or heard is to be given equal weight.[4] Scylax reports the existence of oddities like the Skiapodes, people whose feet are large enough to function as sunshades, and the Otoliknoi, people who wrap themselves in their outsized ears.[5] He does not claim to have witnessed these bizarre phenomena, but seems, nevertheless, to have accepted stories about them in good faith. Both Hecataeus and Herodotus relied on Scylax for their own accounts of India, yet they were in no position to judge from independent observation, or even corroborative evidence, which parts of his book were to be trusted. It is not much help that Hecataeus and Herodotus were honest logographers (i.e., accurate reporters of stories), or that Herodotus explicitly warns his readers that he does not believe everything he is told. It is the credibility of the stories themselves which is at issue.

Uncritical, misleading nonsense swarms in the work of Ctesias as well, but he had less justification.[6] He lived in Persia for years, had access to the imperial court, wrote a history of Persia, and had ample opportunity to verify the truth of weird stories. On top of this, he was trained in medical science at one of the brilliant schools of the age, located in Cnidus, his birthplace. Given these circumstances, one might reasonably expect from him an uncommonly developed respect for fact and a critical attitude, yet it is this same man who reported having seen at the Persian court a creature (Martikhora) much like a lion, with a human face, and a barb-throwing tail. Some scholars have made brave attempts to rescue Ctesias from a bad reputation, finding shadowy realities in his fables, and noting valuable material in his work on the geography, material culture, and customs of northwestern India.[7] This solicitude is understandable, for Ctesias "marked ... the extent of the knowledge gained regarding India before the time of Alexander," and his was the only systematic treatise accessible to the Greeks.[8] The man's deliberate mendacity prompted E.R. Bevan's belief that "his contribution seems to have been the most worthless of all those which went to make up the classical tradition," a harsh but deserved condemnation anticipated long ago by Aristotle.[9] If the Indica had been laughed out of court by the ancients, this critique would be superfluous. As it turned out, according to Sarton,

the _Indica_ "was for a long time the main source of Hindu lore in
the West."[10] The phrase "Hindu lore" must be taken casually, for
the work is quite innocent of significant comment on religious or
philosophical subjects.[11]

Out of three prominent men who wrote memoirs after Alexander's
conquests, two have failed to sustain good reputations for report-
ing.[12] Onesicritus, pilot for Admiral Nearchus on the Indus journey homeward when Alexander split his forces, is suspected of arbitrary untruthfulness.[13] Aristobulus, another general officer,
may have known a good deal, but waited until old age to set down
his recollections; moreover, what was probably a flagging memory
had to fight its way through a literary style swayed by rhetorical
fashions of the time.

Naive, uncritical, and untruthful writing about India was not
without its exceptions. Herodotus and Nearchus were less suscepti-
ble to the fantastic, and certainly less inclined to lie outright,
than either Scylax or Ctesias. But even in surviving narratives
uncluttered by allusions to monsters and marvels, one finds not
the slightest hint of conversance with Indian thought.[14] Among
all these writers, with the qualified exception of Megasthenes,
the usual fare seldom rises above a rudimentary assortment of more
or less accurate facts about geography, customs, war, politics,
and exotica. Of all these early reports, that of Herodotus is perhaps the most objective and fair-minded.[15] But he extracted his
information from the _Periodos Gēs_ /Description of the Earth/ of
Hecataeus, and in the midst of valuable material on the size, popu-
louness, and ethnic diversity of India, he has nothing to say on
the topic of ideas. It seems that the Indians whose ways are described were rude peoples inhabiting frontier regions, not the more
cultivated population of the interior, which may account in part
for the great traveler's ignorance of a luxuriant Indian mythology.

The fullest, most reliable account of India written by a Greek
in the ancient world was the work of a Hellenistic diplomat. Megasthenes was at the royal court of Pataliputra from 302 to 291 B.C.
as the emissary of Seleucus Nicator.[16] Although his book appeared
too late to influence Greek thought down to the time of Aristotle
(d. 322 B.C.), its contents illuminate what an intelligent Greek
with good opportunities might have learned about the Indian mind.
The narrative covers a lot of ground on the topics of law, custom,
government, social organization, and war. Most pertinent, however,
is the material on philosophic doctrines and religious practices,
which is important enough to quote in full.

> The Brahmans have the greatest prestige, since they
> have a more consistent dogmatic system. As soon as they
> are conceived in the womb, men of learning take charge
> of them. These go to the mother and ostensibly sing a

charm tending to make the birth happy for the mother
and child, but in reality convey certain virtuous
counsels and suggestions; the women who listen most
willingly are held to be the most fortunate in child-
bearing. After birth, the boys pass from one set of
teachers to another in succession, the standard of
teachers rising with the age of the boy. The philoso-
pers spend their days in a grove near the city, under
the cover of an enclosure of due size, on beds of
leaves and skins, living sparsely, practicing celibacy and abstinence from flesh-food, listening to
grave discourses and admitting such others to the discussion as may wish to take part. He who listens is
forbidden to speak, or even to clear his throat or
spit, on pain of being ejected from the company that
very day, as incontinent. When each Brahman has lived
in this fashion thirty-seven years, he departs to his
own property, and lives now in greater freedom and
luxury, wearing muslin robes and some decent ornaments
of gold on his hands and ears, eating flesh, so long
as it is not the flesh of domestic animals, but abstaining from pungent and highly-seasoned food. They marry
as many wives as possible, to secure good progeny; for
the larger the number of wives, the larger the number
of good children is likely to be; and since they have
no slaves, they depend all the more upon the ministra-
tions of their children, as the nearest substitute.
The Brahmans do not admit their wives to their philosophy. If the wives are wanton, they might divulge
mysteries to the profane; if they are good, they might
leave their husbands, since no one who has learnt to
look with contempt upon pleasure and pain, upon life
and death, will care to be under another's control.
The chief subject on which the Brahmans talk is death;
for this present life, they hold, is like the season
passed in the womb, and death for those who have cultivated philosophy is birth into the real, the happy,
life. For this reason they follow an extensive discipline
to make them ready for death. None of the accidents,
they say, which befall men are good or evil. If they
were, one would not see the same things causing grief to
some and joy to others - men's notions being indeed like
dreams - and the same men grieved by something which at
another moment they will turn and welcome. Their teaching about Nature is in parts naive; for they are more
admirable in what they do than in what they say, and
the theoretic proofs on which they base their teaching
are mostly fable. In many points, however, their teaching
agrees with that of the Greeks - for instance, that the
world has a beginning and an end in time, and that its

40

shape is spherical; that the Deity, who is its Gover-
nor and Maker, interpenetrates the whole; that the
first principles of the universe are different, but that
water is the principle from which the order of the world
has come to be; that, beside the four elements, there is
a fifth substance, of which the heavens and the stars
are made; that the earth is established at the centre
of the universe. About generation and the soul their
teaching shows parallels to the Greek doctrines, and on
many other matters. Like Plato, too, they interweave
fables about the immortality of the soul and the judgments inflicted in the other world, and so on.

As to the Sarmanes, the most highly honored are
called "Forest-dwellers." They live in the forests on
leaves and wild fruits, and wear clothes made of the
bark of trees, abstaining from cohabitation and wine.
The kings call them to their side, sending messengers to
enquire of them about the causes of events, and use their
mediation in worshipping and supplicating the gods.
After the Forest-dwellers, the order of Sarmanes second
in honor is the medical - philosophers, as it were, on
the special subject of Man. These live sparely (sic),
not in the open air indeed, but on rice and meal, which
every one of whom they beg and who shows them hospitali-
ty gives them. They know how by their simples (sic) to
make marriages fertile and how to procure male children
or female children, as may be desired. Their treatment
is mainly by diet and not by medicines. And of medi-
.cines they attach greater value to those applied exter-
nally than to drugs. Other remedies, they say, are liable to do more harm than good. These too, like the
Brahmans, train themselves to endurance, both active
and passive, so much that they·will maintain one posture without moving for a whole day. Other orders of
Sarmanes are diviners·and masters of incantations and
those who are versed in the lore and the ritual concerning the dead, and go through the villages and the
town, begging. Others again there are of a higher and
finer sort, though even these will allow themselves to
make use of popular ideas about hell, of those ideas at
any rate which seem to make for godliness and purity
of life. In the case of some Sarmanes, women also are
permitted to share in the philosophic life, on the condition of observing sexual continence like the men.[17]

These fragments of Megasthenes may be taken as the apogee of
the ancient world's knowledge of Indian thought before the second
century A.D. What can one learn from them? How do they measure up
both as a source of information and insight with regard to ideas?

First, one might note the external, crudely descriptive character of Megasthenes' observations, which in their brevity can hardly be said to scratch the surface of a complex and ancient religio-philosophical tradition. Such a sparse recitation of facts, unsupported by extended comment and analysis, is not likely to have had more impact than the arousal of curiosity, even had the material been available to educated Greeks as early as the sixth century B.C.

Second, Megasthenes reveals his outlook as a good Greek by saying that "their (the Brāhmans) teaching about Nature is in parts naive," and that "the theoretic proofs on which they base their teaching are mostly fable." The Greek taste was for argument and proof in philosophy.[18] Brahmanical reverence for the ultimate authority of the Vedas, coupled with the insistence that students be properly reticent, submissive, and pliable, would have struck most thoughtful Greeks as a poor way to seek truth.

Third, Megasthenes does not discuss cosmological and metaphysical notions on their own merits, which implies a shallow grasp of Brahmanical thought, but rather picks on those beliefs having a casual resemblance to certain Greek ideas. Godfrey Barber is close to the truth in the judgment that "his Greek background in philosophy and myth made him an unreliable observer, inventing parallels between two different cultures."[19]

Perhaps Megasthenes knew more than his predecessors about the religion and thought of India (like them, however, he describes monsters with a straight face), but he does not seem to have known much or to have known it well, in spite of his relative superiority. There are remarks on frugality, self-immolation, vegetarianism, austerities, self-control, celibacy, readiness for death, the indifference of good and evil for man, mendicancy, sorcery (yogic powers?), and other such matters, but no mention of Ātman, Brahman, samādhi, Nirvāṇa, māya (though it is implied vaguely in the notion of the body as a prison), or the nature of reality as one without a second, an indissoluble unity. On a more general level, as Dahlquist argues, some important inferences can be drawn from Megasthenes concerning the status of Indian religion and mythology. For example, Hinduism had not yet coalesced, Krishna had not yet become a prominent figure among the revered deities, the avatar concept may have been unknown, Indra had not been displaced as yet by the trimurti, and the basic plans of the Mahabharata and the Puranas were not fixed.[20]

An assumption that Greeks were well-informed about Indian thought must survive the skepticism of Strabo, probably the best informed man of his era. His account of India in the Geography brings together fragments from a large group of earlier writers with astuteness and measured criticism. Megasthenes, Onesicritus,

42

Ctesias, Nearchus, and others are compared with one another to emphasize the conflict of opinion. Strabo does not accept the word of a source at face value, and says that certain "statements of Megasthenes are mythical and refuted by many writers."[21] Since Megasthenes was a leading authority on India, and since the more important fragments are preserved in Strabo, his judgment carries substantial weight. Although second, third, or even fourth hand, Strabo's description of India is the best, in a critical sense, to survive the ancient world; his clear rationality would accept only what was "nearest to credibility."[22] He is informative about the sources extant at the close of the Hellenistic age, and writes in a manner that is fair-minded, comprehensive, discreet, and erudite. Strabo was no mere physical geographer. His writings sought to convey a total picture of each region discussed, and he was attracted uncommonly to philosophy, history, archeology, and human custom. How, then, did Strabo assess the state of knowledge about India in the latter half of the first century A.D.?

He urges the reader

> to hear accounts of this country with indulgence, for
> not only is it farthest away from us, but not many of
> our people have seen it; and even those who have seen
> it, have seen only parts of it, and the greater part
> of what they say is from hearsay; and even what they
> saw they learned on a hasty passage with an army through
> the country.[23]

There are examples of men together on the same expedition who witnessed much the same events and sights, or in other ways had similar experiences, "yet all frequently contradict one another. But if they differ thus about what was seen, what must we think of what they report from hearsay?"[24] These reservations are not intended only for Greek writers of earlier times: "Moreover, most of those who have written anything about this region in much later times, and those who sail there at the present time, do not present any accurate information either."[25]

Strabo died around 21 A.D., and was working on a full revision of the Geography as late as 18 A.D. Hence we can assume reasonably enough that he would have revised Book XV if information of unusual value had come to his attention.[26] Most of his research was done at the famed library of Alexandria, the scholarly crossroads of the ancient world, where discussion and consultation with resident or itinerant ment of learning might accompany the study of manuscripts. If gymnosophists or Brahman writings were to be found at Alexandria, is it likely that a man as thorough as Strabo would be unaware of them? This point is a needed corrective to the suggestion that a rich collection of eastern manuscripts may have perished with the library, thus leaving posterity no more than a

43

hint of vanished oriental treasures pregnant with wisdom.

The third promising source is the colorful biography of Apollonius the Tyanian, composed by Flavius Philostratus (ca. 175-245 A.D.) for the philosophical minded Julia Domna, wife of Septimius Severus and mother of Caracalla, shortly before 217 A.D. Philostratus was a clever rhetorician and esthete with a taste for antiquarianism. His philosophical interests were shallow but lively, and G.R.S. Mead, a proponent of the existence of a universal spiritual reality, warns his readers "to expect a sketch of the appearance of a thing by one outside, rather than an exposition of the thing itself from one within."[27] Philostratus based his account on some letters attributed to Apollonius, a memoir by Damis, one of Apollonius' followers, and a mass of legend, anecdote, and tradition, all culled from the "archives" of cities visited by Apollonius. The method used to write the biography was not critical in any sense; it was frankly rhetorical in the mode of the time, which means the author wished to tell an attractive, edifying story by elaborating the source material stylistically, even to the point of inventing speeches. As a result, it is hard to separate the hand of Philostratus from his sources.[28]

The career of Apollonius spanned most of the first century A.D. He died or disappeared shortly after the assassination of Domitian in 96 A.D. If one ignores the element of romance in Philostratus, whose writing abounds with wonders, miracles, and psychic feats, Apollonius can be acknowledged as a genuine celebrity among the humble and lordly folk of his time. His reputation was for prodigious travels, philosophic-religious eclecticism, eloquent sermons, moral rectitude, and longevity. He was at once ritualist and sage, reformer and moralist. He had a devoted following and wrote treatises on sacrifice, divination, and Pythagoras. Much the same description applies to a number of pagan philosophers and wise men who flourished in the first century A.D. Apollonius is of special interest because of his alleged association with Indian seers and holy men during a visit to India. If it is granted that such a visit took place, though for how long or how extensively remain unknown, the question remains as to the impact on his own views and the temper of his age.

A key to understanding Apollonius can be found in the context of his philosophical purpose and style. The close of the Hellenistic period and the advent of the Pax Romana found Mediterranean civilization afflicted with pessimism, doubt, and a malaise of irresolution. The balanced humanism of Pericles, Sophocles, and Aristotle, the organic ideal of the polis, the pursuit of manifold excellence - all of this no longer seemed an achievable ideal. A loss of confidence in the possibilities of creative fulfillment in this world, helped along by the spectacle of Roman conquest and brutality, sent people in droves to the mystery religions, which offered indubitable revelations, refuge from earthly shocks, and comforting assurance of personal immortality. Philosophical inquiry, secular moral discipline, social consciousness, and the study of physical nature receded before the alluring vision of a New Jerusalem. A putative temple of the spirit loomed amid cults of the Ancient Near East and Greece. Unearthly hopes were bred in Syria, Babylon, Egypt, Asia Minor, and golden Hellas to counter the anxiety of an "increase in sensitiveness, a failure of nerve."[29]

Parallel with this ardor for religious certitude and salvation, corrupted as it was by superstition, magic, and divination, there developed a philosophical movement which sought to fortify mind and spirit against adversity. The solution of Epicurean, Stoic, and Cynic doctrines to the capriciousness of life was to transform men into fortresses of discipline, forebearance, and resignation. Rigorous moral training and philosophic wisdom, combined with a reduction of material and psychological needs, would prepare a good man to endure with serenity a bad world, by making him relatively impervious to pain, disappointment, persecution, and death. Such was the philosophic mission of Epicurus, Zeno, Seneca, Epictetus, and a score of lesser teachers. Greek thought abandoned theoretical inquiry for practical morality; metaphysical reflection deferred to ethical training; thinkers became preachers occupied with the diagnosis and treatment of ruffled souls. Dill is right that "it has perhaps been too little recognized that in the first and second centuries there was a great propaganda of pagan morality running parallel to the evangelism of the Church."[30]

Apollonius of Tyana expressed freely the spirit of both revivals: religious and philosophical. He was a missionary with a foot in each camp, a colorful representative of the first century Greco-Roman ethos. The beliefs he held before and after going to India do not show much alteration. Philostratus elaborates on his Indian adventure, yet, according to Mead,

> what Apollonius heard and saw there, following the invariable custom in such circumstances, he told no one, not even Damis, except what could be derived from the following enigmatical sentence: "I saw men dwelling of the earth (sic) and yet not on it, defended on all sides, yet without any defense, and yet possessed of nothing but what all possess."[31]

Onesicritus or Megasthenes could have made the same observation, probably with less opaqueness and mystification. There is not much reason to infer from Philostratus or any other source that Apollonius succumbed to the lure of Indian thought. In doctrine and temperament, philosophical style and religious bent, he nelonged securely in his Greco-Roman environment. The influence of Pythagoreanism accounts for his vegetarianism, linen garb, long hair, habits of abstinence, and "system of wisdom."[32] Divination, visions, miraculous healing, and communication with the spirit world were commonplace with "holy men" of the ancient world, who were expected as a matter of course to possess supernatural powers. Apollonius was no exception.[33] His dietary preferences seem to have originated less with a belief in reincarnation than with a fear of pollution from animal flesh. He refused meat because "it was unclean," and preferred fruit because of its purity.[34] Like other philosophical missionaries of his time, Apollonius shunned theoretical discussions and chose instead to discourse on the efficacy of gentleness (even to the beasts), self-restraint, forgiveness of injuries, self-examination, and philosophy as a medicine of the soul, a path to goodness.[35] He asked in his prayers for righteousness among men and obedience to the laws.[36] In spite of this religious eclecticism, Apollonius was in many respects identifiable as a good Greek, especially in those passages of Philostratus where he defends Greek deeds and heroes.[37] These manifestations of Greekness, however, may be attributable to the unmistakable Grecophilism of Philostratus.[38] Apollonius' surviving letters and sayings often express stoic sentiments, as in a letter to P. Valerius Asiaticus on the death of his son. His meditation on death as a transition from becoming to being is full of stoic consolation.

> It would be a disgrace for such a man as you to owe
> your cure to time and not to reason, for time makes
> even common people cease from grief ... If there is a
> law in things, and there is one, and it is God who
> has appointed it, the righteous man will have no wish
> to try to change good things, for such a wish is self-
> ishness, and counter to the law, but he will think
> that all that comes to pass is a good thing.[39]

This passage might have been written on the Roman frontier by Marcus Aurelius.[40] When Apollonius spoke to the grieved and distressed, he spoke, whatever the "wisdom" he absorbed from India, in the context and language of Greek philosophy, not that of the Upanishads.

The writings of Apollonius show no palpable Brahmanical or Buddhist influence. Could it be that his Indian lore was transmitted in oral teaching to the "Apollonians," an intimate circle of disciples and companions? Might these followers have heard from their master the secret teaching of the Brahmans, preserved it, and passed it on in their turn? Unfortunately for this viewpoint, Apollonius left no school, and instructed no one to perpetuate his teachings or mission. He was a striking religious individualist, quite indifferent to organized religion and creedal tradition.[41] The most distinguished of his disciples, Musonius, spoke and behaved like a philosophic missionary of the Hellenistic age, arming himself with self-knowledge and righteousness, and exhorting others to do the same.[42] Only the faintest echo of India comes from him.

The last source inviting comment is the provocative treatise of Saint Hippolytus. His Refutation of All Heresies, long known as "Philosophumena," was for some time attributed to Origin (185-254 A.D.), though mistakenly.[43] One of the refutations, embodied in a laconic text, deals with a heretical sect called the "Encratites": That is the error, the vain opinion of the Encratites and how they have established their dogmas, not after the Sacred Scriptures, but out of themselves, and after the gymnosophists of India."[44]

The Encratites were disciples of the Assyrian, or perhaps the Syrian, Tatien (ca. 165 A.D.). Their doctrines are confidently declared by Filliozat to be Upanishadic, and he suggests specifically the Maitri Upanishad as the source used by Hippolytus to prepare his refutation.[45] In general, Hippolytus expounds "gymnosophist" ideas about the illusory status of the phenomenal world (māyā) the necessity of austerities if one is to apprehend intuitively the oneness of the individual soul (Atman) with the universal soul (Brahman), and the undifferentiated, nameless character of ultimate reality.[46] In this scheme of things, there is no place for personal salvation through the intercession of a divine being. For Hippolytus, the person of Christ was obliterated by the assertion that "this whole world is Brahma," or that "in the universal dissolution he (man) attains the unity of the Person - yea, of the Person."[47]

Unfortunately, the specific source consulted by Hippolytus is not mentioned in his text. Megasthenes was used, but his book shows no awareness of the mystic formula "That art Thou." Whether or not one believes that Hippolytus read the Maitri Upanishad must depend on how persuasive one finds the elucidation of doctrinal parallels in Filliozat's article. While he seems to have established a convincing parallel, I am left uneasy and skeptical without a visible text of unequivocal Indian origin. More to the point, however, is this question: where did the Encratites come by their ideas, for Hippolytus may have had no other "source" than familiarity with the tenets of a pagan or heretical sect? Filliozat argues for a transmission of ideas from Brāhmans of the Deccan.[48] Hippolytus refers to the "Tagabena" River of that region. But the Deccan is not mentioned in earlier sources, and Brāhmans of northern India were notably cryptic and reticent about the communication of higher truths to foreigners of uncertain motive. Filliozat concedes that for the period down perhaps to the first century A.D., classical writers display little understanding of Brahmanical ideas, a long historical association notwithstanding.[49] On the other hand, the opening of southern India to extensive Roman trade enlarged significantly the opportunities for intellectual as well as material commerce. It was the Brāhmans residing along the Tagabena who were the source of religious and philosophical doctrines infiltrating Rome in the first half of the second century A.D., and maybe even earlier. The sure presence of Upanishadic notions at Rome signifies a breakthrough for scholars long receptive to the hypothesis of serious

exchanges between India and the West, but hampered by the elusive-
ness of respectable evidence.

Let us summarize Filliozat's case for a breakthrough and ask
what it means for the viability of the Indian hypothesis.

(1) Considering the drift and content of Hippolytus' refutation, it is no longer reasonable to deny the currency of authentic
Brahmanical ideas at Rome in the second century A.D.

(2) One must admit also the existence of a sect professing
doctrines identical with some of those found in the Upanishads, a
sect well known to a Father of the Christian Church.

(3) One can no longer maintain, as was so long the case, that
Brāhmans jealously guarded their spiritual knowledge as a class
secret. Brāhmans of southern India, whatever their intentions, were
unable to check the diffusion of esoteric doctrines beyond their
immediate circle, or beyond the borders of India, a fact supported
by recent identification of an Upanishad in Indonesia. In any case,
the image of the tight-lipped Brāhman is probably overdrawn. The
Chāndogya Upanishad says instruction should not be witheld from individuals merely because they lack socially acceptable parentage;
a sincere desire for truth is a higher recommendation than pedi-
gree.[50] To clinch the issue, Brāhmans had no monopoly on philosophical parts of the Vedas. "Sophists" were conversant with mystical
doctrines while being more accessible for questions and discussion.

(4) Thus a movement of Indian thought into the Greco-Roman
world must have had greater latitude in the first two centuries of
the Christian era, a crucial period for the gestation of the Judao-
Christian tradition.

(5) All of the foregoing ought to encourage a reappraisal of
Philostratus' Life of Apollonius of Tyana. Apollonius may well
have known a good deal about Indian thought through direct or indirect contact with Brahmans of the Deccan.

(6) Most cogent, however, is the implication for Neo-Platonic
mysticism, for the long suspected influence of Indian thought on
the Enneads is at once simplified and reinforced. Plotinus may have
had access to the unknown source used by Hippolytus.[51] If so, the
consequences may have been momentous, for much Greek philosophy entered Christianity through the medium of Plotinus.

Clearly the Refutation of Hippolytus is the most impressive
of all extant classical sources relating to Indian thought. But
how great a burden of inference and plausible speculation can it
support? Points one through four might be conceded without necessitating acceptance of the inferences contained in points five and

six. Something is known about Indian ideas at Rome in the second century A.D. Extrapolation backward into the first century from a few pages of the Refutation has some justication, but not much, because there is really so little to go on. Hippolytus ought to make one cautious about rejecting out of hand some awareness of Indian thought in religious circles of the first century, but there is no compelling reason to modify or abandon judgments reached earlier on the Indian material in Strabo and Apollonius. Since Hippolytus wrote well after the beginnings of the Christian movement, his unknown source has no demonstrable relevance for the mainstream of Greek philosophy and religion, or for Christianity before Plotinus. Hippolytus' purpose was to refute doctrines of the Encratites. Doubtless his treatise had the approval of other prelates and was circulated to discourage theological error. Obviously he was hostile to unitary theories in philosophy and religion; one can learn from Adolf Harnack's History of Dogma that other theologians shared this antipathy for uncompromising oneness.

The question of Plotinus presents greater difficulties. His residence at Rome (ca. 245 A.D.) coincides roughly with the composition of the Refutation. But it is not known that he discovered the Upanishads in the manner of Hippolytus, whatever that was, only that he lived in the same city about the same time. It is enchanting to visualize Plotinus perusing an Indian text (presumably in Greek or Latin translation), conversing with a learned "Sophist" steeped in Indian religious lore, and then undertaking the transformation of Greek philosophy in light of his own mystical experiences, confirmed or even inspired by the transcendental wisdom of the Upanishads. Putting enchantment aside, the relationship of his thought to Indian ideas is an important issue for the later development of Christian theology, and the Refutation of Hippolytus unquestionably gives the issue a fresh dimension. But it proves absolutely nothing, and even Filliozat admits that the Hippolytean critique is too flimsy to have swept Plotinus off his feet into a foreign view of ultimate reality; whatever its source, his view appears to be out of line with the central march of Greek metaphysical speculation. More will be said on this topic in a later chapter.[52]

In summary, classical sources lack the necessary abundance, variety, and credibility to justify positive inferences about the transmission of Indian myth and thought to Greek or Christian sages of the ancient world. There is enough, perhaps, to allow a bit of diverting speculation, but diverting speculation should not be confused with probable inference.[53]

1. Jean Filliozat, "La doctrine des brâhmanes d'après saint Hippo-
   lyte," Revue de l'histoire des Religions (July-December, 1945),
   59-91.
2. CHI, I, p. 425.
3. George Sarton, A History of Science: Hellenistic Science and
   Culture in the Last Three Centuries B.C. (Cambridge: Harvard
   University Press, 1959), p. 197.
4. "In fact, in speaking of India or any other little-known country, a writer in these days had to drag in all that popular
   legend associated with it or he stood little chance of being
   listened to." Mead, p. 60.
5. Scylax of Caryanda was a Greek sea captain who sailed down the
   Indus to its mouth at the command of Darius the Great (522-
   486 B.C.) and wrote subsequently the first Greek book that we
   know of on India. The Periplus of Scylax was a later compila-
   tion of ca. 360-347 B.C. Herodotus alludes to him: Histories
   iv.44. On all of this, see George Sarton, A History of Science:
   Ancient Science Through the Golden Age of Greece (Cambridge:
   Harvard University Press, 1952), pp. 298 f, 522-523. Although
   Scylax is the earliest navigator of the Indus on record, Sarton believes it "certain that many people had sailed down the
   Indus, across the Arabian Sea, and up the Red Sea before the
   fifth century." Ibid., p. 299.
6. Ctesias of Cnidus (ca. 400 B.C.) wrote two works: Persica and
   Indica, parts of which survived in later summaries, chiefly
   that of Photius of Constantinople (ca. 858 A.D.). Ibid., p.
   327.
7. See Lassen's "Revue of the Reports of Ktêsias Concerning India," in McCrindle, Ktêsias the Knidean, pp. 65 ff.
8. Ibid., p. 91.
9. CHI, I, p. 397. Aristotle, History of Animals viii. 28.
10. Sarton, Ancient Science Through the Golden Age, p. 329.
11. Filliozat is content to leap beyond untrustworthy sources: "if
    the work of Ktesias is fantastic, it does not follow that noth-
    ing serious could have been brought from India." The Classical
    Doctrine of Indian Medicine, p. 246. One must ask, without re-
    liable sources how can it be known that something "serious"
    passed to the classical world from India, and how does one dis-
    cover what that something was?
12. Sarton discusses the five ancient histories of Alexander's cam-
    paigns which have survived. The most important is Arrian's,
    from the second century A.D. It was based largely on Megas-
    thenes, Nearchus, and Aristobulus. Sarton, Hellenistic Science
    and Culture, p. 173.
13. On Alexander's captains and their reports of India, see CHI, I,
    pp. 398 ff. A quaint but still useful book is William Vincent's
    The Voyage of Nearchus From the Indus to the Euphrates (London:
    1797). The Oxford Classical Dictionary (Oxford: Oxford Univers-

ity Press, 1949), p. 600, cited hereafter as OCD, refers to Onesicritus' "honest and trustworthy chronicle."

14. Tarn says that "the Brahman was the natural enemy of the Greek invader," because the Greeks were associated or even identified with the Kshatriyas, the warrior-administrators of the four tiered Indian class system, with whom the Brahmans were in competition for social primacy. The Greeks in Bactria and India, pp. 173 ff. This point is worth noting. Since the Brahman priests were traditional custodians of religious texts and secrets, it seems unlikely that they would communicate freely with what appeared to be Greek counterparts of their immediate rivals for prestige and power.

15. Herodotus Histories iii. 38, 94, 98, 106, and vii. 65, 86.

16. McCrindle believes that "the work of Megasthenes - in so far as it is part of Greek literature and of Greek and Roman learning - is, as it were, the culmination of the knowledge which the ancients ever acquired of India." Megasthenes and Arrian, p. 27.

17. Quoted in CHI, I, pp. 419 ff. Cf. Strabo Geography xv. 59-60. For references to philosophy and religion in Strabo, see Ibid. xv. 58-66, 68, 70-71, 73.

18. Indian mythology is renowned for its tangled luxuriance, which stands well apart in style from Greek mythology. Martin Nilsson observes "how the distinguishing feature of the Greek mind, its rationalism, led to a selection, a purification, and a remodelling of the too fantastic elements in the folk-tale material." A History of Greek Religion (2nd ed. rev.; New York: W.W. Norton and co., 1964), p. 49. In a thorough and important book on Megasthenes, Allan Dahlquist defends the Greek ambassador's impartiality: "The suspicion that Megasthenes has been guilty of some form of interpretatio graeca has shown itself to be entirely unjustified." Megasthenes and the Indian Religion: A Study in Motives and Types (Stockholm, 1962), p. 288. While Dahlquist's work forces a closer look at Megasthenes' reports, the overall vindication seems a bit overdrawn. Even if one can safely eliminate his Greek bias as an intervening factor, the question of how much he knew and how well he knew it, in the realm of ideas, remains up in the air. Dahlquist has promised a second book on Megasthenes and Indian philosophy, which could open up a new perspective.

19. OCD, p. 553. Cf. Strabo Geography xv. 59.

20. Dahlquist, pp. 285-288. On the trustworthiness of Megasthenes, see T.S. Brown, "The Reliability of Megasthenes," American Journal of Philology, 76 (1955). Cf. Dahlquist, p. 26.

21. Strabo Geography xv. 58.

22. Ibid. xv. 10.

23. Ibid. xv. 2.

24. Ibid.

25 Ibid. xv. 3.

26. Sarton, Hellenistic Science and Culture, p. 421.

27. Mead, Apollonius of Tyana, p. 56. See also Osmand de Beauvoir Priaulx, "The Indian Travels of Apollonius of Tyana," Journal of the Royal Asiatic Society, 17 (1860), 70-105.
28. Mead, p. 61.
29. Gilbert Murray, Five Stages of Greek Religion (New York: Doubleday Anchor Books, n.d.), p. 119.
30. Samuel Dill, Roman Society From Nero to Marcus Aurelius (New York: Meridean Books, 1956), p. 346.
31. Mead, p. 86. Philostratus The Life of Apollonius of Tyana iii. 15; vi. 11.
32. Ibid. i. 32.
33. Mead, pp. 110-118.
34. Philostratus Life of Apollonius i. 8.
35. Ibid. iv. 3; vii. 31.
36. Ibid. iv. 40.
37. Ibid. iv. 30, 44; v. 22.
38. Mead, p. 143.
39. Quoted in Mead, p. 151.
40. Marcus Aurelius Meditations ii. 3; v. 8; xii. 31.
41. Mead, p. 130.
42. Dill, pp. 248-249.
43. Hippolytus, Philosophumena, or Refutation of All Heresies, English trans. F. Legge (London, 1921). For the Greek text, see Hippolytus, Philosophumena, sive Haeresitum Omnium Confutatio, ed. Patrice Cruice with Latin translation (Paris, 1860).
44. Quoted in Filliozat, "La doctrine des brâhmanes ... ," 70.
45, Ibid., 79.
46. Ibid., 65-78, for Filliozat's analysis of Upanishadic themes in Hippolytus.
47. Maitri Upanishad 4.6., in Robert E. Hume, The Thirteen Principal Upanishads (2nd ed. rev.; Oxford: Oxford University Press, 1931). All subsequent citations from the Upanishads are from Hume.
48. Filliozat, "La doctrine des brâhmanes ... ," 81.
49. Ibid., 60. I believe Filliozat to be mistaken in holding that Strabo would have passed up philosophical information, but he is right about Diodorus Siculus and Arrian.
50. Chāndogya Upanishad 4.4.
51. Filliozat, "la doctrine des brâhmanes ... ," 83.
52. Ibid.
53. In a valuable discussion of relevant texts, R.C. Majumdar concludes "that we must dismiss from our mind the notion that the statements of classical writers have any special claim to be regarded as true or authentic, and based on ascertained facts. In particular, the older generations that preceeded Strabo were ... very uncritical, and therefore much less reliable than writers like Strabo and Arrian." The Classical Accounts of India (Calcutta, 1960), p. xxv. In a convenient summary of what is to be found in classical texts on the subjects of religion and philosophy, Baijnath Puri says "we must doubt the aptness

and inclination of the Greeks to learn of the Orientals." <u>India in Classical Greek Writings</u> (Ahmedabad, 1963), p. 259. The summary is on pages 55-98.

CHAPTER IV

THE LURE OF PARALLELS: MONISM AND
PLURALISM, INDIAN AND GREEK

Most of the classical writing about India which has survived
is superficial, externalized, patchy, and bereft of instructive
philosophical content. The rare exceptions must be used with care,
lest a few helpful passages be overworked and exaggerated out of
all proportion to their worth. It is doubtful that Greek literature
on India inspired varied elements of Greek religion and philosophy,
or that fitful visits of Greeks to regions of the Indus provoked a
spiritual revolution back home.

The independent cohesion of the Greek intellectual tradition
from Homer to Aristotle is not seriously threatened by its alleged
"parallels" with Indian thought. Reminders are needed that parallels are often misleading.[1] In philosophy, science, and religion,
genuine parallels may shed light on generically related historical
experiences, convergent lines of thought within different cultural
frameworks, or similar but independent conceptual developments. It
is the growing mass of loose parallels which is weakening the fibre
of thought, a tedious cataloguing of parallels in comparative religion and philosophy which has bordered on the obsessive. When
known historical relations between societies are dim, when textual
evidence falters, the student in search of primal truths understood
by people everywhere turns with relief to the paralells. Unfortunately, the source of this relief is dubious. .

In the first place, the intricate context of sophisticated
conceptual systems should take precedence over any single idea in
them. Parallels between ideas which have been wrenched from context are more often than not illusory. Greek and Chinese "humanism,"
for instance, manifest a cluster of similar features when they are
removed from the respective historical and valuational contexts of
Greek and Chinese civilizations.[2] More rigorous analysis would show
that the two humanisms do not have the same consequences for either
reflection or action; they do not reflect, in Radhakrishnan's epitome, the "same view of life." The chasm between apparent and real
affinities is more emphatic in the case of Indian (Brahmanical and
Buddhist) and Greek ideas. A host of ostensibly neat parallels between Indian, Greek, and Christian thought is due to a careless
handling of context, stemming either from obliviousness or inad-
vertence. This freewheeling methodology, ironically enough, con-
ceals a marked positivistic bias. Collectors of parallels divorce
the part from the whole, juggle ideas like discrete atoms, or like
interchangeable parts. Bhagavan Das's The Essential Unity of All
Religions is a perfect type of this disguised positivism in comparative religion. His book, whose intentions are surely spiritual, is
rife with the "cold abstraction" so often imputed to Western thought

55

by its Eastern critics. Das's book develops a passionately religious theme in a methodologically positivist way, surely an ironic association of ends with means.

Second, even where parallels can be shown to exist, they reveal nothing in themselves about mutual influence. Without corroborating evidence from history, archeology, linguistics, and relevant texts, they are explained most simply as alluring coincidences.

Third, inordinate fascination with parallels detracts from the uniqueness and intrinsic richness of various cultural traditions, whose differences of content and valuation illustrate the manifold potentialities of humanity. Rather than try to isolate a cognitively mystical core in the great religions and philosophies, one might prefer to examine in a critical spirit the historical alternatives between which a self-conscious individual might choose. One might study other civilizations and their views of life to understand better the workings and virtues of one's own tradition. One might seek on a purely individual basis to build from comparative studies a spiritual and intellectual synthesis consonant with one's own needs and experience. There are still other possibilities, and most would require a respectful acknowledgement of differences in the religious and philosophical content of the world's cultural traditions. There is wisdom in Johann Gottfried Herder's view that cultural diversity is good, and that every people has an original identity shaped by language, tradition, and the fullness of historical experience. So long as they are not destructive, these differences are enriching, like the perfumes and colors of many species of flowers in an immense garden. The same perspective is not inappropriate to spiritual experiences, which need not be of one kind to be valuable.

The purpose of what follows is not to glorify the "Greek miracle" and demean Indian thought. The analysis trys to avoid a culturally invidious spirit. Moreover, there is no intention of implying that people are trapped in their cultural milieus like insects in amber, or that trans-cultural syntheses may not be feasible and desirable. Those issues are of profound interest, but they are not the issues we wish to take up here. Now, the integrity of specific parallels calls for a long and close examination.

Let us begin with the least convincing and problematic case of similarities. There is plausibility in the occasional suggestion that the Milesian and Eleatic belief in a unifying principle beneath the flux of the sensible world derived from the more ancient monistic speculation of the Vedic hymns and the Upanishads.[3] In rebellion against the polytheism and mythological literalness of Homer and Hesiod, so the argument goes, may have responded to intimations of a unitary theory sounding from India through the Persian Empire, or percolating into the busy, cosmopolitan ports of the

Ionian cities.[4] The simplicity of the idea might have seemed to a
few Greeks a fruitful alternative to the radical pluralism of Greek
mythology, thus becoming the organizing principle of an intellectual revolution. While this line of argument has not been pressed
enthusiastically, it is worth glancing at as an example of the formidable gap separating the pre-Socratics as philosophers and religious thinkers from the mystical rishis of the Upanishads.

The hypothesis has an immediate and somewhat sweeping appeal,
but there is much that stands against it. Most importantly, the
seeds of philosophical monism were already present in the Greek
tradition. Werner Jaeger has argued that Greek monism and rationalism are implicit in Greek mythical ideas. "There is no reason," he
writes, "why we should not look upon Hesoid's Theogony as one of
the preparatory stages of the philsophy to come."[5] Hesiod was the
first to organize a bewildering multiplicity of deities into a sem-
blance of rational order. In so doing, he favored the god Eros,
"fairest among the deathless gods," who is given the distinction
of initiating a chain of divine procreation.[6] As the power inspir-
ing a union of Heaven and Earth, themselves mighty gods, Eros was
the primal cause binding together all forces and objects in the
universe. He was a cosmic power in the pantheon of gods, primus in-
ter pares, and since all the other gods were beholden to him for
their existence, they were bound by something like natural law, although Hesiod characterizes this law "as a god among gods rather
than as one ruling principle."[7]

Here are three ingredients of the Ionian revolution: a rational ordering of phenomena in the universe, by arranging the gods in
a hierarchy; a single creative principle, Eros, postulated as the
ultimate source of all becoming; and the suggestion of a central
governing power, or natural law.[8] To these elements the Ionians
added a rational skepticism tempered by a respect for experience
of the sensible world. The result was the birth of western philosophy and the beginnings of natural science.

> The impulse which makes the Ionian philosophers of nature
> seek to comprehend the world in universal terms takes a
> form that is utterly and unmistakably their own. The He-
> siodic type of rationalism, with its interpretation and
> synthesis of the traditional myths, has given way to a
> new and more radical form of rational thinking, which no
> longer draws its content from the mythic tradition, nor
> indeed from any other, but takes its point of departure
> from the given realities of human experience.[9]

Although the pre-Socratics took the sustained order of nature
as their touchstone of truth, explanation, and purpose, their philosophical naturalism still retained a substantial religious element. For Jaeger, the puzzles of change and diversity suggested to

reflection a master principle, and only this principle, being the source of all becoming, seemed at that time worthy of the epithet "Divine." This was a "philosophical idea of God."[10] Gregory Vlastos believes this formulation is misleading and has too much of the occult about it. He stresses the unique association of religious ideas and natural philosophy in the thought of the _physiologoi_: "they alone, not only among the Greeks, but among all the people of the Mediterranean world, Semitic or Indo-European, dared transpose the name and function of divinity into a realm conceived as a rigorously natural order and, therefore, completely purged of miracle and magic."[11]

This "rigorously natural order" was, moreover, postulated of a _material_ reality, a point marking off vividly the divergence of Greek and Indian monism.[12] The pre-Socratics appear to have shared in common the assumption that spatial existence is a necessary condition of being.[13] Even the Boundless (_Apeiron_) of Anaximander is is spatially conditioned material substance, a speculative, logical extension of the unitary principle Thales attributed to water. Aristotle regarded the Apeiron as an anticipation of his own "indeterminate matter."[14] Here is a frank materialism accompanied by belief in a self-generating, self-sustaining, self-operating Kosmos which emerges through the agency of necessity.[15]

The temptation to find hints of Indian monism in Milesian thought ignores its secular, rationalistic, speculative, and tentative outlook. The Milesians proposed cosmogonical hypotheses open to criticism and modification, systems of thought inviting correction, not myths demanding solemn acquiescence. Greek philosophers from Thales to Democritus were able to question and test their predecessors. These materialist cosmogonies were progressive and fruitful. The idea of primordial matter anticipates the law of the conservation of matter, and Anaximander's "use of the mechanical analogy completes the picture of the scientific approach which distinguishes Ancient Greece from all that went before."[16] Viewed, therefore, from the general perspective of assumption, content, objective, and result, Greek monistic speculation is not comparable, except on the weakest analogical grounds, to a vague notion of "oneness," to the Brāhman "Science of the Self (_Adyatmavidya_), which is the religion and philosophy of India."[17]

The thought of Thales and Parmenides raises some minor questions of possible oriental influence and mystical tendencies. Thales' identification of water as the primal substance has some parallels in the Vedas, but it is futile to suppose that such parallels are indicative of a historical relationship.[18] Legendary accounts of Thales' oriental travels cannot be trusted; it seems doubtful that he visited Egypt and Babylonia, much less those regions close to India.[19] His account of _physis_ is essentially a speculative hypothesis, whereas the Vedic allusions to water are in mythical form,

58

and water myths occur in many cultures.[20] Indeed, the relation of
water to life is so obvious to experience that Thales may well have
decided on his primal substance through the empirical method of observing the world around him.[21] But if one must have oriental influences, Kirk and Raven stand behind the probability that Thales'
idea of the earth floating on water came from Near Eastern sources,
"possibly Egyptian," which does not, of course, entail necessarily
a trip to Egypt.[22]

Like some of the Upanishadic mystics, Parmenides repudiates
as illusory the shifting qualities and quantities of the phenomenal world, but in contrast to the incorporeal Universal Soul ex-
tolled by the rishis, he reasons his way relentlessly to a block
universe of imperturbable matter.[23] From the Milesian assumption
that all existence is material, Parmenides deduces that what is
non-material - namely space - cannot exist.[24] In Karl Popper's
view, change is the seminal problem of Greek cosmology. Parmenides
believes it is impossible to give a rational, logically consistent
account of change, of how change can occur without loss of identity, and therefore denies that it occurs at all, in what is "the
first hypothetico-deductive theory of the world."[25] Parmenidean
being is comparable to the left-hand column of the Pythagorean Table of Opposites, whose attributes reflect reason rather than sense.
Based on the distinction between odd and even numbers, the left
side encompasses: one, odd, male, being, determinate, square,
straight, right, light, and good; the right side includes: many,
even, female, becoming, indeterminate, oblong, crooked, left, darkness, and bad. Kirk and Raven see Parmenides as a former Pythagorean who seems to reject Pythagorean dualism and grapples with the
paradoxes of being and becoming from the perspective of abstract
reason.[26] His philosophical poem may be regarded as a critique of
Pythagoreanism. Whatever Parmenides' motive, however, his thought
developed organically from the problems and speculations of earlier Greek philosophers.

But there is in Parmenides' poem an affective coloring which
seems irrelevant to its logical arguments. The Prologue conveys a
strong impression of supernal revelation, as goddesses drive the
philosopher-poet in a chariot "towards the light," where "it is
divine command and Right" that he should "inquire into everything."[27]
Raven asks: " ... is it not permissable to imagine that Parmenides,
swayed perhaps by a deeper respect for the good principle than his
'fellow-Pythagoreans' revealed, may have been driven along the
road from darkness into light by a basically religious desire to
vindicate the good principle against the bad?"[28] Furthermore, "the
ultimate triumph of his logical faculty over his emotion should not
blind us to the possibility that an emotional impulse underlay his
unemotional reasoning."[29] These interpretations cohere roughly
with Radhakrishnan's belief that "supporters of pure monism recognize a higher power than abstract intellect which enables us to

feel the push of reality."[30] He detects "echoes" of this attitude in Parmenides.

Even if there is no serious issue of direct or indirect influence on Parmenides from Indian sources, may we not affirm that Parmenides and monists of the Upanishads share the same spiritual outlook? Both maintain that reality is one, and that man's purpose, in some sense, is to know it; vidyā (knowledge) and avidyā (ignorance) seem very close to Parmenides' Way of Truth and Way of Seeming. The plausibility of this identification rests on oversimplifications which weaken most analogies between Indian and Greek ideas. The religious significance of Parmenides' thought still awaits a consensus among scholars, but it is probably misguided to interpret him as a "mystic." Guthrie cautions us that Parmenides' Prologue may have no more importance than being a respectful obeisance to traditional rhetoric and imagery.[31] Both Jaeger and Vlastos see Parmenides as a philosopher using religious forms of expression to formulate a view of the world purged of the irrational, arbitrary sentiments found in cult religion.[32] His objective was not magical control of nature or mystical disengagement from it, but rather a philosophical understanding of it by means of inquiry and cricicism. While giving the religious element in Parmenides its due, and acknowledging that religious and philosophical content are properly separable only for analytical purposes, one should be aware of the "ultimate triumph of his logical faculty over emotion." Eleatic monism is rooted in discursive argument and an insistence upon distinctions. Early Indian monism commonly stresses the psychological rather than the cosmological point of view; true "knowledge" (vidyā) is achieved by abandoning distinctions and distrusting argument.[33]

Most students of Greek philosophy regard the pluralistic doctrines of Empedocles, Leucippus, and Democritus as a natural development out of an impasse which befell Ionian monism.[34] The stubborn problem of how many things could be differentiated out of one thing required a new approach. The path taken was to posit a plurality of substances to explain the variety of the world. If one wishes to take the trouble, however, parallels can be found in the Indian tradition, with the inevitable hint of diffusion and influence. Empedocles' four elements – earth, air, fire, and water – had a counterpart in the materialism of Ajita Kesakambalin, who denied the spiritual absolutism of later Vedic thought and affirmed the utter finality of death, saying: "Man is formed of the four elements ... When he dies earth returns to the aggregate of earth, water to water, fire to fire, and air to air, while the senses vanish into space ... When the body dies both fool and wise alike are cut off and perish. They do not survive after death."[35]

If one accepts the earliest dates assigned to Empedocles (ca. 493-433 B.C.), his career overlaps Ajita's in time, who was a contemporary of Gautama Buddha (died ca. 486–473 B.C.). Did one man know of the other? Could one have learned from the other, by either direct ot indirect means? While all things are possible, this particular event is not probable.[36] With Empedocles, the "four roots" are more likely a result of taking the familiar Greek "opposites" – hot and cold, wet and dry – and assigning to them the status of tangible substances.[37] As for Ajita, he breathed a philosophical atmosphere in which the idea of cosmic process organized around four or five basic elements was already venerable.[38] Ajita and his fellow materialists applied a radical interpretation to a well-known concept.

It is ironic that in the case of Empedocles a Greek philosopher was the religious seer, while the few Indian thinkers with whom he might be compared were materialists or atheists. He was both a philosopher and a magic working shamam.[39] The views expounded in On Nature and in the Purifications are apparently incompatible, the one being mechanistic, the other spiritual. The former work was conceived by a "thorough materialist," the latter by a man who believed in "a divine self alien to the body."[40] There is more to say about these remarkable treatises in the next chapter. It is enough at this point to contrast the religiosity of Empedocles with the mocking unbelief of Ajita.[41]

An element theory of genesis and change in nature was also a prominent feature of ancient Chinese cosmology, which sought to explain the existence and modification of varied phenomena as a complementary oscillation of yin and yang (passive and active principles respectively), or as a cyclical movement based on the successive dominance of five elements (earth, wood, metal, fire, and water).[42] The great antiquity of this doctrine confirms its originality with the Chinese, who are not likely to have communicated it to India, with which China had no known intercourse until the accession of the Han Dynasty (206 B.C.-220 A.D.).[43] The Chinese theory has an exceptionally rich identity in historical context, projecting, as it does, the image of a harmoniously functioning cosmos, a self-contained, self-operating, self-sufficient organism whose various parts form a natural hierarchy of Heaven, Earth, and Man, the whole governed by moral as well as physical laws.[44] All of this is far more absorbing and wondrous than any stark parallel one might be able to establish between element theories.

Greeks, Indians, and Chinese, without exception, had enough imagination to abstract an element theory out of relatively common experiences of the natural world and its transmutations. Much the same can be said of the atomic hypothesis espoused by Leucippus and Democritus (5th to the 4th centuries B.C.), which has been compared with the atomism of Vaiśeṣika (from a Sanskrit word meaning "particularity"), one of the six classical systems of Indian philosophy. Vaiśeṣika arose probably in the sixth and fifth centuries B.C., and was given a systematic exposition by Kanāda (or Kāśyapa) around 300 B.C.[45] It affirms the particularity of ultimate reality, which is said to consist of immutable atoms imperceptibly small. The Greek and Indian theories agree generally on the primacy of changeless units, elusive to ordinary perception, which explain and rationalize the flux. But there are crucial differences worth spelling out.

As to origin, Greek atomism arose in response to problems created by sixth century metaphysical speculation: the relation of the one to the many, and of change to permanence. Aristotle tells us that Leucippus believed he had hit upon a hteory consistent with human experience of change and multiplicity and Parmenides' logical demand for an irreducible reality that is - both eternal and unchanging.[46] Vaiśeṣika seems to have been a defensive response to the radical phenomenalism of Buddhism, specifically the doctrine of impermanence (anicca) and its denial of a soul, or self, that endures.[47] Although Vaiśeṣika is not without skeptical overtones, it has a spiritual slant wholly absent from the nearly contemporary doctrine of the Greeks, which is a mechanistic system uncongenial to incorporeal gods and souls. The principle of moral law (dharma) pervades the reasoning of Vaiśeṣika.[48] The atoms of Leucippus are distinguished from one another on quantitative grounds, whereas those of Vaiśeṣika differ qualitatively.[49] The atoms of Leucippus produce their effects chiefly through motion, whereas those of Vaiśeṣika are primarily at rest.[50] In the scheme of Leucippus, consciousness and "self" are due to varying arrangements of atoms in the void, while in Vaiśeṣika, souls are regarded as co-eternal, independent existences.[51] The upshot is that both systems converged on an idea "that wise men, trying to reconcile the unity and relative stability of nature with its ceaseless changes, were bound to make sooner or later."[52] The bare idea, however, was used and elaborated quite differently in each case.

The atomic theories of Jainism and Buddhism are earlier than the Greek version, but they are even more divergent than Vaiśeṣika in the matter of details. Unlike Greek atomism, the Jain view attributes qualities to matter and undertakes an elaborate analysis of how atoms combine into aggregations and molecules.[53] In the last instance, atoms cohere because of negative (roughness) and positive (smoothness) qualities. The Greek theory has atoms generating varied phenomena by dint of their collisions and juxtapositions. Description and explanation are indebted to quantitative variables like number, weight, size, and position. The Jain conception of matter views karma as one of its forms. Influxes of karma impregnate the soul (jīva) and weigh it down, thus necessitating reincarnation until the soul can be divested of its karmic burden. Once this goal has been achieved, salvation is realized as the soul rises to the top of the universe, where it basks in an eternity of omniscient bliss. The religious element in Greek atomism is minimal, if not completely absent. Moreover, the Greeks are unequivocal pluralists, whereas Jainism is a form of materialistic monism, in that all manifestations of consciousness contain matter. The only exceptions are time, which is described as nonextended, and the liberated jīva, which is extended but paradoxically devoid of matter.[54]

Buddhist atomism negates all eternal substances, including material substances. According to Stcherbatsky, the Buddhists "pictured the world as a photoplay consisting of unique flashes of light. Strictly speaking, there is no matter; there exists only forces."[55] The flashes, however, are not detectable in nature. They form the irreducible base of complex atoms which may be composed of up to eight distinct parts: four primary forces (earth, water, fire, and air, corresponding to reflection, adhesion, heating and movement), and four secondary qualities (color, taste, smell, and touch), all of which, in the last analysis, are flashes. Mental and moral events in Buddhist cosmology are not dependent on "physical" events; they are not, in effect, to be regarded as mere epiphenomena rising like smoke from the fire of material circumstances. In contrast, Greek atomism is materialist in the most fundamental sense. Dr. Samuel Johnson would have no trouble stubbing his toe on one of Leucippus' atoms. Finally, Buddhist cosmology and phenomenological analysis are firmly subordinated to the problem of defining the psychological conditions for the individual's release from attachment to the flux. Explaining the composition and dynamics of the world order is not the central purpose of Buddhist "science."

The emphasis of Indian atomism, whether Vaisesika, Jain, or Buddhist, is on the qualitative rather than the quantitative aspects of phenomena, whereas the reverse is true of Greek speculation.[56] Even if one assumes that Greek philosophers had access to reliable accounts of Indian atomism, there is not much doubt that their own formulations turned out differently both in detail and spirit.[57]

1. Edward Conze, "Buddhist Philosophy and its European Parallels," Philosophy East and West (April, 1963), 15-17, 20-21. See also Conze's "Spurious Parallels to Buddhist Philosophy," Ibid. (July, 1963), 105-115.
2. See Raphael Demos, "Similarities and Contrasts Between Chinese and Greek Attitudes, Ibid. (April-July, 1961), 53-56. Many important distinctions can be worked out of Hajime Nakamura's Ways of Thinking of Eastern Peoples: India-China-Tibet-Japan, trans. Philip Wiener (Honolulu: East-West Center Press, 1964), Part II.
3. Rig-Veda x. 29. 3., in Sarvepalli Radhakrishnan and Charles Moore, eds., A Source Book in Indian Philosophy (Princeton: Princeton University Press, 1957). Unless otherwise indicated, all future references to Indian religious and philosophical texts, with the exception of the Upanishads, are taken from this source. See also the Brihadaranyaka Upanishad 4.5.15.
4. On Ionia's network of trade, see Sarton, Ancient Science Through the Golden Age, p. 164.
5. Werner Jaeger, The Theology of the Early Greek Philosophers (London: Oxford University Press, 1947), p. 14. I do not know if anyone has yet proposed that Hesiod was a Brahman in Greek dress, but it may be prudent to cite Jaeger's conclusion that "Hesiod's Theogony is already Greek in content and spirit," which is not the same as saying that Hesiod escaped foreign influence. On the basis of parallels between the Theogony and the Hittite Kumarbi-tablet, G. Kirk and J. Raven believe that "some of the contents of the Theogony are of non-Greek origin and of a date far earlier than Hesiod's immediate predecessors." The Presocratic Philosophers (Cambridge: Cambridge University Press, 1957), p. 36.
6. Hesiod Theogony, p. 87.
7. Jaeger, The Theology of the Early Greek Philosophers, pp. 16-17.
8. Jaeger expounds Hesiod's "three essential elements of a rational cosmogony" somewhat differently in Paideia: The Ideals of Greek Culture, trans. Gilbert Highet, 3 vols. (Oxford: Basil Blackwell, 1945), I, 65. But the central point remains intact. Gregory Vlastos believes that Jaeger exaggerates the role of Eros in the Theogony, and fails to take account of serious gaps in "the natural pattern of sexual generation," which is not comparable with the idea of natural law. "Theology and Philosophy in Early Greek Thought," The Philosophical Quarterly, 2 (April, 1952). 100 n.
9. Jaeger, The Theology of the Early Greek Philosophers, p. 18. W.K.C. Guthrie believes that the Hesiodic theogony underlies the philosophical doctrine of multiplicity emerging from oneness and returning to oneness: "The familiarity of this pre-philosophical conception may well have influenced Thales and his successors in

64

the direction of monism - it is almost impossible to believe that it did not." A History of Greek Philosophy, 3 vols. (Cambridge: Cambridge University Press, 1962), I, 69-70.

10. Jaeger, The Theology of the Early Greek Philosophers, p. 174.
11. Vlastos is critical of Jaeger for using the term "theology," because it obscures "the actual relation of beliefs of the pre-Socratics to those of contemporary religion." "Theology and Philosophy in Early Greek Thought," op. cit., 116. The pre-Socratics were free intellectually of cult religion when thinking about nature, but their ideas retained, nevertheless, a unique conception of divinity: "To present the deity as wholly immanent in the order of nature and therefore absolutely law-abiding was the peculiar and distinctive religious contribution of the pre-Socratics, and it should be put in the forefront of any account of their religious thought. They took a word which in common speech was a hallmark of the irrational, unnatural, and unaccountable and made it the name of a power which manifests itself in the operation, not the disturbance, of intelligible law." Ibid., 116-117.
12. Aristotle Metaphysics i. 983b. See also John Burnet, Early Greek Philosophy (London: Adam and Charles Black, 1930), pp. 80, 197.
13. D. O'Brien, Empedocles' Cosmic Cycle: A Reconstruction From the Fragments and Secondary Sources (Cambridge: Cambridge University Press, 1969), p. 242. Plato was the first to challenge the assumption that space is a condition of being.
14. Burnet, p. 55. In the fragments, we read: "The Non-Limited is the original material of existing things." See Kathleen Freeman, Ancilla to the Pre-Socratic Philosophers: A Complete Translation of the Fragments in Diels, Fragments der Vorsokratiker (Cambridge: Cambridge University Press, 1962), p. 19 (all subsequent pre-Socratic citations, unless otherwise noted, will be taken from Freeman's translation). As to the notion of infinity in Anaximander, Paul Seligman suggests that what is meant is not the infinite of mathematics, or a religiously conceived infinite, "but there is the possibility that he meant 'spatially infinite' in a weaker, poetical sense, just as we speak of an endless expanse in order to convey an idea of its vastness." The Apeiron of Anaximander: A Study in the Origin and Function of Metaphysical Ideas (London: Athlone Press, 1962), p. 33.
15. Guthrie, I, 140-142 f. Radhakrishnan emphasizes that in the Upanishads "the forms and energies of the world are not final and ultimate," nor or they "self-originated or self-maintained." Indian Philosophy, I, 97.
16. Samuel Sambursky, The Physical World of the Greeks, trans. M. Dagut (London: Routledge and Paul, 1956), pp. 7, 15. The Ionian philosophers could have abandoned their monism and materialism without giving up their belief in "nature," because the former were speculative, scientific doctrines. R.G. Collingwood, The Idea of Nature (Oxford: Oxford University Press, 1945), p. 46. On this last important point, see also Karl Popper, Conjectures

and Refutations (New York: Basic Books, 1963), chapter 5.

17. Ananda K. Coomaraswamy, The Dance of Shiva (New York: Noonday Press, 1957), p. 9.

18. Vedas x. 190. 1; x. 129. 3. " ... in the beginning this world was just water." Brihadaranyaka Upanishad 5.5.1.

19. D.R. Dicks rejects evidence that Thales visited Egypt and Babylonia: it is "late and unreliable and we are not entitled on the strength of it to build up elaborate theories about his travels and the knowledge he is supposed to have acquired on them." "Thales," Classical Quarterly (November, 1959), 306.

20. See Charles H. Long, Alpha: The Myths of Creation (New York: George Braziller, 1963), pp. 193–216.

21. W.D. Wightman, The Growth of Scientific Ideas (Edinburgh, 1950), p. 10. Cf. Aristotle Metaphysics i. 983^{b}20.

22. Kirk and Raven, p. 77. Cf. Seligman, p. 143, who cautions that "when all is told the doctrine of Thales is not a mere rehash of Oriental beliefs."

23. Francis M. Cornford, "Parmenides' Two Ways," Classical Quarterly (January, 1933), 103.

24. See Guthrie, I, 113. O'Brien denies that Parmenides could dispense wholly with space: "Parmenides has, as it were, stripped his one being of all the attributes, time, change, and movement, which he thought belonged to the sensible and in that sense the material world. But for something to exist he still supposed that it must exist in space. To be but not to be extended in space is a possibility of which Parmenides seems not to have been aware." Empedocles' Cosmic Cycle, p. 240.

25. Popper, Conjectures and Refutations, p. 146. Moreover, Parmenides may be said to have "fathered theoretical physics." Ibid., p. 79.

26. Kirk and Raven, p. 277. Also see Popper, p. 78.

27. Freeman, p. 41.

28. J.E. Raven, Pythagoreans and Eleatics (Cambridge: Cambridge University Press, 1948), pp. 23–24. Good and bad refer, of course, to the Table of Opposites.

29. Ibid., p. 24.

30. Radhakrishnan, Indian Philosophy, I, 37.

31. " The mythical elements of the prologue are for the most part traditional. Most of the phrasiology is borrowed from Homer and Hesiod. The goddess who instructs the poet corresponds to the Muse of the epic writers." Guthrie, II, 10.

32. Jaeger, The Theology of the Early Greek Philosophers, p. 97. Gregory Vlastos, "Parmenides' Theory of Knowledge," Transactions of the American Philological Association, 77 (1946), 74 ff.

33. Radhakrishnan, Indian Philosophy, I, 145, 196.

34. After Parmenides, who pushed metaphysics against a wall by arguing that "if this one really is, we must give up the idea that it can take different forms ... , the leading men were all pluralists." Burnet, p. 197.

35. Quoted in Dale Riepe, The Naturalistic Tradition in Indian

<u>Thought</u> (Seattle, Washington, 1961), p. 36.

36. Jean Przyluski believes that the theory of elements originated in Iran and spread from thence to Greece, India, and China. "La théorie des éléments et les origines de la Science," <u>Scientia</u>, 54 (1933), 1-9.

37. Burnet, p. 228.

38. <u>Brihadaranyaka</u> <u>Upanishad</u> 2.4.12. Also see Radhakrishnan, <u>Indian</u> <u>Philosophy</u>, I, 277 f.

39. "Empedocles represents not a new but a very old type of personality, the shaman who continues the still undifferentiated functions of magician and naturalist, poet and philosopher, preacher, healer, and public counsellor." E.R. Dodds, <u>The</u> <u>Greeks</u> <u>and</u> <u>the</u> <u>Irrational</u> (Berkeley: University of California Press, 1963), p. 146. For Jaeger, Empedocles is "a philosophical centaur, so to speak - a prodigious union of Ionian elemental physics and Orphic religion." <u>Paideia</u>, I, 295.

40. See Frgs. 3, 28, 29. Cf. Frgs. 51, 56. See Guthrie, I, 318.

41. Ajita's was the Lokayata doctrine, that only this world (<u>loka</u>) exists. An interesting body of materialist texts are in Radhakrishnan and Moore, <u>Source</u> <u>Book</u>, pp. 228-249. On Lokayata, also see Riepe, pp. 58-59.

42. Derk Bodde "Harmony and Conflict in Chinese Philosophy," in Arthur Wright, ed., <u>Studies</u> <u>in</u> <u>Chinese</u> <u>Thought</u> (Princeton: Princeton University Press, 1953), pp. 21 f.

43. Fung Yu-lan, <u>A</u> <u>History</u> <u>of</u> <u>Chinese</u> <u>Philosophy</u>, trans. Derk Bodde. 2 vols. (Princeton: Princeton University Press, 1952), I, 159-169.

44. Bodde, p. 20.

45. Radhakrishnan, <u>Indian</u> <u>Philosophy</u>, II, 178-179.

46. Burnet, p. 335. A good discussion of what went wrong with Greek monism is in Collingwood's <u>The</u> <u>Idea</u> <u>of</u> <u>Nature</u>, 40-41, 51. Parmenidean monism, though logically rigorous in denying reality to change and multiplicity, was too hard on the demands of common sense.

47. Radhakrishnan, <u>Indian</u> <u>Philosophy</u>, II, 177.

48. Vaiśeṣika <u>Sutra</u> i. 1; iii. 2.18, 21. On Leucippus and Democritus, see Burnet, 334-349.

49. Vaiśeṣika <u>Sutra</u> i. 1.5, 6.

50. Ibid. i. 1.17, 18, 19.

51. "Democritus carries his materialistic conception of the universe to such extremes that he even imagines the human soul ... to consist in atoms, namely of a peculiar kind of small, spherical, and smooth particles." E.J Dijksterhuis, <u>The</u> <u>Mechanization</u> <u>of</u> <u>the</u> <u>World</u> <u>Picture</u> (Oxford: Oxford University Press, 1961), pp. 11-12. Cf. Radhakrishnan, <u>Indian</u> <u>Philosophy</u>, II, 226.

52. Sarton, <u>Ancient</u> <u>Science</u> <u>Through</u> <u>the</u> <u>Golden</u> <u>Age</u>, p. 225. Riepe holds that: "so far as parallels between early Greek thought and Vaiśeṣika are concerned, ... the closest parallel is between Empedocles and Vaiśeṣika." <u>The</u> <u>Naturalistic</u> <u>Tradition</u>, p. 242.

53. Tattvarthadhigma Sutra v. See Riepe, p. 96, and Radhakrishnan, Indian Philosophy, II, 313, 317-318.
54. Riepe, p. 98. Radhakrishnan, Indian Philosophy, II, 316.
55. Th. Stcherbatsky, "Scientific Achievements of Ancient India," Indian Studies, 10 (July-September, 1969), 323.
56. Riepe, p. 96.
57. This is a good place to remind the reader that classical scholars and specialists in Greek philosophy do not always agree on what their subjects say and mean. In this chapter, and in the two chapters that follow, we shall nearly always be in the presence of "schools of thought" on most big issues, and even smaller ones. It would be an unnecessary distraction from the main purposes of this study if I should give space to a running commentary on all the differences that crop up between scholars and attempt to take sides. It is not my task to take a position on all the disputes which might arise. Fortunately, there is no need for such a tactic. Where authorities are appealed to, it is enough that they be established and respected, and that they present viewpoints for which evidence and argument are presented. We are looking for viable alternatives to various assertions of the Indian hypothesis. If those alternatives are forthcoming and if they have strong scholarly support, then we need not be content with the claims of the Indian hypothesis. Both Burnet and Cornford explain Greek philosophy in its Greek context, so it matters little if Burnet sees the pre-Socratics as proto-scientists and Cornford sees them as rational theologians.

CHAPTER V

THE LURE OF PARALLELS: THE MYSTICAL TRADITION,
INDIAN AND GREEK

The intellectual and spiritual achievement of classical Greece
has been described as rationalistic, humanistic, naturalistic, and
this-worldly. It was in Hellas that the self-conscious individual
came into his own. Greek ideals marked a radical departure from
those of Near Eastern societies, whose cultural traditions ranged
over some three and a half millennia. In Sumer, Akkad, Assyria,
Babylon, Persia, and Egypt, the institution of sacred kingship and
the sway of arbitrary, inscrutable gods inhibited the play of the
mind. The active, self-conscious person, aware of his powers and
eager to display them, was rare, for only the gods could create, and
man's ordained place was to serve, obey, and revere their often ca-
pricious wills.[1]

In the Greek context, human possibilities surpassed timorous
conditions of obedience, humility, and resignation, which left too
little scope for individual genius. There is no precedent in world
literature for the confidence that radiates from a passage of the
Illiad, which urges men "to strive always for excellence and to sur-
pass others."[2] Thereafter the Greek world teemed with distinguished
individuals, who in the course of a few centuries left a baffled
posterity an immensely original cultural treasure: tragic drama,
pure mathematics, political democracy, authentic historical writing,
systematic political theory, an array of poetic and other literary
forms, the first triumphs of science, and a conception of art whose
influence has never disappeared.

There was, however, another side to the Greek experience, the
side Radhakrishnan believes was "a decisive break with the Greek
tradition of rationalism and humanism." This "mystical" aspect of
the Greek mind was preoccupied with deliverance of the soul from
the prison of the body, the godly and wicked predilections of man,
attainment of divinity through purification, rebirth in another
world, or on another plane of existence, immortality of the soul,
the wheel of life and death, the search for a higher life among initiates who are the custodians of secret, spiritually efficacious
rites and doctrines, and other such matters. Here the ultimate purpose of all human striving is satisfaction for a spiritual thirst;
a desire for release from earthly limitations becomes the central
fact of human existence.

Nilsson describes the centuries before the Persian wars as a
time when "maenads in their ecstasy raged in the woods and fields,
Orphics preached that man's sinful nature must be subdued and purified by mortifications to avoid punishment in the other world," and

69

"the land was full of prophets, wandering seers, collectors of ora-
cles, Bakis, the Sibyl and their like, workers of miracles, and puri-
fying priests. Some composed poems about the origin of the world and
of the gods, some took no nourishment, some could send their souls
wandering free from their bodies."[3] Are mysticism and rationalism
in Greek thought incompatible? Is it possible that the incongruous,
"alien" branches of Greek civilization - the orgiastic, ascetic,
·ecstatic, and otherworldly - were grafted onto the main trunk from
the outside? While a cautious student might balk at giving India
even indirect credit for the beginnings of Greek philosophy, he
might be persuaded easily enough to give her some credit for the
mysticism found in Orphism and Pythagoreanism, in Empedocles, Heraclitus, and Plato. The parallels in these cases seem striking. Perhaps even the skeptic would be tempted to make concessions.[4]

It cannot be denied that some ideas in Brahmanical thought are
present in Greek religion and philosophy, nor is it deniable that
they hang together in a pattern remarkably like that found in the
Upanishads, all of which may or may not imply something more at work
than coincidence. The issue really depends on how the key ideas were
understood by the Greeks, and on whether or not they are explainable
in a Greek context. Pythagoreans, devotees of Orphism, Empedocles of
Acragas, and much later, Plato, believed in key notions of the "mystical tradition"; these included a soul imprisoned in the body, the
round of rebirths, the possibility of immortality by means of purification, and a sharp division of material from non-material reality. Socrates also has been fitted into this tradition because of his
appeal to a "god" within and his commitment to the care of the soul.

Still, it is well known that such mystical ideas have turned
up across the globe, and there is not much reason to believe that
they spread from a primordial center. The idea of each person having
a soul, spirit, a non-corporeal essence or copy of the physical body is universal in pre-literate societies and advanced cultures. It
is a device for helping consciousness reach beyond the grave and its
disquieting mysteries. Belief in transmigration of the soul appears
in cultures everywhere, and seems to occur naturally to the human
mind at a stage when the world is perceived as bursting with spiritual forces and agencies.[5] The dead are not distinguished clearly
from the living. The life of the tribe is thought to continue in the
spiritual being of its dead members.

This life, which is perpetually renewed, is reborn out of
that opposite state called 'death,' into which, at the
other end of its arc, it passes again. In this idea of reincarnation ... we have the first conception of a cycle of
existence, a Wheel of Life, divided into two hemicycles of
light and darkness, through which the one life, or soul,
continuously revolves.[6]

70

In response to the uncertainties of death, many peoples have taken comfort in myths of rebirth and resurrection.[7] The cycle of the seasons, entailing a periodic death and rebirth of vegetation, alternations of sterility and fecundity, is the root experience of a great mythic theme formed around the figures of Inanna and Tammuz, Isis and Osiris, Cybele and Attis, Aphrodite and Adonis, Demeter and Persephone. The drama of a god's death and resurrection was enacted throughout the Near East, being the medium in which immortal life and divine transfiguration were sought.

Underlying many of these ideas is a type of consciousness arising from mankind's experience in remotest time. In earlier stages of cultural development, the Greeks had in their midst, like all other known peoples, the shaman, whose "neurotic-epileptoid consciousness" facilitated intercourse with ill-conceived powers associated with disease, portentous dream states, and death.[8] Everything not understood or subject to human control - the forces of nature, unpredictable human violence, the frustration attending thwarted goals, material deprivation, precarious health - lay within the shaman's purview. His inner fever and exceptional sensitivity, manifested often as trance, seizure, or hallucination, thrust him, or so it seemed, into a supernatural dimension of the world which yielded knowledge and power.[9] A seizure might resemble death and rebirth. Fabulous visions might suggest to the prosaic onlooker the shaman's transformation into a beast, or the journey of his soul beyond the body to supernal regions.[10]

The priest of advanced agricultural societies was more bureaucratic, socialized, and subject to institutional controls, but his descent from shamanistic religion is unmistakable. Desiring wealth, power, or a respectable calling, hieratic priesthoods avoided the psychic eccentricities of the classic shaman while continuing to probe the supernatural by means of an inherited shamanistic formula, "a formula which is the projection of a neurotic-epileptoid mind."[11] Greek literature is familiar with the shaman and his works: the healer and wonder worker, the prophet and seer, busy manipulating nature, living without visible sustenance, roaming the earth in animal form.[12] Greeks may have learned of shamanistic religion in Scythia or Thrace, perhaps during exploratory missions around the Black Sea area in the seventh century B.C.[13]

There is a close affinity between shamanism and the mystical tradition. Both lay down much the same conditions for spiritual insight and potency: suffering or asceticism; isolation from the common life of man; avoidance of select foods, acts, and thoughts (taboos); purification as a corollary of solitude and avoidance; exceptional, revelatory psychic states; rare powers of healing, levitation, clairvoyance, and precognition; various soul powers, such as bilocation (temporary separation of soul and body), reincarnation, and immortality; and the secret transmission of these doctrines and practices to carefully chosen disciples.

In Greece, the earliest organized manifestation of these ideas is in Orphism, the vehicle of mystic rites associated with the death and rebirth of Dionysus, founded allegedly by the miracle-working shaman Orpheus. There is no evidence that Orphism was one thing, that all Orphics shared the same beliefs, or that a homogeneous body of Orphic literature circulated around Greece. Only a tentative description of "Orphism" can be attempted.

The sect held man to be part bad and part good, half human and half divine, a legacy from the remote time when the Titans rebelled against Zeus, slew his son Dionysus-Zagreus, and were in turn destroyed by a thunderbolt from the hand of the vengeful father. Man's dual nature, body and soul, was a consequence of his creation by a divine hand from the ashes of the Titans. In the Orphic view, overcoming evil and realizing the divine was a matter of ritual purification, and to a lesser extent, of righteousness. Those who fell short on either count were doomed after death to an unpleasant fate in the underworld, a gloomy place of retribution. In so far as Orphics were concerned with justice, punishing the wicked and impure, rewarding the virtuous and pure, their notion of justice was one common to Greek tradition: punishment conceived as retribution or payment in kind (diké).[14] They added to it a promise of suffering in another world, the possibility that offensiveness in the next world might force a soul back into this world for chastisement, and the idea that a short cycle of existences in both worlds, viewed as counterparts of one another, might be conditional to a soul's claim on immortal bliss.[15] The stress on purification belonged to a taboo mentality coursing through Greek religion in the late archaic period. The powers and spiritual forces could not be approached or communicated with, propitiated or supplicated, without due regard for appropriate rules and rituals governing the attitudes and behavior of initiates. Proximity to the supernatural implied awareness of human limitations, of the religious subject's condition - his purity or impurity - in the presence of the divine.[16] This cluster of religious conceptions, in Nilsson's phrase, "is the combination and crown of all the restless and manifold religious movements of the archaic period."[17]

Where Orphism was not directly indebted to Greek religious tradition, its doctrines may well have been original creations, whatever their surface agreements with those of other cultures.[18] But it would not do to omit the strong probability of shamanistic influences from northern Greece accounting for much in the spirit of Orphism, whose home was in Thrace.[19] Dodds suggests that the acute problem of divine justice in the late archaic period may have been relieved by an appeal to reincarnation.[20] In the tribal, family dominated social structure of archaic Greece, inherited guilt was the divine means of punishing transgressions. In a later and more individualistic social order, where blood guilt haunting successive generations became unacceptable, reincarnation held out the prospect of retribution only for the guilty party. The tense Greek spirit of the archaic period needed, perhaps, only a nudge from shamans of the north to stimulate a fresh doctrine on the origin of evil, the nature of retribution, and the source and consequences of guilt. The Orphic doctrine of the soul has a distinct shamanistic coloring, although one must be careful not to assume that a clear, unambiguous conception of "soul" existed in the Greek world. A characteristic of what Gilbert Murray has called the "Inherited Conglomerate" was a bewildering chaos in Greek literature and thought about the precise nature of the soul, which might be described variously as a person's breath, an amorphous shape in Hades, an interred but sentient corpse, or a daemon inhabiting the body.[21] If Orphics believed in something independent of the body capable of reincarnation, bilocation, and immortality, they need not have received the idea from India. Northern shamanism may have been the source, but Nilsson argues for an independent origin, and goes so far as to hold that Eleusinian and Orphic conceptions of immortality developed on Greek soil independently of one another. One might suppose that the former borrowed from the latter, being so close geographically and sharing a similar cultural tradition, yet Nilsson persists that "the same idea grew up independently in two different quarters."[22]

Radhakrishnan surveys "common" Indian and Orphic theories of the soul, and believes that "if we add to them metaphors like the wheel of birth and the world egg, the suggestion of natural coincidence is somewhat unconvincing."[23] Orphic ceremonies utilized wheel symbolism, which also appears frequently in Buddhist iconography. In Orphic rites, an initiate may have been obliged to step into and then out of a circle as an act of purification.[24] What this act meant is not clear, but the likelihood that wheel ritual came from Egypt, or perhaps from Crete, is far less problematic. Hero of Alexandria tells us that "in Egyptian sanctuaries there are wheels of bronze against the door-posts, and they are moveable so that those who enter may set them in motion, because of the belief that bronze purifies."[25] Moreover, wheel and circle are metaphors related organically to the round of the seasons, belief in successive passages of the soul beyond and back to the body, the alternation of life with death, the shape of the sun and the moon, which to the ancients were abodes of divinity. They are ciphers natural to a cyclical description of the world's movement, and even to a shaman's solitary withdrawal and return. Wheel imagery is not an exclusive possession of Indian religions, because they did not hold a monopoly on the most dramatic experiences of human life. As for Orphic cosmology, which postulates a great world egg as the origin of the universe and its activity, similar formulations are to be found not only in India, but in Africa, Polynesia, and Japan as well.[26]

Do Orphism and Indian religions share the same view of life?

73

One cannot deny that in a sense they do, but the assertion is basically vague and misleading, and overlooks significant disparities.
In the Upanishads, a dualistic conception of body and soul is frequently enunciated; however, this parallel to the Orphic distinction
is merely a stage along the way to a more radical doctrine, or it
can be seen as a reflection of the mixed, inconsistent, irregular
content of the more than one hundred Upanishads. What stands out as
distinctively "mystical" in the Upanishads is the Ātman-Brahman formula, that the two are one, and that all duality is illusion and ignorance. The ultimate goal of the religious life is compared to a
dreamless sleep:[27] "An ocean, a seer alone without duality, becomes
he whose world is Brahma."[28] In this view of salvation, only the
undiscriminated Ātman-Brahman is real.[29]

Orphic doctrine, so far as it can be made out, seeks immortality for the individual soul, which delivers itself from a truly ex-
istent prison of matter. The participant in the drama of salvation
is an enduring soul which partakes of divinity. The body, and the
sensible world where it dwells, are transient, unreliable, and offensive, but they have a firm ontological status. Orphic mysticism
contrasts with Upanishadic mysticism, therefore, in being dualistic,
and in disengaging the soul from the world in a different manner. In
its state of immortality and bliss, the Orphic soul does not cease
to exercise cognitive and conative functions, nor does there cease
to be a distinction between the individual soul and all other souls.
There is no hint in Orphic texts of the All, of the one without a
second.[30]

Orphism has a peculiar style which is at odds with the serene
detachment of monistic rishis in the Upanishads. Ecstasy, emotional
uplift, and sustained moral feeling are qualities which give Orphic
theology a slant binding it to the world of man, even though its
focus is on the realm of the gods. In the Upanishads, feeling and
moral action in the world are forms of attachment; they must be
abandoned if union with Brahman is to be achieved. Ethical behavior
has only instrumental value in the task of disengagement; once in
samādhi, no distinctions arise to cause moral problems, for one is
beyond good and evil, pleasure and pain.[31] Orphism and Theravada
Buddhism are even more emphatically at variance, because the latter
makes a point of denying the existence of a permanent entity (the
doctrine of anatta, or no-soul, no-self) amidst the flux of existence.[32] Even if early Buddhism is interpreted as a variant of Upanishadic ideas, as Radhakrishnan is wont to do, the difficulties
raised up to this point remain in force.[33]

That leaves Jainism, and in this case there are some real parallels, though not exact ones by any means. Both Orphism and Jainism
taught immortality and transmigration of the individual soul, the
distinction between matter and spirit, and the necessity for spiritual discipline. Thereafter, the differences become paramount.[34]

First, the Orphic soul is confined to man and its numbers are finite. The Jain soul (jīva, or "life") is found everywhere - in rocks,
trees, water, fire, wind, plants, animals, and man - and its numbers
are infinite, although each particular soul is finite; all of these
souls, even that of a dust mote, feel pain. Second, Orphic souls are
very much like spiritual counterparts of finite, earthly personali-
ties, whereas Jain souls, when completely purged of karmic matter,
are omniscient mirrors of the universe. Third, the Orphic scheme of
deliverance is nonrational, being ecstatic possession by the god.
Orphic blessedness is sensual in quality, reminding one that Dionysus, god of the vine and the table, is the saviour, a fact prompting
Plato to call Orphic salvation "an eternal intoxication." The Jain
scheme, in contrast, is remarkably logical, even cut and dried. It
entails an intricate cosmology, and a classification of beings and
souls which can properly be associated with one another. Deliverance
from the wheel of rebirth comes with the elimination of karmic matter
accumulated by past injuries inflicted on other ubiquitous souls, and
with the prevention of new influxes of matter. Full success with this
cleansing program releases the soul automatically from its karmic
sheath and floats it to the roof of heaven. Fourth, Orphics believed
in rewards and punishments. The unpurified could expect retribution
in the underworld, a consequence resting on moral as well as theological premises. The whole idea has a highly personal ring, like a
judge sending a criminal to prison. Jains, on the other hand, believed that karma is self-sufficient in the sense of being an impar-
tial cosmic law of cause and effect; it determines mechanically and
efficiently the exact degree of imperfection in a given soul, and
then assigns it with equal detachment to its deserved place on the
scala perfectionis. This viewpoint was not designed to arouse fear
of god, but to encourage greater piety and caution in the next life.
Fifth, because man's flesh came from the ashes of the Titans, the
murderers of Dionysus, Orphic dualism was ridden with guilt; a desire to atone for something like original sin led to a repudiation
of the body. Jain dualism is a highly objective analysis of the relation of souls to karmic matter. Sixth, and last, Orphic doctrine
demands justice, the righting of wrongs. Hence there is a positive
moral element in Orphic theology. Jain ethics are essentially negative and calculating, the object of the moral life being to minimize
influxes of karmic matter. With all of this said, it is not easy to
see just how Orphism and Jainism approximate the "same view of life."

Orphism had about it an exclusiveness and fanatical smugness
which alienated all but a select circle of followers. Among those
who may have been attracted to its worldview was Pythagoras, although no means exist for establishing such a connection.[35] The
cult aspect of Pythagoreanism was quasi-shamanistic, with the familiar apparatus of vegetarianism, asceticism, reincarnation, clannish-
ness, and transmission of secret doctrines. Pythagoras himself was
reported as having received the soul of an earlier shaman.[36] Thus
the religious framework of the Pythagorean order, whatever may have

been its affiliations with Orphism, was part of the wonder-working, superstitious, emotionally charged climate of the sixth century Greek world, in which the shamanistic temperament had a bright future.[37]

The idea that Pythagoras visited India, and acquired there his religious convictions, is based entirely on legendary travels, after which he supposedly settled in Croton to found a religious brotherhood. There are no grounds for his tour of Egypt and Babylon, much less grounds for one of India.[38] Nor is there evidence that he imbibed the wisdom of Indian gymnosophists. In fact, nothing at all of substance is known about the man's life, and not much more can be scraped together about his personal views.[39] Pythagoras, in effect, must be distinguished from Pythagoreanism.

Apart from the familiar elements of shamanism, what made the Pythagorean order different from similar taboo-ridden sects of the period was a new conception of purification. Pythagoreans taught that spiritual freedom lies in purging the soul by means of philosophy or "science."[40] Mathematics and cosmology were cultivated along with asceticism and the avoidance of taboo practices. From simple experiments with the manipulation of pebbles, representing numbers in various spatial relationships, the Pythagoreans were persuaded to see numbers at the heart of reality. Just as the "nature" of a particular tone can be described as the geometrical patterns traced out by a vibrating string, so everything that exists has an essence in the form of a distinctive geometrical shape. The nature of anything, that which makes it behave as it does, is not in the material of which it is made, as the Ionians had argued, but in its geometry, and in its numerically harmonious relationships to other things in the cosmos.[41] This idea of kosmos, of a mathematically ordered system of reality, was quite original and very influential. Two thousand years later, Kepler and Galileo applied the idea to the motions of bodies.

But the Pythagoreans do not seem to have been interested in measuring or mathematizing the physical world for the sake of knowledge. They aimed to purify the soul of its dross, to break the round of rebirths by meditating on the mathematical unity of all things.[42] The immortality of the soul can be understood as the soul attaining a harmony analogous to the harmony of the cosmos.[43] Needless to say, this is a strikingly intellectual notion of immortality which seems incompatible with the introspective, psychologically oriented doctrines of the Upanishads.

A dedication to the principles of science characterized the highest and best of the Pythagorean's "three lives": the lover of knowledge as opposed to the seeker of gain, or the seeker of fame and honor, a Homeric value more central to Greek culture. This division of mankind into three categories of attitude and vocation has an obvious parallel with the Vaishyas, Kshatriyas, and Brāhmans of India, respectively the traditional classes whose dharmas were to buy and sell, fight and govern, and tend the sacred lore of the Vedas. The similarity, however, does not run deep.

Pythagoras, or his followers, apparently got the idea from observing three types of people commonly seen at the Olympic games: the hawkers of dainties ensconced in their stalls, the glory-loving participants, and the spectators who were content to look on. This rude typology of man was not, so far as can be judged, a crucial element in Pythagorean cosmology, but rather a didactic means of clarifying the true vocation of man. Individuals are not born into one group or the other as a consequence of moral failings in a previous life. In the Hindu frame of reference, however, the separation of men into varnas, or classes - serf, merchant, warrior, and priest - was no arbitrary human action. It was mandated in social and religious spheres by the very constitution of the universe.[44] A purveyor of sweetmeats at the Olympic games might see the light and submit himself to the Pythagorean brotherhood, and in time master the "science" of the soul well enough to achieve release from bondage on the tyrannical "wheel of birth." No unregenerate Indian could hope for such expeditious redemption from karma. In the course of any man's lifetime, he could not hope to bridge the gap between classes, at least in principle. Only death and the action of karma could effect a transition from one mode of life to another. Furthermore, and here the gap between Brahmanism and Pythagoreanism is wide, the road to salvation was not a purificatory contemplation of incorporeal geometrical harmonies, which would have to be self-willed, but a regimen of austerities aimed at breaking down ego consciousness, a program of disciplines to transcend all thinking and willing. Incorporeal as the Upanishadic view of reality may be, Pythagoras probably would have found it odd and unattractive. In a reality of absolute monism, there would be no place for serious meditation on numbers, which Pythagoras and his followers defended as the worthiest occupation.[45]

This last point calls for further comment on two levels. The mysticism of the Upanishads praises the infinite and indeterminate as the ultimate reality. This reality is beyond description, explication, analysis, or understanding because its non-duality closes the gap between subject and object upon which cognition depends.[46] Pythagoreanism, on the other hand, taught explicitly that evil is a manifestation of the infinite, and good a manifestation of the finite. The monistic perspective was rejected and dualism affirmed.[47] Even the distinction between soul and body did not entail belief in a supreme being toward whom the soul strives. Pythagoras, it seems, was no theist, unless one takes kosmos to be his god.

Second, the spiritual concerns of Pythagoras were bound to criticism and inquiry. His style of "spirituality" does not resemble that of the rishi in quest of samadhi, nor does it have about it a

77

quality of devotionalism. Heraclitus has sharp words for Pythagoras' method. The former searched for truth within himself, a strategy at least analogous to the inwardness associated with Indian mysticism.[48] In contrast, Pythagoras "practised research most of all men," and was "original chief of wranglers," a man of extensive learning.[49] Heraclitus spurned Pythagoras precisely because the latter searched beyond himself for truth, specifically in the works of Homer, Hesiod, the poets, Anaximander, travellers, and men of science.[50] There is nothing in Pythagorean doctrine to suggest a progression from inquiry to the deliberate and systematic abandonment of inquiry, such as one finds in the famous dialogue between Uddalaka Aruni and his son Śvetaketu in the Chāndogya Upanishad.[51]

Empedocles, a champion of pluralism in Greek thought, was also an inhabitant of that shamanistic religious atmosphere which gave rise to the Orphic mysteries. He produced a work titled Purifications, had a reputation as a sorcerer and seer, and speaks in the fragments of his own partial incarnations.[52] The background of his conviction is not hard to discern. For a brief period he was a member of the Pythagorean order, but was expelled for "stealing discourses."[53] The specifically mystical content of Empedocles' teaching forms the basis of his physical theory, which, in part, was an effort to deal with the paradoxical metaphysics of Parmenides. Radhakrishnan is impressed by Empedocles' description of himself as an exile from heavenly bliss, doomed to be tossed from one material state to another in various incarnations for a period of "thrice ten thousand years," a beleaguered journey ending with the soul's reunion with the "God" from whom it was separated when it trusted the separative power of "insensate strife."[54] On the face of it, Empedocles' spiritual posture is in conflict with his pluralistic materialism. There is an abnormal tension, as Radhakrishnan puts it, between the mystical and rational impulses of Empedocles' thought, intimating the presence of India's spiritual influence, or expressing, at least, a view of human destiny identical with that of the Upanishads.

The materials of intellectual history are nearly always complex, elusive, and full of surprises. This is true especially with Empedocles, whose religious and philosophical ideas in their mutual relations are subjects of inconclusive debate among specialists. But it is still arguable, on respectable grounds, that religion and cosmology belong together in his thought. One can discount at once the probability of any direct Indian transmissions. Empedocles' doctrine of the soul is traced more readily to Orphism (i.e., the Second Olympian Ode of Pindar) and Pythagoreanism.[55] The question of indirect transmission would return us simply to a discussion of Orphism and Pythagoreanism, which, as we have seen, can be accounted for satisfactorily in a Greek context. As for Empedocles' cosmology, he shared the pre-Socratic "world-picture": "the spherical kosmos of warring opposites lapped in the circumambient divine which in a more or less adulterated form penetrates the cosmic sphere."[56]

Scholars are divided on the relation of mysticism to reason in Empedocles. Burnet and Vlastos believe that his two poems, Purifications and On Nature, are irreconcilable.[57] On the other hand, a formidable body of opinion affirms a coherent relationship between the two poems.[58] Guthrie sums up a central point relevant to Radhakrishnan's mysticism versus reason formula:

> Regarding rationalist and mystic as contrasting and mutually exclusive terms, we are apt to classify our Greeks as belonging to one or the other class - the Milesians on one side of the fence, the Orphics on the other, with a disapproving frown for Empedocles because he insists on keeping one leg on each side. Surely what Empedocles should teach us is that we in a period of thought before such distinctions had any meaning all shared a common background which was neither rational nor mystical exclusively.[59]

Empedocles shared with Sir Thomas Browne a capacity for living like a "great and true Amphibium ... in divided and distinguished worlds," and made no formal distinction between spiritual and material.[60] Perhaps, as Kirk and Raven suggest, the cycle of the soul in the Purifications provided a model for the cosmic cycle expounded in On Nature.[61] Following this line of interpretation, the thought of Empedocles can be viewed as a unity, and by so doing, it can be thrown into rather sharp contrast with the religion and philosophy of the Upanishads.

Cornford notes that:

> The driving power, the cause of Empedocles' system is not only, or chiefly, intellectual dissatisfaction with Parmenides' theories, but a profound belief that a somewhat different interpretation of the mystic view of the soul and God provides a scheme which, when we use it to interprete nature, leads to conclusions not so paradoxically at variance with the sense-data and with Ionian science as those of Parmenides.[62]

That is to say, one can view Empedocles' objective as simultaneously religious and scientific. Parmenides had argued that the One, the only reality, could not enhance its self-sufficient perfection by spawning a world of change and evil, for the two modes of being are incompatible. The One's immutability, plenitude, and timelessness contradict the transient panorama of the senses. This train of reasoning ends with a rupture between reason and experience, a troublesome contradiction which Parmenides resolved to his own satisfaction by rejecting the phenomenal world as an illusion.[63] Empedocles was not content with an either/or position. Whatever logic may say about the motionless oneness of the world, experience shows it

to be a vividly pluralistic continuum of change.[64] He tried to reconcile permanence and change in a single cohesive system capable
of giving both the spiritual and the empirical a legitimate place
in the world. Although his system was original, its components were
drawn freely from the religious and philosophical climate of the
time.[65]

Think of the world process as a cycle of alternating movements
between two poles: the Reign of Love and the Reign of Strife. At
the top of the cycle all the elements are evenly mixed in the Sphere
by the harmonizing power of Love, which circulates throughout the
whole (Love and Strife are conceived as spatial and corporeal powers). Encircling the Sphere is the menacing stream of Strife, ex-
cluded from contact with either Love or the elements. But the order
of nature will not permit homogeneity and quietude to dominate the
cosmos, and Strife is called upon to penetrate the Sphere and initiate the cycle. The restless wheel of Time and Justice will not remain still.[66] Strife pours into the Sphere and the elements begin
to separate, the process of differentiation continuing apace until
it is consummated in the Reign of Strife at the opposite pole, with
Love streaming around on the outside. In the continuum of mixture
and separation between the two extremes, the objects of the world,
including man and the gods, come into existence and pass away, their
various natures being determined by appropriate combinations of the
four elements and the two forces. This first pulse of the cycle is
a descent from light into darkness (an Orphic contrast), a lapse
from a zenith of goodness to a nadir of evil, which is culminated
when the elements are completely divorced from one another and Love
is flowing around the victorious Sphere of Strife.[67] The process is
reversed when Love flows into the Sphere and initiates the upward
swing toward light and union, bringing about the creation of a new
world.[68]

Empedoclean reality is one in so far as the "four roots" constitute an eternally shifting plenum, allowing change and unity to
coexist, and many in so far as the irreducible elements are capable
of generating multiplicity. There is being in that the elements are,
always have been, and always will be. There is becoming in that nothing remains forever what it is except the elements and the two forces.[69] Everything that comes into existence has something of the
divine in it. On the downward and upward swings of the cosmic cycle
the unity of Love is violated; it is mixed with Strife and the elements, in the countless permutations which occur between the two
points of rest. For Empedocles, the soul is identified with Love in
its unbroken state. Exposing a mystic's taste for unity, he expresses a hunger for the primal bliss which existed before the soul
placed its trust in "insensate strife." Evidently the soul is at
peace only when freed altogether from polluting contact with Strife
and the four elements, a condition that obtains, oddly enough, at
the lowest ebb of the cosmic cycle, in the Reign of Strife, which

Cornford terms the hemisphere of night.[70] Unity at the upper end, in the hemisphere of day means something quite different, for although Love is free of Strife, it is blended with the elements; thus the idea of unity can refer only to their intermingling without discord or separative tendencies.

In the Purifications, Empedocles speaks of the soul as an immortal daemon which transmigrates, and of himself as just such an immortal, passing through numerous incarnations in preparation for a return to bliss with the gods. As Kahn has pointed out, the notions of "soul" in each poem can be reconciled only if one identifies the daemon with divine Love, and interpretes the cosmology as an effort to make a place for spirit in a world of matter, to legitimize an immortal, transmigrating Pythagorean soul in an Ionian world of unstable material substances.[71] Empedocles applies the Parmenidean "law of the conservation of matter" to the soul, which assures its permanence as well as that of the elements. His approach to the soul can be viewed as a synthesis of Pythagoreanism, Ionian physical science, and Eleatic logic. Perhaps the taboos and exhortations of the Purifications are to be understood as means of facilitating the separation of pure from impure, or perhaps they are simple guides for living in accordance with the nature of things as revealed by reason and experience.

If those scholars who are prepared to follow this line of argument are right, then no schism of reason and mysticism exists in the thought of Empedocles. The apparent contradiction is due, in part, to the composition of two poems for different audiences. On this premise, it is clear that (a) his ideas are much indebted to Greek predecessors and contemporaries, and that (b) his pluralism and materialism are integral to his ideas of "soul" and "salvation," which have no true analogues in the Upanishads, or in any other Indian text down to his time. If the arguments for a synthesis of the two poems are wrong, and the Purifications is, indeed, a world apart from On Nature, then it is still clear that (a) Empedocles drew his spirituality from the wells of Orphism and Pythagoreanism, and that (b) his spiritual universe is a plurality of gods and souls for whom there is good and evil, and for whom there must be a material world to provide a basis for purity and impurity. Even his most original idea, that of a nonanthropomorphic deity both invisible and incorporeal, assumes the necessity of a physical universe in which the sacred mind (phrēn) can disport itself.

Empedocles wrote about cosmology as well as religion, and if one inclines to the interpretation that the former served the interests of the latter, the fact remains that he wished to make the operations of nature intelligible, a motive which invests his philosophy with a quality of rationality quite alien to Indian transcendentalism, and far in advance of the tentative cosmological speculation ventured in either the Vedas or the Upanishads.[72]

Now we shall turn to Marlow's suspicion of Buddhist influence on Heraclitus (fl. 500 B.C.). Does coincidence explain the formulation about the same time of two cosmologies which hold impermanence as a central doctrine?

Early Buddhist thought discovered in change, and in human attachment to its manifestations, the cause of suffering and rebirth, whose cessation, the condition for quietude and bliss, requires a resolute disengagement of consciousness and body from the flux.[73] Because the Buddha's views on change were not clearly set forth, several schools of thought on the issue eventually appeared: the world as a stream of sensations alone; the world as consciousness alone; the world as a void.[74] The nature of the phenomenal world was not, it seems, an urgent question for the Buddha, but rather a potential distraction from the diagnosis and cure of suffering.[75] The Buddhist conception of change is negative and pessimistic, for impermanence (anicca) is the field upon which craving (tanhä) provokes all the ills of existence.[76] While one lives in attachment to the flux, there can be no hope of peace or fulfillment transcending the moment. While the flux is quite real, it is by repudiating it in the discipline of the Eightfold Path that one attains enlightenment (Nirvāṇa) and experiences no further rebirths.

In the dynamic cosmology of Heraclitus, change and reality are one and the same; nothing lies beyond the flux. It is, as in Buddhist cosmology, uncreated and eternal, containing within itself law, wisdom, soul, harmony. Its elements are transformed incessantly out of and into one another, with Fire presiding as the Logos. Embodied in Fire is the soul-substance which flows through the world. It differs from other elements as a matter of degree, being the least corporeal substance in nature, and "souls have the sense of smell in Hades."[77] Oneness for Heraclitus is a seamless flow of transformations, the raging, eternal Fire.[78] Oneness also means a harmony of opposites: "harmony consists of opposing tension, like that of the bow and lyre."[79] Within the universal stream of change is found all wisdom and knowledge. The way to enlightenment is not withdrawal, meditation, or trance, but broad inquiry and experience of the world: "those things of which there is sight, hearing, knowledge; these are what I honor most."[80]

Cornford argues that Heraclitus was a mystic in rebellion against the rationalism and "mechanism" of Ionian philosophy.[81] While there is much to be said for this view if one concentrates on those aphorisms which mention soul, God, rebirth, and the like,[82] a reading of Heraclitus' views on such matters in context easily shows how remote were his ideals from those of Brahmanism or Buddhism. First, he was a saucy individualist who commented with irony on the follies of men.[83] Second, he admired the old Homeric standard that publically acknowledged excellence is the highest good: "the best men choose one thing rather than all else: everlasting

fame among mortal men. The majority are satisfied, like well-fed
cattle."[84] In the whirling sand of this suffering world, a Buddhist
saw fame among mortal men as so much worthless chaff, a symptom of
chronic immersion in samsāra (the cycle of existence): "Come, look
at this world resembling a painted royal chariot. The foolish are
sunk in it; for the wise there is no attachment for it."[85] Third,
there is in Heraclitus a patent animosity toward the mystery religions, a distaste for shamanistic pretensions, and, by inference,
a self-conscious distance from the mystical tradition: "Night-
ramblers, magicians, Bacchants, Maenads, Mystics: the rites accepted by mankind in the Mysteries are an unholy performance."[86] Finally, he was no admirer of the Pythagoreans or their founder.[87]

That shamanistic traits appear in Heraclitus merely shows that
no thinker can evade wholly the prevailing zeitgeist of his age. If
parallels must be drawn, there is an impressive one with the modern
conception of matter-energy equivalence, and another, perhaps more
exotic one, with the Chinese theory of cosmic harmony maintained by
an alternation of opposites: the yin and yang. In the Upanishads,
Uddalaka analyzes the qualities of phenomenal existence as manifestations of fire, or heat.[88] The Mundaka Upanishad makes generous
use of fire imagery to describe ultimate reality.[89] The first two
parallels are obviously coincidental. The second pair cannot be
taken seriously because of the diverse aims of Heraclitus and the
sages of the Upanishads. The aim of the latter, according to Radhakrishnan, "was not science or philosophy, but right living."[90]
The aim of Heraclitus was wisdom, and for him this meant science
and philosophy, the keys to "understanding the world's operation."[91]

What of Heraclitus' belief in the soul and the divinity of a
higher truth? What of his mystical tendencies? If a connection between Heraclitean and Buddhist conceptions of impermanence are open
to dispute, the gap between the Heraclitean and Upanishadic versions
of "soul" is virtually unbridgeable.

In the fragments of Heraclitus, the phenomenal world is reality. There is no human destiny outside the activity of the world.
The soul, like everything else, is Fire.[92] Moreover, the soul has
at least part of its essential being in motion, as do all things in
nature.[93] It has a unique principle of growth in which its self-
realization takes a readiness for the unexpected, a perceptive at-
tunement to the flux, a recognition that change, not fixity, is the
law of life: "We must not act and speak like men asleep."[94] Soul
must pursue the fullest, most intense activity, all the while bearing within itself an element of discord. As Wheelwright puts it,
"that soul is a more or less accidental product of the natural world
and that soul is somehow significantly self-determining are two warring but ineradicable truths about the soul, which an awakened intellect will always hold in unresolved tension."[95] Fulfillment
means action, climbing toward "light, dryness, and intellectual

awareness."[96] From this perspective we can understand why Heraclitus honored most "those things of which there is sight, hearing, knowledge," since there can be no wisdom without their help.

Heraclitus' conception of soul has no counterpart in Christianity or Brahmanism. The Christian soul is incorporeal and imperishable, salvation being a transcendent state in which it is freed of all physical limitation.[97] In the Upanishads the call is for disengagement from the mutable aspects of experience, which are consistently assigned a lesser reality than Brahman. Any dependence upon knowledge or wisdom in a temporal, worldly sense is a mark of delusion. Deliverance from the wheel of rebirth demands a repudiation of "sight, hearing, knowledge." Heraclitus proclaims change as the ineluctable law of reality, the only law within which humanity can aspire to fulfillment. In contrast, the rishis lament

> the drying up of great oceans, the falling away of
> mountain peaks, the deviation of the fixed pole-star,
> the cutting of the wind cords (of the stars), the
> submergence of the earth, the retreat of the celestials
> from their station. In this sort of cycle of existence
> (samsāra) what is the good of enjoyment of desires,
> when after a man has fed on them there is seen repeatedly his return here to earth?[98]

Two more radically different attitudes toward change can hardly be imagined.

Like most of the pre-Socratics, Heraclitus had a religious interest as well as a desire to provide a rational account of nature's changing spectacle. As Karl Popper has emphasized, his cosmology is a speculative hypothesis which bases reality in change, but Heraclitus also speaks of the "divine," the Logos "which is present in all things and discoverable by all observers if only they will open their eyes and their minds to the fullest possible extent."[99] Logos is the all-pervading essence of things, the ultimate principle of the world, the supreme desideratum of the awakened intelligence.[100] Such a grand principle merits the epithet "divine," a name commonly given to gods and supernatural forces by ignorant men.

Heraclitus imputes divinity to the rational, self-sufficient, lawful operation of the world. The Logos has "permanence" in the sense that lawfulness does not pass away in the flux.[101] Perhaps he intended the divinity of his world order to be taken seriously as a possible object of worship, if only by the enlightened few capable of wisdom and understanding.[102] There is a vague tinge of mysticism in Heraclitus' remark: "That which is wise is one: to understand the purpose which steers all things through all things."[103] But when all religious and mystical interpretations

have been wrung from the idea of Logos, it remains a rational concept, the process of the world, and the highest object of understan-
ding.104 As we have already observed, the general idea of cosmic
order appears in all high cultures, hence there is no imperative
need to associate the Logos of Heraclitus with the rita of the Vedas.
In various notions of Brahman as cosmic order in the Upanishads,
there are fundamental departures from the view of Heraclitus. Realization of Brahman in mystical oneness takes precedence over understanding the cosmic process. Most telling is the consistent pull
away from the flux to a mode of reality whose character, if one
may call it that, is antithetical to change and motion.

The case for Heraclitus as mystic rests on three grounds.
He appeals to inwardness: "I searched into myself."105 He spoke
with a dramatic sense of inspiration, "and it is no metaphor to call
his style oracular."106 Finally, it is likely that Heraclitus was
not content with knowing about the Logos, but held that one must encompass it somehow within oneself.107 On all three counts he can be
described as a mystic only in the loosest sense, if one means by
"mysticism" the submergence of individual consciousness in some un-
namable reality, usually with the help of drugs or some meditative
discipline.108 Heraclitus may have searched within, but he also
searched without, and one would expect a man of his intellect and
curiosity to embrace both fields of inquiry. He differs from the
sages of the Upanishads in that his introspection contributed to the
formulation of a rational cosmology. His oracular manner was not un-
common among the pre-Socratics and may be attributed to the influence of powerful religious traditions and rhetorical forms. The
closest he comes to a kind of mystical identification is in the
notion of rousing the fire of the soul to the intensity of the cosmic fire, or the idea that reality is apprehended to the extent that
one is attuned to the Logos. But we do not find in Heraclitus, as
we do in the Upanishads, the warning that participation in the divine, or union with it, requires the annihilation of the discriminating intellect, nor does he suggest that meditative discipline is
a necessary condition for spiritual insight.

If there is any element of mysticism in Heraclitus' conception of the upward way towards light, it is at any
rate a mysticism, not of sleep, but of waking alert-
ness. Heraclitus has nothing in common with the type of
mystic who thinks to achieve participation in the divine,
and thus to find truth, by going into a trance. In sleep
and trance there is nothing but a private world of
dreams.109

Before turning to Plato, it is worth pointing out that Burnet,
Cornford, Jaeger, Kirk and Raven, and Vlastos have produced signi-
ficant work on the pre-Socratics, yet not one of them believes that
Indian ideas influenced Greek philosophy and religion. In fact, one

of them neatly turns the tables by saying that "everything points to the conclusion that Indian philosophy arose under Greek influence."110

The philosophy of Plato is tempting game for those who see an historical or substantive connection between Indian and Greco-Roman-Christian thought. Radhakrishnan singles out Plato as the penultimate example of the Greek mystical tradition, telling us that he rejected rationalism for the ineffable vision of the sage.111 Along with B.J. Urwick, Radhakrishnan proposes that so many parallels with the Upanishads in one man's work cannot be mere coincidence.

Plato believes in the immortality, preexistence, and reincarnation of the soul; he teaches the contingent reality of the sensible world; he distinguishes rulers, defenders, and producers (Cf. Brāhmans, Kshatriyas, and Vaishyas); he recognizes a tripartite soul with the functions of reason, activity, and appetite (Cf. the Indian rajas, sattva, and tamas); there is an ens realissimum, the Form of the Good, which is perceived intuitively (Cf. the unitive experience of Brahman known as samādhi); he characterizes reality as eternal, perfect, and incorruptible, and distinguishes genuine from pseudo-knowledge (once more, Brahman, and the contrast of vidyā and avidyā); he praises philosophy, with its goal of intuiting the Good, as man's highest vocation. When one takes into account also his frequent denigration of the sensible world, there is apparent reason for at least a strong suspicion that the great Athenian was a student, either directly or indirectly, of Brāhmans or Brahmanical writings. The evidence is sufficiently imperfect to allow a measure of freedom in this kind of speculation. While most Plato scholars reject an Indianized Plato, it is still not rare for authors in other fields, especially comparative religion and philosophy, to flirt with those speculations, and still a larger group - writers like Guénon, Coomaraswamy, and Aldous Huxley - has been prepared to assert an identity of outlook, a shared spiritual perspective, in Plato and the Upanishads. The problem is not, therefore, a dead horse, but one that invites a better refutation than an impatient, curt growl that Plato's thought is vintage Greek.

If Plato were in touch with Indian philosophers, it is not probable that he went to them. His sole reference to travel mentions only Italy and Sicily; thus he journeyed west, not east. A trip to Egypt cannot be ruled out, but there is no good evidence for it.112 In the surviving record Plato's biography is obscure up to the age of sixty, the fullest episode being his brief experience as tutor to Dionysus in Syracuse.113 The adventure with Dionysus is in the controversial Seventh Letter,114 and the most important traditional material on his early life is summarized in Diogenes Laertius (Lives iii. 6), whose value for Plato is assessed by J.E. Raven:

86

The one and only suggestion of the slightest reliability
to emerge from Diogenes' entire account of the first
half of Plato's life is that at the age of twenty-eight
Plato withdrew to Megara, with others of the Socratic
circle, and stayed there for an unspecified length of
time.[115]

Many of the dialogues in which "mystical" doctrines occur were composed before he was fifty, the period of his life least accounted
for.[116] Since nothing of significance can be learned about Plato's
alleged exposure to Brahmanical teachings from biographical facts,
we must search for clues in his doctrines.

Plato's dialogues are a great watershed of Greek religion and
philosophy. They make use of numerous ideas developed by his predecessors. While concerned with abstract issues of metaphysics,
epistemology, and logic, they are also concerned with the political
and moral crisis which overtook Athens as a result of the disastrous
Peloponnesian War (431-404 B.C.). In Plato's generation, anarchy and
unreason seemed to poison everything of value, the sickness reaching
something of a climax with the trial and execution of Socrates (399
B.C.), an event of capital importance in young Plato's development
as a philosopher. Mathematics, metaphysics, and logic were his talents, and "it is difficult to believe that government was his chief
interest."[117] Yet he faced a crisis of values in his chaotic Greek
environment, and tried to resolve it by finding a new basis for morality and political authority. In effect, he did not philosophize
in a cultural vacuum. In the Republic and the Laws, even though he
went from a state governed by men to one governed by laws, his larger purpose was a bedrock of principle upon which a just state might
be founded. The tint of mysticism in Plato's metaphysics should not
deflect one from recognizing his life-long struggle with man's fate
as a social being in general, and with the political fate of Athens
in particular.

In the developed Hindu scheme of things, the life-course of the
individual is divided into four ideal stages: that of pupil (brahma-
carya), the householder (gārhasthya), the forest dweller (vānapras-
tha), and the wandering ascetic (sannyāsa).[118] The first two stages
discharge one's obligations to society, the third is transitional to
the fourth, and the fourth is devoted to achieving mystical union
with the world soul. While the eclectic Bhagavad-Gītā attempts to
reconcile worldly activity with spiritual detachment, chiefly by
the device of activity without regard for fruits, or karma yoga, it
is still maintained that the highest knowledge leads beyond the
field of action.[119] Without embarking at this point on a discussion of Plato's views on the career of the soul, it is instructive
that when he was in the twilight of life, past the eighty year
mark, he was not practicing yoga, retiring to the forest, or con-
centrating all his powers on detachment from the world. Rather he

was absorbed in the composition of the Laws. The old philosopher was still giving hard thought to the political, economic, legal, ethical, and religious foundations of the state.[120]

The antecedents of Plato's major ideas seem to be wholly Greek. His distress over the prospects of enduring truth being found in the unstable world of sense experience was owed probably to Cratylus, a disciple of Heraclitus who took seriously the proposition that "you cannot step twice into the same rivers," and limited himself, consistently enough, to pointing and grunting when he wished to communicate, on the assumption that nothing very definite can be said of a flux.[121] Plato's response to this challenge was the proposal that reality is a timeless realm of intelligible Forms, an idea most likely indebted to the Pythagorean doctrine that the true nature of things is the geometrical patterns they form in space.[122] Mathematics played an active role in the formulation of Pythagorean cosmology and theology. Plato's metaphysics and theory of education also reserve an exalted place for mathematical studies, which are able to direct the soul's "eye" away from the material world to unobstructed contemplation of the Forms. It is significant that Plato's Academy was, at least until the Alexandrian renaissance, the chief source of mathematical and astronomical inquiry in the Greek world.[123] There is a tenuous parallel with Brahmanism here, for the serious student of Vedic literature was expected to discipline himself in grammar and logic; in the fourth century B.C., grammatical studies were brought to a level of precision and rigor by Panini.[124] If the spirit of the Academy was summed up in the admonition, "Let none enter who knows not geometry," then a similar spirit for the Brahmans might have been expressed in the words, "Let none enter who knows not grammar."

Plato's division of the soul into three parts is traceable to the Pythagorean idea of Three Lives.[125] His separation of knowledge (of the Forms) from opinion (about phenomena)[126] has its counterpart in Parmenides' Truth (that reality is an eternal plenum) and Belief (that the flux is real).[127] And so it goes. Virtually all of Plato's doctrines can be attributed to the interaction of his unique genius with the controversies of his predecessors and the disheartening failures of Athenian polity. Since historical evidence does not support Indian influence on him, we are left with the claim of significant parallels between his philosophy and certain ideas in the Indian tradition down to about the fourth century B.C. If the most crucial of those parallels can be proved inconclusive, then the historical case for outside influence will be weakened further, and Plato's membership in a worldwide mystical tradition will have to be viewed as doubtful.

Let us begin with Plato's theory of knowledge, specifically the method by which knowledge is acquired, its sources, and its proper objects. In the Vedas, what counts for knowledge is the words and procedures defining the right execution of ritual and sacrifice. The universal law (rita) governing men and gods is bound closely to the performance of sacrifice, and is seen also as a mandate for moral rectitude and as a source of the necessity underlying natural phenomena.[128] Radhakrishnan's claim that rita "corresponds to the universals of Plato" is moot.[129] There is a resemblance in that rita and Plato's Forms give all aspects of reality their being and coherence, but the differences are great enough to nullify any true correspondence between the two.

For the Vedic seers, knowledge comes predominantly from tradition, and reveals itself in details of ritual and the effects of sacrifice as surely as in the rhythms of nature. True knowledge is found in the Vedas, with the structure of ritual providing a legitimate object of knowledge. The Vedic concept of rita is colored by "the spirit of an age in which all intellectual activity is concentrated on the sacrifice, describing its ceremonies, discussing its value, speculating on its origin and significance."[130] For Plato, the true objects of knowledge are the abstract Forms, not tradition, ritual, or a body of literature transmitted orally. His method is not memorization or exact transmission of traditonal learning, but the practice of dialectic, described in the Republic (534E) as "the coping-stone as it were, placed above the sciences," a philosophical method embracing analysis and synthesis.

There are still other differences. Rita bestows material advantages and good fortune as the expected consequences of sacrifice.[131] Plato has no interest in sacrificing to the gods or to any other kind of divinity, and where prayer is discussed in the dialogues, the wise man is depicted as not asking for, or wanting, material benefits.[132] The Forms of Plato require no special protection at the hands of the supernatural, while rita must be upheld and guarded by deities.[133]

The mystical doctrines of the principal Upanishads are even more remote from Plato's thought than the ritualism of the Vedas.[134] There is, however, some common ground. Both wish to identify a foundation of being which sustains and contrasts with time, change, and sensuous experience. Both agree on the desirability of living in accordance with knowledge of such a permanent source of being, and both concede that their respective notions of being are, in the end, quite ineffable. Nevertheless, severe qualification will be necessary shortly in all of these areas of agreement. It is much more difficult to find points of agreement on the key issues of how one knows, the source of knowledge, and the object of knowledge. We shall now take up each point in turn.

The Upanishads affirm that intuition is the ultimate source of the highest knowledge.[135] The method by which one comes to know the ground of all being is some form of meditative discipline

as opposed to rational inquiry.[136] The supreme object of knowledge
is the Self, which is equated with Brahman, the indescribable, inexplicable , all-pervasive reality concealed behind the mask of
distinction and duality.[137] The Self, or Ātman, is the touchstone
of all lesser things: "the Soul, indeed, is this whole world."[138]
Some Upanishads distinguish between a phenomenal and a supra-pheno-
menal Brahman, a lower and a higher reality, but the main line of
speculation upholds Brahman as an ineluctable unity.[139] Knowledge
of the imperishable, not to be confused with knowledge of the world,
is inaccessible to reason or empirical inquiry, for "this Soul (atman) is not to be obtained by instruction, nor by intellect, nor
by much learning."[140] It is not a characteristic of Ātman or Brahman that they are intelligible; they cannot be grasped in the do-
main of reason. They are not objects of knowledge in the sense of
providing criteria for truth or falsehood, or of requiring such
criteria as a condition of knowledge.

It follows from this conception of knowledge that duties in
the spheres governed by ethics, politics, and social life are secondary. The highest good is not moral knowledge and action, nor is
it the creation of the best state, the most rational social order.

> Whatever ethics we have in the Upanishads is subsidiary
> to this goal (i.e., union with Brahman). Duty is a means
> to the end of the highest perfection. Nothing can be sat-
> isfying short of this highest condition. Morality is valu-
> able only as leading to it.[141]

Plato departs radically from this transcendental theory of
knowledge in holding that the permanently real is intelligible. The
Forms constitute a realm of intelligible objects. Their intelligibility resides in their power to vindicate both fact and value to
the satisfaction of reason. They are transcendent only in the sense
of being eternal and incorruptible, in contrast to the sensible
world of appearances, and not in the sense of being inaccessible
to thought. Moreover, there are as many Forms as there are classes
of objects in the universe (lower Forms like bricks and higher Forms
like justice). At the summit of Plato's ontological pyramid is the
Form of the Good, the ultimate source of being, which invests all
the lesser Forms with their reality. On the latter depends the integrity, reliability, and substance of the phenomenal world. Phenomena "participate" in the Forms just they, in turn, participate
in the Good. Obviously the Good seems to approximate the epistemological ideals of the Upanishads, but some caveats soon will be
in order.

Plato views the rational faculty of the soul as the source of
knowledge. He agrees with the Upanishads that sense experience is
incompetent to penetrate the vitals of reality, but rather than appealing to non-discursive intuition, he turns to rational inquiry

of a special type. Dialectic is Plato's method of exploring and
defining reality. The largely ethical concerns of Socrates are ex-
panded in the dialogues to include a science of the real, on the
premise that reality is not only intelligible but demonstrable. In
the early dialogues, dialectic is a method of examination by question and answer. Its purpose is to discover the "virtue" which all
moral behavior in a certain class shares in common.[142] This argu-
mentative method is in the service of moral arete, or the highest
excellence of the soul. Plato does not pretend to have uncovered
these ideal types - courage, piety, temperance, and the like. His
results are negative, but in the positive sense that we become aware
of how little we know about virtue.

In the Republic, dialectic becomes a means of ascent through
stages to a vision of the Good. The ascent demands prolonged, exhaustive intellectual training and years of practical experience
in worldly affairs.[143] Formal study is dominated by mathematics,
because it is the science which mirrors most accurately the nature
of the Forms.[144]

In the Sophist, dialectic is pursued with slight reference to
virtue or the Good, and is concerned rather with the irreducibles
of reality, those things which cannot be divided beyond a certain
point.[145] Here the dialectic assumes its most analytical role.
What Plato may have had in mind, as a long-range program, was the
reduction of mathematics to logic (perhaps in the spirit of White-
head and Russell's Principia Mathematica), the introduction of precision into the study of phenomena by geometrizing natural science,
and closure of the gap between fact and value by transforming truths
of fact into truths of reason.[146] Among other things, physics would
become something more than "a likely story." Dialectical inquiry
would consummate itself by pressing beyond the creation of philosopher kings and care for the soul to a synoptic vision that necessity makes things what they are, that everything is for the "best"
when seen from the perspective of intelligible science.

Although Plato's method has no analogue in the Upanishads, his
quest for unity is certainly echoed there.[147] Another point of con-
vergence is that the Good will not yield to dialectic, nor is it de-
finable in rational propositions. Being the source of all predi-
cates, it cannot be assigned a predicate. As with Brahman, one must
adopt a language of negation: "it is not this, it is not that"
(neti-neti), or use, as Plato does, analogies and myths.[148] Plato
says that "the power and capacity of learning exists in the soul
already," a belief which approximates to some extent the equivalence of Ātman-Brahman, in that ultimate "knowledge" is found in
the Self and not outside it.[149] On all of these points, however,
important differences separate Plato and the Upanishads.

First, the Platonic intuition of the Good is something of a

rational intuition, for it is the rational part of the soul which does the perceiving, or has the vision.150 Second, the vision of the Good can be interpreted as a perception of cosmic intelligibility, an outcome of experience with lesser stages of intelligibility, helped along by learning and thought. That is to say, one does not unite with Brahman without the assistance of yoga, and one does not have a vision of the Good without the aid of dialectic.151 Third, Plato does not treat the Good consistently as an end in itself. but is inclined rather to see it as an essential condition of the good life. While all worldly value depends on the Good, the world is not to be renounced. In the Upanishads, renunciation is not only a condition for deliverance but is frequently set forth as an ideal in its own right.152 The Platonic ideal is not one of renuncation. Cutting through his mystical tendencies is a steady commitment to ethics and the secular values of social and political life. A vision of the Good makes one the most valuable citizen; it is not a reprieve from living sanely in a community of men, nor is it an invitation to cultivate withdrawal.153

Plato believed in the pre-existence, immortality, and reincarnation of the soul. The respective meanings intended by Plato and the sages of the Upnaishads, as indicated by substantive usage in the texts, do not have much in common. A consensus in the Upanishads is that "soul," or Self in that context, is precisely the same as Brahman, the ultimate reality.154 On the other hand, in Plato there is no occasion, in his cosmology or theology, when a multiplicity of souls gives way to one universal soul.155 His drift is to specify the existence of a supremely good soul, the "best" which lords it over the others.156

The essence of a soul is described in the Phaedrus and the Laws as capacity for self-movement. Whatever can move itself is immortal because the motion will never cease. Things whose motion is generated from the outside must eventually suffer the fate of coming to rest, which is the same as death. Soul is the origin of life and motion (interchangeable terms) and therefore is immortal and pre-existent.157 In the Upanishads, motion is nearly always associated with a lesser mode of reality.158 The exception is Uddalaka in the Chāndogya Upanishad, who "held a hylozoistic and perhaps even materialistic view of the world."159 In the Upanishads, Brahman is still like the mind of the yogin who has succeeded in quieting the swirl of empirical consciousness. In Plato, the intrinsic motion of the world soul is at the core of reality.

More fundamental than any other consideration is Plato's insistent appeal to reason as the arbiter of his views. Mystical consciousness has little interest for him, especially with regard to the nature of souls, for whose existence he constructs detailed arguments. Their reality, he believes, can be demonstrated, for they are not objects of intuitive experience; they are intelligible entities accessible to thought. Compare, for example, the arguments for immortal souls in the Phaedo with the bare assertions of the Upanishads.[160] Plato wishes to persuade, the Upanishads are content to announce.

In the majestic myth of the Phaedrus , whose substance varies little from the Myth of Er in the Republic, the souls are led by the gods in a procession around the course of the heavens, at midpoint between the flawed world of man and the impeccable abode of the Forms.[161] As they make the celestial circuit, these divine ones impart order to the world. But their true purpose is to abandon the familiar track from time to time and gaze at the Forms on "the plain of reality," after which they resume their round in the heavens and try to shape the world in accordance with the remembered vision. This myth recalls Orphic ideas, such as the account of souls falling to earth and losing their wings, which cannot be recovered until ten thousand years of reincarnations have been endured by the offender. The difference is that Plato's rhapsody about gods and souls is backed up with strong reasoning in the Laws.[162] The point is that his gift for mythical imagery should not be allowed to obscure the weight he gave to rational demonstration.[163]

In way of illustration, it is not mystical experience but intellectual considerations which lead him to postulate the existence of an "evil" soul to explain the presence of disorder (earthquakes, irregularities in planetary orbits, and the like) in the world. If serene motions produce order, then erratic motions must be responsible for disorder; the one is just as necessary theologically as the other.[164] In this penchant for intellectual tidiness, we do not feel the presence of the Upanishads but of the Pythagoreans. Some of Plato's beliefs are no doubt mystical after a fashion, if one means otherworldly by "mystical." But they are at the same time rationalistic, in that he expounds them with a persistent regard for standards of intelligibility.

It is easy to misunderstand the function of myth in Plato's philosophy. He did not have to cope with truths so spiritually profound that reason failed and the symbolic power of myth came to the rescue. Indeed, this interpretation is itself a myth.

> The notion, common since the days of Neo-Platonism, that myth is the appropriate form in which to symbolize truths too sublime for rational comprehension, is entirely foreign to Plato. It is precisely when he is dealing with what he regards as the ultimate realities that his language is most 'scientific' and least mythical.[165]

The myths of the Gorgias, Republic, Phaedo, and Phaedrus function in Plato's thought neither as allegorical representations of "higher"

truth nor as revelations of supernal reality. They are philosophical fables superior to traditional myths about the gods, which, to
Plato's discontent, often depicted the gods as foolish, degenerate
beings. They serve as a means of bridging the realms of feeling and
reason. The superiority of the philosophical myth lies in its conformity to the conclusions of philosophic reason. By itself, the
myth is powerless to stimulate conviction; it can only hint to the
affective side of human nature the truths of philosophy in the form
of "a story shaped at will."[166] Just as Plato tried to reconstruct
the foundations of knowledge and society, so he tried to create a
new mythology which would portray the virtue of the gods, but a
virtue he believed that only dialectic could establish beyond doubt.
In an imaginative, almost playful, vein, his mythologizing brings
to the unphilosophical mind some notions of the soul and its destiny, and suggests the distinction between appearance and reality.

> But never does he acknowledge a truth that reason cannot
> grasp, that lies beyond its reach, because reason is
> 'fragmentary.' The myth, shaped in accordance with rea-
> son, brings to the realm of the passions the light of
> the intellect.[167]

For Plato, there is no meaningful knowledge of reality or cultivation of the soul without the active participation of reason. In
the Kena Upanishad, Brahman is "that which one thinks not with
thought."[168] In the history of Indian religion and philosophy, one
cannot find a maker of myths like Plato; "the mythology of India
serves its function as the popular vehicle of the esoteric wisdom
of yoga experience and of orthodox religion ... the tales are not
the products of individual experiences and reactions."[169] Platonic
myths grow from the soil of reason; Indian myths are collective
evocations of profuse worldly manifestations of an inexpressible
absolute. They bypass rather than illustrate reason.

Plato's doctrine of the soul has little in common with that of
the Upanishads, which insist on a general view of soul that is unitary. It is not mistaken to say that Plato also thinks of the soul
as somehow a unity, but he goes on to make some crucial distinctions
on behalf of his social and political theory. While a man is alive
he has three souls. The Timaeus distinguishes the rational soul,
which is seated in the brain and is immortal, the spirited soul,
seated in the thorax, and the appetitive soul, seated in the abdo-
men.[170] This model is set out more dramatically in the Phaedrus,
where the three souls, or "parts" of the soul, appear symbolically
as a charioteer (reason) driving two horses, one noble and coura-
geous (spirit), the other gross and base (appetite).[171] The last
two perish with the mortal body. The rational soul survives, but
hardly bears any resemblance to the kinds of immortality proclaimed
in the Upanishads.[172]

The highest good for Plato is cultivation of the rational soul, though not to the exclusion of other faculties.[173] When the individual dies, it is intellect alone that is able to contemplate the timeless Forms. In short, it is intellect that becomes immortal.[174] Radhakrishnan's account of various forms of immortality in the Upanishads leaves one with an impression of vagueness. The fate of the soul is tossed between "liberation devoid of any activity, perception, thought or consciousness" and "a state of activity, full of freedom and perfection."[175] By comparison, Plato's doctrine has the lucidity of the Greek atmosphere. Whatever synthesis one might be able to build from interpretations of immortality in the Upanishads, it is not likely that a glorification of reason would be the outcome, nor has this ever been so in philosophical speculation based on the Upanishads.

One should not make too much of Plato's transcendentalism. In the Phaedrus he ranks seers below traders and athletes, while philosophers schooled in reason rank first in his hierarchy of human types.[176] For someone treading the path of the perennial philosophy, he was remarkably capable of development, change, and exploration.[177] Judging from the Laws, he seems to have decided that the ideal of philosopher kings is unworkable in a too imperfect world, a change of heart forced upon him by experience of men, not immersion in mystical oneness. In that last work of his, we hear no more of intuitive visions, of the Good or anything else. He draws the blueprint of a grim, repressive, closed society (a Sparta rather than an Athens) whose stock in trade is official lies, censorship, heresy trials, and harsh sanctions, all reflecting a profound disillusionment with the educability of the ordinary person. Philosophy is for the few, laws and organized religion for the many. The voice of the Laws, whatever else it may be, is not the voice of a transcendentalist.

The question of what kind of god Plato believed in has been much discussed. In the Timaeus he says that "the father and maker of all this universe is past finding out; and even if we found him, to tell of him to all men would be impossible."[178] An agnostic might just as well say this as a seer of the Upanishads, although one cannot deny close verbal resemblances between the Timaeus and some of the Upanishads.[179] But Plato was concerned with what is possible: the demonstration of certain religious principles, their enforcement by law, their inculcation through education, and the fusion of religious and civic life. The capstone of his life's work was a cult to insure the stability of the social order, based on the worship of celestial bodies.

This joint cult -in place of the expected cult of Zeus - expresses the union of old and new, Apollo standing for the traditionalism of the masses, and Helios for the new 'natural religion' of the philosophers; it is Plato's

95

last desperate attempt to build a bridge between the
intellectuals and the people, and thereby save the unity
of Greek belief and Greek culture.[180]

Plato's religion belongs in the world, and is entangled with it.

The mystical aspect of Indian thought is quite antithetical
to the critical tradition of Greek philosophy as developed by the
pre-Socratics. But Indian mysticism does not have much in common
as well with the "transcendentalism" of Phythagoras, Empedocles,
and Plato, all of whom were committed to the explanatory adventures
of Greek rationalism. What they all shared together, whatever the
religious significance of their thought, was the critical outlook.
Their mode of philosophizing invited questions, revisions, doubt,
and further inquiry. All is not derived from some divine source,
duly certified for certainty and permanence, even though Greek philosophy was obsessed with the problem of change. In the Upanishads
it is said: "That which is the finest essence - this whole world
has that as its soul. That is Reality. That is Ātman (Soul). That
art thou ... "[181] Xenophanes replies: "Truly the gods have not revealed to mortals all things from the beginning; but mortals by
long seeking discover what is better."[182]

1. See Henri Frankfort et al., _Before Philosophy_ (Baltimore: Penguin Books, 1949), pp. 126-127, 218-219.
2. Quoted in Moses Hadas, _The Greek Ideal and Its Survival_ (New York: Harper and Row, 1960), p. 18. Cf. Jaeger, _Paideia_, I, 6-7.
3. Martin Nilsson, _Greek Piety_, trans. H.J. Rose (London: Oxford University Press, 1948), p. 29.
4. Erwin Rohde has spoken of "a drop of alien blood in the veins of the Greeks." Quoted in Dodds, _The Greeks and the Irrational_, p. 139.
5. "The world appears to primitive man neither inanimate nor empty but redundant with life; and life has individuality in man and beast and plant, and in every phenomenon which confronts man – the thunderclap, the sudden shadow, the eerie and unknown clearing in the wood, the stone which suddenly hurts him while on a hunting trip." Frankfort, p. 14. On the prevalence of belief in immortality and reincarnation of the soul, and the probable origins of these beliefs, see Paul Radin, _Primitive Religion: Its Nature and Origin_ (New York: Dover Publications, 1957), pp. 269-288. See also Erwin Rohde, _Psyche: The Cult of Souls and Belief in Immortality Among the Greeks_ (New York: Harcourt, Brace, 1925), pp. 346-347.
6. Francis M. Cornford, _From Religion to Philosophy_ (New York: Harper Torchbooks, 1957), p. 161.
7. There is excellent material in Joseph Henderson and Maud Cokes, _The Wisdom of the Serpent: The Myths of Death, Rebirth, and Resurrection_ (New York: George Braziller, 1963). Also useful is James Frazer, _The New Golden Bough_, rev. and ed. Theodor Gaster (New York: Mentor Books, 1959), part IV.
8. Radin, p. 110.
9. In general, see Mircea Eliade, _Le Chamanisme et les Techniques archaïques de l'extase_ (Paris: Payot, 1957), and N. Kershaw Chadwick, _Poetry and Prophecy_ (Cambridge: Cambridge University Press, 1942), chapter VI, entitled "The Spiritual Journeys of the Seer." Chadwick mentions Thrace, "where manticism appears to have been highly cultivated." _Ibid._, p. 11.
10. Joseph Campbell, _The Masks of God: Primitive Mythology_ (New York: Viking Press, 1959), pp. 258 f.
11. "This formulation ... consisted of three parts: first, the description of his neurotic temperament and his actual suffering and trance; second, the description of his forced isolation, physical and spiritual, from the rest of the group; and third, the detailed description of what might best be called an obsessive identification with his goal. From the first arose the theory of the nature of the ordeal through which he must pass; from the second the insistence upon taboos and purifications; and from the third the theory either that he was possessed by the goal or that he was possessed of the goal." Radin, p. 132.

12. Dodds, p. 141.
13. W. Ruben has argued that Greek and Indian notions of reincarnation may have had a common origin in shamanistic practices of Central Asia. Acta Orientalia, 27 (1939), 164 f. Erwin Rohde notes that "the ascetic ideal was not absent even from Greece. It remained, however - in spite of the influence it had in some quarters - always a foreign thing in Greece, having its obscure home among sects of spiritualistic enthusiasts, and regarded in contrast with the normal and ruling view of life, as a paradox, almost a heresy." Psyche, pp. 302-303. Some evidence points to the north of Greece as the source of shamanistic practices, which enables one to accept Rohde's judgment without relying on the remoter hypothesis of Indian influence. Like most of the elusive topics discussed in this essay, the concept of "Greek shamans" is controversial. James A. Philip believes that "in Greece we have no evidence for any such institution. There is word for 'shaman' and no record of the practices characteristic of shamanism." What Philip has in mind when he refers to practices is the institution of the soul-journey which the shaman undertakes at the behest of the entire community and not for his own edification. Guided by this criterion, we find that the "most important common characteristic" one would expect to distinguish northern and so-called "Greek" shamans does not occur among the latter. Pythagoras and the Early Pythagoreans (Toronto: University of Toronto Press, 1966), pp. 160-161. The argument is well taken, but it is clear, nevertheless, that shamanistic traits occur among the Greeks. The evidence for transmission from the outside is slight, so there is passive reason for being content with the hypothesis of an independent cultural development.
14. Nilsson, Greek Piety, p. 35. On the subject of Orphism, I am especially indebted to W.K.C. Guthrie's work of synthesis, Orpheus and the Greek Religion: A Study of the Orphic Movement (New York: W.W. Norton and Co., 1966).
15. No source from the classical period attributes belief in transmigration to Orphism. Moreover, one cannot be sure that so-called Orphic poems were even in existence before the time of Pythagoras. Dodds, p. 149.
16. Nilsson, Greek Piety, pp. 83 ff.
17. Ibid., p. 28. See also Nilsson's "Early Orphism and Kindred Religious Movements," Harvard Theological Review, 28 (1935), 184.
18. Nilsson, A History of Greek Religion, p. 216.
19. Rohde has surveyed the major evidence on Greek shamanism in Psyche, pp. 327 ff. Scholars dispute the place of origin, some placing it in Macedonia, others in Thrace. Guthrie is probably right in saying that "the matter is of comparatively little importance." Orpheus and Greek Religion, p. 63.
20. Dodds, p. 150.
21. Nilsson, A History of Greek Religion, p. 102-104. Dodds, pp. 179 f.

22. Nilsson, A History of Greek Religion, p. 213. In Homer, there is no unitary conception of the soul, but rather three faculties: thymos (emotion), noos (perception, and psyche (life or breath). Bruno Snell, The Discovery of the Mind: The Greek Origins of European Thought, trans. T.G. Rosenmeyer (New York: Harper Torchbooks, 1960), pp. 14-15. It should be emphasized that various notions of "soul" may have been held by Orphics, reflecting a general confusion among Greeks on the issue. In general, one should be cautious not to identify Greek cults with one another. See George Mylonas, Eleusis and the Eleusinian Mysteries (Princeton: Princeton University Press, 1961), p. 288. But this caveat does not mean there was interpenetration. "It is even likely, since the representatives of Orpheus taught at Athens and it was open to every Athenian (indeed to every Greek) to become an Eleusinian initiate, that many a man was initiated at Eleusis who was also an Orphic." Guthrie, Orpheus and Greek Religion, p. 153.

23. Radhakrishnan, Eastern Religions and Western Thought, p. 138.

24. Jane Harrison, Prolegomena to the Study of Greek Religion (Cambridge: Cambridge University Press, 1922), p. 592.

25. Ibid., p. 590.

26. Charles H. Long, Alpha: The Myths of Creation (New York: George Braziller, 1963), pp. 113 ff. Jaeger says that "while the conception of the world egg is not Hesiodic, we have evidence of its presence elsewhere on Greek soil. It is so closely in accord with the early zoomorphic feeling for nature that there is very little likelihood of its being derived from the Orient." The Theology of the Early Greek Philosophers, p. 65. Cf. Nilsson, A History of Greek Religion, p. 216, and Kirk and Raven, p. 47.

27. Brihadāranyaka Upanishad 4.3.

28. Ibid. 4.3.32.

29. Svetāsvatara Upanishad 1.16. Cf. the translation and commentary of Swami Nikhilananda, The Upanishads, 4 vols. (New York: Harper and Brothers, 1952), II, 86. In the later history of Indian thought, two schools of thought contested the nature of Brahman. Vedanta sought "to establish the attributeless Brahman as Ultimate Reality," a position defended by Shankara. The Qualified Non-Dualistic School of Rāmānuja argued for "the ultimate reality of Brahman as endowed with benign qualities only and free from all blemish." Ibid., I, 27. Nikhilananda's attempt to resolve this distinction leans strongly toward non-duality. Ibid., 49-50. So does my own reading of the Upanishads.

30. The precise nature of the Orphic's final bliss and salvation is not discernable in extant sources, unless one chooses to focus on fairly late traditions. As Rohde observes: "Complete escape from the world of birth and death is distinctively anticipated for the pious Orphic ... The other and positive side completing this negative promise is not clearly supplied for us by any fragment. We never even hear distinctly of the return of the indivi-

dual soul to the one Soul of the World; though certain Orphic
myths – probably of late origin – seem to suggest such a doctrine of Emanation and Remanation (sic)." Psyche, p. 359. Nilsson tells us that "the Orphic imagined the life of the blessed
in the other world as a banquet of the holy or, literally translated, as a 'carousal'." A History of Greek Religion, p. 218.
For Cornford, "the soul in its pure state consists of fire, like
the divine stars from which it falls; in its impure state,
throughout the period of reincarnation, its substance is infec-
ted with the baser elements, and weighed down by the gross ad-
mixture of the flesh." From Religion to Philosophy, p. 197.
Guthrie hazards the most elaborate inferences. The final hope
was "to become one with the divine mind which is at the same
time the fiery aither, at once the encompasser and the orderer
of the universe." The Greeks and Their Gods (Boston: Beacon
Press, 1950), p. 325. Aer was an impure substance surrounding
the earth as far as the moon, aither a purer substance, the
home of divinity and possibly divine itself, filling the region
beyond the moon. "Those, then, who believed the soul to be immortal and divine, were naturally inclined to suppose it made
of an imprisoned spark of aither, which when set free would fly
off to rejoin its like." The soul is said "to fly to the stars,
or become a star, for the aither is the substance of which the
stars, existing as they do in these pure outer regions, are
made." Orpheus and Greek Religion, p. 185. In an article, Guthrie argues that Orphic salvation is "the bliss of escape and
reunion, which is the only true immortality. Retention of Individuality means that the soul is still airy, still clogged with
the lower elements within the kosmos. The final goal, like that
of every true mystic, is the utter loss of self in the infinity
of the divine." "The Presocratic World Picture," Harvard Theological Review (April, 1952), p. 94. Without pausing to dispute
with Guthrie the loss of self being "the only true immortality,"
it can be noted that two worlds are distinguished, and that the
soul, even on the total absorption hypothesis, is absorbed into
a substance. Evidently the Orphics, like the pre-Socratic philosophers, required a tangible, spatially located being.

31. Some Upanishads attribute real existence to plurality. The phenomenal world is sometimes said to be contained in Brahman,
while at other times Brahman is said to rule over a world that
emerges from and returns to Brahman. Moreover, plants and animals have souls as well as people. Das Gupta, A History of Indian Philosophy, I, 51. The Orphics distinguished the physical
from the spiritual, while in the Upanishads dualistic speculation has a strongly monistic flavor. "The Upanishads require
us to look upon the whole world as born of God as the self of
man is." Radhakrishnan, Indian Philosophy, I, 214. Radhakrishnan was a Vedantist. Cf. Nikhilananda, I, 39-42.

32. Edward Conze, ed., Buddhist Texts Through the Ages (Oxford:
Bruno Cassirer, 1954), p. 74.

33. Radhakrishnan accepts the Buddhist analysis of the empirical
    self, but is convinced that Gautama did not reject the Ātman;
    he simply refused to discuss what was beyond discussion. For
    Radhakrishnan, "the spirit of the Upanishads is the life-spring
    of Buddhism." Indian Philosophy, I, 362, 387. In reply to this
    reduction of Buddhism to "the spirit of the Upanishads," I am
    in agreement with Junjirō Takakusu that "Brahamanism, as it was
    represented in the Upaniṣads, was a philosophy of 'Thatness'
    (Tattva) and was based on the theory of the reality of Being
    ... Buddhism, on the other hand, was a philosophy of 'Thusness'
    (Tathātā) - things as they actually are - and started with the
    theory of becoming, admitting no ātman, individual or universal,
    and no eternalism whatever ... The Buddha's rejection of the
    Brahmanistic principles was thus complete. All the fundamental
    Brahmanistic elements were wiped out and completely eliminated
    from Buddhism." "Buddhism as a Philosophy of 'Thusness'," in
    Charles A. Moore, ed., The Indian Mind (Honolulu: East-West
    Center Press, 1967), pp. 86-90.
34. On Jainism, see A.L. Basham's comments in Theodore De Bary, ed.,
    Sources of Indian Tradition (New York: Columbia University
    Press, 1958), pp. 49-54. Also see Y.J. Padmarajiah, A Compara-
    tive Study of Jaina Theories of Reality and Knowledge (Bombay,
    1956). Relevant Jain texts are in Radhakrishnan and Moore, eds.,
    Source Book, pp. 252-260. On Orphism, also see Ivan Linforth,
    The Arts of Orpheus (Berkeley: University of California Press,
    1941), who, in my judgment, adds little to Guthrie, although
    he does analyze the evidence exhaustively.
35. Extant biographies of Pythagoras from the hands of classical
    authors - Diogenes Laertius, Porphyry, Iamblichus - are un-
    trustworthy and often spurious. Even Aristotle, the best au-
    thority, is "already fabulous to a degree." Sarton, Ancient
    Science Through the Golden Age, p. 199. On the relations of
    Orphism and Pythagoreanism, see Guthrie, Orpheus and Greek Re-
    ligion, pp. 217-221. Guthrie confesses the difficulty of know-
    ing whether Orphism or Pythagoreanism came first, but concludes
    that "it nevertheless seems most likely from the character of
    the two systems, and in particular from the fact that Pytha-
    goreanism takes up Orphism into itself, but has as well an in-
    tellectual system to reinforce it, that Orphic dogma was al-
    ready formulated, at least in its main outlines, when Pythagor-
    as founded his brotherhood ... the most natural assumption seems
    to be that Pythagoras had the mythological solution before him,
    and realizing its religious value but impressed by the claims
    of the intellect as well, evolved as a complementary scheme his
    mathematical conception of reality." Ibid., p. 220.
36. Diogenes Laertius Lives of Eminent Philosophers viii. 4. The
    idea of "soul" in Pythagoreanism is not confined to that which
    transmigrates from one life to the next. It can also mean (1)
    motes in the air, (2) an "attunement," and (3) that which moves
    the motes. Kirk and Raven, pp. 261-262.

101

37. Pythagoreans staggered beneath a weight of taboos so great, one wonders how they ever found time from obeying the rules to experiment with mathematical ideas. Burnet, p. 96, and Guthrie, A History of Greek Philosophy, I, 183. With regard to the "religious revival" of the sixth century, its foremost characteristics - magic, rites of purification, cults of the dead, ecstatic communion with a god - had a long earlier history, predating, as Rohde is at pains to show in Psyche, the Homeric epics, which are virtually free of cultism and orgiastic religious striving. See the discussion in Guthrie, The Greeks and Their Gods, pp. 295 ff.

38. Sarton, Ancient Science Through the Golden Age, p. 201. Cf. Guthrie, A History of Greek Philosophy, I, 173, 252.

39. Vlastos says that "apart from the doctrine of transmigration and the belief that 'things are numbers,' the only idea we can credit to him with any measure of probability is the conception of the world in terms of a duality of principles, the finite and the infinite, the first being the principle of good, the second of evil." "Theology and Philosophy in Early Greek Thought," Op. cit., 111.

40. Burnet, p. 92.

41. Collingwood, The Idea of Nature, pp. 50-54. Collingwood points out that the idea of reality as a mathematical harmony can be misunderstood, for the Pythagoreans believed in a reality which is perceivable; that is, bodies are composed of line, point, and surface, all of which are substances, not abstractions. Cf. Raven, Pythagoreans and Eleatics, pp. 53-55.

42. "The genius of Pythagoras ... lay in his concentration on the formal element as real and permanent, and dismissal of the physical and individual as accidental." Guthrie, A History of Greek Philosophy, I, 317. Cf. Collingwood's interpretation, my note 48 supra.

43. Guthrie, A History of Greek Philosophy, I, 315.

44. See Heinrich Zimmer, Philosophies of India, ed. Joseph Campbell (New York: Meridean Books, 1956), p. 152. Also see Manu Smriti i. 31.

45. It is convenient to use the general term "Pythagoreanism" when comparing its doctrines and outlook with that of the Upanishads, but there were, of course, schools of Pythagoreans, some of whom stressed religious and cult elements, and others who concerned themselves more exclusively with science and mathematics. Pythagoreanism had its religious and philosophical branches, with combinations and permutations in between. Guthrie, A History of Greek Philosophy, I, 193. Happily, for purposes of this study, it has not been necessary to cast myself into what Vlastos has called "the bottomless pit of research in Pythagoreanism."

46. Brihadāranyaka Upanishad 4.5.15. Again, the reader must be reminded that the Upanishads are not a coherent treatise on the metaphysics of monism. They contain diverse materials which were incorporated later into several systems of Indian thought, even

though the Ātman-Brahman doctrine is persistent and striking. Also, the latter underwent a tortuous development. See the intelligent, succinct comments of A. Barth, The Religions of India, trans. J. Wood (Delhi: S. Chand and Co., 1969), pp. 67-76.

47. "Pythagoreanism not only rejects the monistic concept of nature axiomatic in the physiologoi, but implicitly condemns the highest principle as evil." "Theology and Philosophy in Early Greek Thought," Op. cit., 112.

48. Frg. 101.

49. Frgs. 129, 81, 40.

50. See Philip, p. 178.

51. Śvetaketu is brought gradually to the realization that speech, mind, conception, thought, meditation, understanding, strength, food, water, heat, space, memory, hope, and vital breath (in that order) derive from Soul, which is "this whole world," and outside the sphere of "research" as Pythagoras understood it. Chāndogya Upanishad 7-8.

52. Frg. 117.

53. Diogenes Laertius Lives viii. 54.

54. Frg. 115.

55. See O'Brien, p. 250; Kirk and Raven, p. 348; and Guthrie, A History of Greek Philosophy, II, 252.

56. Guthrie, "The Presocratic World Picture." Op. cit., 101-102. This model is not accepted universally among students of early Greek philosophy, but it has the virtue of providing a clear analysis of the relation of mysticism and rationalism in Greek thought which belies the claim that Greek and Indian mystics were expressing the same view of life and the world.

57. On the Nature of Things (Peri Physeos) and Purifications (Katharmoi). Burnet believes that "the cosmological system of Empedocles leaves no room for an immortal soul, which is presupposed by the Purifications." Early Greek Philosophy, p. 250. For Vlastos, "the two pictures of reality remain not only heterogeneous and contradictory at crucial points; they admit of no rational or, for that matter, even imaginative harmony." "Theology and Philosophy in Early Greek Thought," Op. cit., 120-121.

58. Cornford: "The two poems show us a religious doctrine, and a translation of it into physical terms, which stands out as extraordinarily ingenious and successful." From Religion to Philosophy, p. 240. Jaeger: "The philosopher tries to interpret the fundamental religious facts of Orphic theory in accordance with the supreme principle of his natural philosophy." The Theology of the Early Greek Philosophers, p. 150. Kirk and Raven: "Between the physical poem and the Purifications there are certain remarkable parallels of detail ... But the most remarkable parallel of all is that between the cosmic cycle in the physical poem and the cycle through which the soul passes in the Purifications." The Presocratic Philosophers, p. 348. These arguments are reiterated in H.S. Long, "The Unity of Empedocles' Thought," American Journal of Philology, 70 (1949).

59. Guthrie, "The Presocratic World Picture," op. cit., 103.
60. The Prose of Sir Thomas Browne, ed. N.J. Endicott (New York: Doubleday and Co., 1967), p. 42. Guthrie, A History of Greek Philosophy, II, 260. Cf. Sāṃkhya Kārikā LXVIII.
61. Kirk and Raven, p. 348.
62. Cornford, From Religion to Philosophy, p. 225. The developed evolutionary phenomenalism of the Sāṃkhya Kārikā belongs to an age later than that of Empedocles, but a few of its concepts are anticipated in some of the Upanishads (and even in the Vedas) where the physical world is invested with reality and described in terms of gunas (qualities). Śvetāśvatara Upanishad 5.7. This tendency in the direction of a naturalistic theory of the universe is not, however, systematically united with the mystical content of the Upanishads. Spirit and matter remain distinct, as they do in later Samkhya natural philosophy. See Riepe, The Naturalistic Tradition in Indian Thought, pp. 202-203, for a discussion of Sāṃkhya dualism. There may be a parallel here with Empedocles, if one accepts the view that his mysticism and rationalism are incompatible.
63. "Being has no coming-into-being and no destruction, for it is whole of limb, without motion, and without end." Frgs. 7, 8.
64. In what is commonly regarded as a reference to Parmenides, Empedocles exclaims: But, ye gods, avert my tongue the madness of those men, and guide forth from my reverent lips a pure stream." Frg. 3.
65. The religious elements are chiefly Orphic, or shamanistic, while "the physical system is simply the cosmology of Anaximander, with such modifications as were dictated by Empedocles' religious beliefs, together with the new notion of elements as 'things' which Empedocles had taken from Parmenides and turned against its author." From Religion to Philosophy, p. 241.
66. Frgs. 30, 31.
67. Cornford, From Religion to Philosophy, p. 197. See O'Brien, pp. 1-3.
68. Frgs. 17, 22, 35, 36.
69. Frg. 26. Cf. Śvetāśvatara Upanishad 6.4. Nikhilananda's translation should be consulted, along with the commentary. The Upanishads, II, 131-132.
70. Cornford, From Religion to Philosophy, pp. 232, 239, 251 n. In this interpretation, the soul has two parts; one is immortal, composed of Love, corrupted by Strife during transmigration, and a mortal part (the four elements).
71. See Charles H. Kahn, "Religion and Natural Philosophy in Empedocles' Doctrine of the Soul," Archiv für Geschichte der Philosophie, 42 (1960), 3-35.
72. See Riepe, pp. 25-26, 30-31. Rig-Veda x. 121, 129. Aitareya Upanishad 1.1.1-3. Chāndogya Upanishad 3.19.1-4.
73. Conze, Buddhist Texts, pp. 74-75. Also see Walpola Rahula, What the Buddha Taught (New York: Grove Press, 1959), pp. 30-31, 37-39.

74. Radhakrishnan, Indian Philosophy, I, 381-382. One of the best works on philosophical Buddhism is Junjiro Takakusu's The Essentials of Buddhist Philosophy, ed. Wing-tsit Chan and C.A. Moore (Honolulu: University of Hawaii, 1947). A fine attempt to evoke the worldview of the Buddha is in Zimmer's Philosophies of India, pp. 467-487.

75. These are "questions which tend not to edification." Radhakrishnan and Moore, Source Book, pp. 289-292.

76. Ibid., p. 287. Visuddhi-Magga xvii. Vinaya Pitaka i.14.

77. Frg. 98. Souls vaporize from wetness. Frg. 12. "Soul, then has its natural place somewhere in the area between water and fire, and contains within itself the possibilities of self-transformation in either direction." Philip Wheelwright, Heraclitus (Princeton: Princeton University Press, 1959), p. 62. G.S. Kirk reminds us that "the fragments about god cannot be separated from the physical fragments; for Heraclitus all branches of knowledge were interconnected." Heraclitus: The Cosmic Fragments (Cambridge: Cambridge University Press, 1954), p. 7.

78. Frgs. 12, 49a, 91.

79. Frg. 51. Also see Frgs. 57, 59, 60, 75. Harmony, equilibrium, and balance are integral to Heraclitus' cosmos. "For Heraclitus bow and lyre symbolize the whole cosmos, which without such constant 'warfare' would disintegrate and perish." Guthrie, A History of Greek Philosophy, I, 440. The soul, being fire, is related to the world fire, and the study of soul, institutions, and ideas were "in no way separate from the study of the outside world; the same materials and the same laws are found in each sphere." Kirk and Raven, p. 205.

80. Frgs. 35, 55. In the Buddhist view: "When ignorance has been got rid of and knowledge has arisen, one does not grasp after sense-pleasures, speculative views, rites, and customs, the theory of self." Majjima-Nikaya i.67, in Conze, Buddhist Texts, p. 75. The Buddha honored the Arahant, the one who had achieved detachment from the Five Aggregates, or Grasping Groups - consciousness, matter, sensation, perception, and mental formations. Rahula, What the Buddha Taught, p. 42. Rahula takes issue with my own remark about the Buddhist attitude toward change (in the text just above citation 76): "Buddhism is neither pessimistic nor optimistic. If anything at all, it is realistic, for it takes a realistic view of life and the world." Ibid., pp. 17, 37-38.

81. Cornford, From Religion to Philosophy, p. 184.

82. Frgs. 41, 45, 50, 98, 102.

83. Frgs. 11, 22, 26.

84. Frg. 29. Cf. Suttanipata 920, in Conze, Buddhist Texts, p. 90: "As in the ocean's midmost depth no wave is born, but all is still, so let the monk be still, be motionless, and nowhere should he swell."

85. Dhammapada 13.5.

86. Frg. 14. Also see Frgs. 13, 15, 68.

87. Frg. 40.
88. See Walter Ruben, Geschichte der Indischen Philosophie (Berlin: Deutscher Verlag der Wissenschaften, 1954), p. 88.
89. Mundaka Upanishad 2.1.1. In the Vedas the fire god Agni bears aloft the sacrifices, and was especially revered. Rig-Veda i. 143.
90. Indian Philosophy, I, 145.
91. Kirk and Raven, p. 204.
92. Ibid., p. 205. The soul originates in moisture, however, and attains maturity through vaporization, or the loss of moisture and the acquisition of heat: "we must cultivate the fiery nature of the soul so that when released from the damp fumes of the body it may be ready to rejoin the Logos - fire." Guthrie, A History of Greek Philosophy, I, 448.
93. Kirk and Raven, p. 205.
94. Frgs. 73, 115.
95. Wheelwright, p. 64.
96. Ibid., p. 65.
97. "The phrase, 'the soul,' is likely to carry, for the modern reader, brought up (however loosely) on Christian notions, a suggestion of permanence - which, of course, is absent from Heraclitus' conception." Ibid., p. 64.
98. Maitri Upanishad 1.4. On the nature of soul, the Katha Upanishad is particularly rich. See Nikhilananda, I, 117-190. The drift clearly is toward non-duality. E.g., Ibid., 173-174.
99. Wheelwright, p. 24. There is a vague parallel with the notion of Brahman as intelligence. Aitareya Upanishad 3.5.3.
100. On the multiple meanings of logos, see Guthrie, A History of Greek Philosophy, I, 420-424.
101. Ibid., 479.
102. See H. Frankel, "Heraclitus on God," Transactions of the American Philological Association, 69 (1938), 230-244.
103. Frg. 41.
104. See Popper, Conjectures and Refutations, p. 144.
105. Frg. 101.
106. Guthrie, A History of Greek Philosophy, I, 414.
107. Wheelwright, p. 25.
108. There is a sensible discussion of mysticism in Frits Staal, Exploring Mysticism (Berkeley: University of California Press, 1975). He stresses the need for experiments rather than theory.
109. Wheelwright, p. 25.
110. Burnet, p. 18. Needless to say, his point of view is as objectionable as the one being examined in this study.
111. Eastern Religions and Western Thought, p. 144.
112. A.E. Taylor argues that "the frequent allusions in the dialogues to Egypt and Egyptian customs may be due to reminiscenses of actual travel in Egypt, but can hardly be said to show more knowledge than an Athenian might have acquired at home by reading Herodotus and conversing with traders from the Nile Delta." The Mind of Plato (Ann Arbor: University of Michigan

Press, 1960), p. 11. This book was first published in 1922.

113. A.E. Taylor, Plato: The Man and His Work (6th ed. rev.; London: Methuen and Co., 1949), p. 3.

114. "Almost everything that we can claim to know of the events of Plato's life derives, directly or indirectly, from the seventh of the thirteen letters which have been preserved from antiquity in the corpus of his writings." J.E. Raven, Plato's Thought in the Making (Cambridge: Cambridge University Press, 1965), pp. 19-26. Raven accepts the authenticity of the seventh letter, a point still in dispute. Ludwig Edelstein, for example, concludes that the letter "cannot be genuine," though it is "an interesting and rather important interpretation of Plato's life and doctrine which must go back to the first decades after his death." Plato's Seventh Letter (Leiden, 1966), p. 4. In any event, the letter deals mainly with Plato's adventures in Sicily. See Bluck's tramslation in Plato's Life and Thought (London: Routledge and Kegan Paul, 1949), pp. 152-188.

115. Raven, Plato's Thought, p. 33.

116. Taylor, The Mind of Plato, pp. 26-27.

117. I.M. Crombie, Plato: The Midwife's Apprentice (London: Routledge and Kegan Paul, 1964), p. 181.

118. Manu Smriti vi. 33-34. These stages are called āshramas.

119. Bhagavad-Gītā 14.1-2. Tradition eventually codified four ends of life (purushārtha): dharma (referring generally to the duties associated with one's station in life), artha (dealing with man's economic and political relations within society), kama (dealing with the pursuit of pleasure and beauty), and moksha (spiritual release from the world). The first three ends helped prepare one for the fourth. The apparent conflict between ritual duties associated with dharma and the abandonment of the world required by moksha was healed in the Gītā with the idea of action detached from its fruits (karma yoga). See De Bary, Sources of Indian Tradition, pp. 211-357. The four ends of life have an obvious relationship to the four stages.

120. Taylor, Plato: The Man and His Work, p. 463.

121. Aristotle Metaphysics i. 6. Also see Raven, Plato's Thought, p. 4.

122. According to Dodds, the "majority" of scholars trace Plato's "transcendental psychology" to his contact with Pythagoreans. The Greeks and the Irrational, p. 209. Also see Raven, Plato's Thought, p. 70. Karl Popper argues that an "extra-philosophical" basis for Plato's Theory of Forms, and indeed for his entire philosophy, was the Pythagorean discovery of the irrationality of the square root of two: "the realization that irrational magnitudes ... existed, and that their existence could be proved, undermined the faith of the Pythagorean order, and destroyed the hope of deriving cosmology, or even geometry, from the arithmetic of natural numbers. It was Plato who realized this fact, and who in the Laws stressed its importance in the strongest possible terms, denouncing his compatriots

for their failure to gauge its implications." Conjectures and
Refutations, pp. 86-87.

123. Taylor, Plato: The Man and His Work, p. 504. Taylor remarks
that although other sciences were studied at the Academy, it
was mathematics "which appealed most to Plato himself." Also
see Sarton, Ancient Science Through the Golden Age, p. 436.

124. Basham, The Wonder That Was India, p. 388.

125. Republic 434D-441C. Unless otherwise indicated, all citations
of Plato come from The Dialogues of Plato, trans. B. Jowett
(New York: Random House, 1937). See Taylor, Plato: The Man
and His Work, p. 120 n.

126. Republic 474B-480.

127. Frgs. 4-19. There is also a third way of "seeing" which com-
bines the first two. Kirk, Pythagoreans and Eleatics, pp. 26-
27.

128. Das Gupta, I, 27.

129. Indian Philosophy, I, 79.

130. A.A. Macdonell, quoted in Das Gupta, I, 13. Cf. Radhakrishnan,
Indian Philosophy, I, 128, on Vedic knowledge as "intuitive insight."

131. Rig-Veda ii. 23. 10. Das Gupta, I, 21.

132. Laws 689C-E.

133. Rig-Veda ii. 28. 4. Radhakrishnan, Indian Philosophy, I, 78,
80.

134. It is worth being reminded that skeptical, naturalistic speculations can be found in some of the Upanishads. Riepe, pp. 26-
27. It is likely that Plato would have found such speculations
just as uncongenial as the more prominent and radical monistic ideas.

135. Radhakrishnan, Indian Philosophy, I, 176 f. Brihadāranyaka
Upanishad 4.4.20.

136. Svetasvatara Upanishad 1.3. Many types of yogic discipline
are described in ancient Indian literature, and in the Upanishads are set forth as the path to union with Brahmin. Maitri
Upanishad 6.19-30. On two specific systems of yoga, see Radhakrishnan and Moore, Source Book, pp. 453-485, and Rammurti
S. Mishra, Yoga Sutras (New York: Doubleday, 1973). On the relationship between spiritual disciplines and mystical experience, see Staal, pp. 143-154. What all such disciplines have
in common is an appeal to non-discursive means of achieving
spiritual "knowledge."

137. Radhakrishnan, Indian Philosophy, I, 162.

138. Chāndogya Upanishad 7.25.2. Brihadāranyaka Upanishad 2.4.6.

139. See Hume's discussion of this point, The Thirteen Principal
Upanishads, pp. 36-39.

140. Katha Upanishad 2.23. Brihadāranyaka Upanishad 4.4.21. For
material on the role of thought, see Chāndogya Upanishad 7.5.
1-3. Cf. Śvevāśtavara Upanishad 4.1. On the last example, see
Nikhilananda, II, 106-107.

141. Radhakrishnan, Indian Philosophy, I, 208.

142. Jaeger, Paideia, II, 37, 64, 117. See Julius Stenzel, Plato's Method of Dialectic, trans. D.J. Allan (Oxford: Oxford University Press, 1940), p. 129.
143. Republic 521C-531C.
144. Jaeger, Paideia, II, 311.
145. Sophist 253D. Stenzel, pp. 108, 148.
146. Taylor, Plato: The Man and His Work, p. 293. Republic 511B.
147. See Hume, p. 39. Cf. Republic 443B, 509B, 537C. Also see Stenzel, p. 46, and Taylor, Plato: The Man and His Work, p. 285.
148. Katha Upanishad 4.15. Das Gupta, I, 44. Taylor, Plato: The Man and His Work, p. 287. Jaeger, Paideia, II, 311.
149. Republic 518B. Cf. Brihadāranyaka Upanishad 3.7.3-10. Taittirīya Upanishad 2.8. Chāndogya Upanishad 3.13.7.
150. Republic 511D and 441A.
151. Maitri Upanishad 6.22. Śvetāśvatara Upanishad 1.3. Cf. Taylor, Plato: The Man and His Work, p. 287.
152. Mundaka Upanishad 3.2.5-6. Maitri Upanishad 6.28. Das Gupta, I, 58.
153. Republic 517 and 519D. Cf. Brihadāranayaka Upanishad 3.5., where we read that "Brahmans who know such a Soul overcome desire for sons, desire for wealth, desire for worlds, and live the life of mendicants." Radhakrishnan's insistence that Brahman does not mean "death, stillness, or stagnation" does not blunt the recurrent theme of renunciation as a desirable way of life in the Upanishads. Indian Philosophy, I, 173.
154. Ibid., 157, 171.
155. This point has been disputed. Georges Grube suggests that "the aim of the Platonic philosopher is to live on the universal plane, to lose himself more and more in the contemplation of truth, so that the perfect psyche would, it seems, lose itself completely in the universal mind, the world-psyche." Plato's Thought (Boston: Beacon Press, 1958), p. 148. Grube's dissent is, however, very tentative, thus reflecting the ambiguity of Plato's views on the soul in its relations with reality. "What exactly Plato took the soul to be is not so clear." Crombie, p. 77.
156. Laws 896E-898D.
157. Phaedrus 246A. Laws 893B-896D.
158. See, for example, Iśā Upanishad 1. Brihadāranyaka Upanishad 3.8.8. Chāndogya Upanishad 7.25.2.
159. Riepe, p. 29. In Sāmhkya, souls are liberated when the motion of the three gunas no longer influences them. Das Gupta, I, 248.
160. Phaedo 70C-84B. Cf. Katha Upanishad 4.3, 5-6.
161. Phaedrus 246A-257A. Republic 613E to the end.
162. Laws 896A-897C.
163. See Dodds, pp. 216-217.
164. See Cornford, From Religion to Philosophy, pp. 248-249.
165. Taylor, The Mind of Plato, p. 95.
166. Ludwig Edelstein, "The Function of Myth in Plato's Philosophy,"

167. Ibid., 477.
168. Kena Upanishad 1.5.
169. Heinrich Zimmer, Myths and Symbols in Indian Art and Civilization (New York: Pantheon, 1946), p. 40.
170. Timaeus 69-70. On this point, as well as many others, Plato differs also with Samkhya, which holds that souls are without qualities or parts. Das Gupta, I, 238.
171. Phaedrus 253-254. Cf. Nikhilananda, I, 149, for chariot imagery.
172. Śvetāśvatara Upanishad 1.6-7. Cf. Nikhilananda, II, 76-78. There is more on immortality in Nikhilananda, I, 97-99, 110-112.
173. As Herschel Baker rightly emphasizes, where Plato is concerned with "the health and beauty and well-being of the soul" (Republic 444), he means the development of the whole man in the classic Greek tradition. The Image of Man (New York: Harper Torchbooks, 1961), p. 21.
174. "The realm of the Forms is rational, and Plato's effort has been to show that the soul belongs of right and nature to this realm of Forms." Robert Patterson, Plato on Immortality (University Park, Pennsylvania: The Pennsylvania University Press, 1965), p. 126. The Katha Upanishad contains an extended "chariot image" which ought to be compared with Plato's, for it sheds light on the place of intellect in the Upanishadic notion of ultimate reality. The charioteer in the Katha Upanishad is buddhi, or intellect, or the discriminating faculty. So far there is a clear parallel with Plato. But the function of buddhi is purely instrumental, to control the senses and to avoid evil, harmful actions, to prepare the ground for cosmic consciousness. It is not a constituent of ultimate reality: "Beyond the senses are the objects; beyond the objects is the mind; beyond the mind, the intellect; beyond the intellect, the Great Atman; beyond the Great Atman, the Unmanifest; beyond the Unmanifest, the Purusha. Beyond the Purusha there is nothing: this is the end, the Supreme Goal." Nikhilananda, I, 148-154.
175. Indian Philosophy, I, 240-241. Radhakrishnan admits the fuzziness.
176. Phaedrus 248B.
177. "He pleads the case of all philosophers more subtly, more systematically, more plausibly, more eloquently than their own advocates can state them." Paul Shorey, What Plato Said (Chicago, 1933), p. 56.
178. Timaeus 28C. "The very multiplicity of beings to whom Plato at one time or another attributes the term 'god' or 'divine' raises an important and difficult question: where in Plato's theology is the 'God' by reason of whom Plato deserves to be called a theist?" William Chase Greene, Moira: Fate, Good, and Evil in Greek Thought (Gloucester, Mass.: Peter Smith, 1968), p. 291. In way of answering the question, Greene says "one is forced to the conclusion that Plato's ultimate God is viewed as the impersonal Nous, or in mythical terms as the personal Demiurge, both of which impart their goodness to the world through the

creation of Soul. What is God in himself? Plato will not answer directly ... " Ibid., pp. 292 f. In the sense of a cosmic
or divine mind, Plato identifies Nous, in the Timaeus, as the
principle which brings rational order to nature. Nous is a kind
of universal rational Soul, but it is also more than that. Whatever else Nous may be, it has reason as a distinct and active
part of its being, reason to which all souls aspire as their
true end and immortality. Brahman, compared with Nous, is
"without parts, without action, tranquil, blameless, unattached
... , like a fire that has consumed all its fuel." Svetāsvatara
Upanishad, in Nikhilananda, II, 141. While both versions of
reality may be "ultimate" and in some sense "all-encompassing,"
thus establishing a weak parallel, they do not produce the same
philosophical and theological music, nor do they have the same
consequences for the organization of thought and life.

179. Hume, p. 41.
180. Dodds, p. 221. Plato's effort to restore unity to Greek intellectual tradition is best understood as a response to internal
developments of Greek thought. As Jaeger puts it: "the history
of Greek thought is an organic unity, closed and complete."
Paideia, I, 151.
181. Chāndogya Upanishad 10.3.
182. Frg. 18.

CHAPTER VI

THE LURE OF PARALLELS: INDIAN THOUGHT
AND CHRISTIAN ORIGINS

It is now well-known that a variety of historical forces and
circumstances participated in the shaping of the Christian faith.
At its center was the charismatic personality of Jesus. From the
Jews came monotheism, the ethics of righteousness, a Messianic eschatology promising a Kingdom of God and rectification of wrongs,
and the idea of physical resurrection of the dead.[1] Greek philosophy, in its later Neo-Platonic development, contributed the abstract idea of an unknowable, transcendent God, whose relationship
to the world of matter is achieved through intermediary forces or
beings (i.e., the Logos of the Stoics and Philo Judaeus), the contact of a divine reality with its earthly reflection, or terminal
emanation, and a distrust of sense experience. From Philo came the
allegorical interpretation of scripture, the principle that a text
means something other than what it says.[2] From the mystery religions of the Near East and Greece came many sacramental and cere-
monial practices, as well as the drama of man's fallen soul redeemed and immortalized through the miraculous agency of a resurrected god.[3] The Stoics, whose philosophy Tarn calls "the greatest creation of the /Hellenistic/ age,"[4] bequeathed ideals of
conscience, duty, the brotherhood of man, resignation before divine
providence, and moral improvement through suffering.[5] From Gnosticism, which left a profound mark on Christianity in the first century A.D., came the idea of a redeemer rescuing souls fallen from
light into darkness, pantheons of demons and angels, and the conviction that an evil power is at work in the guise of matter.[6] And
from Rome came the language, legal framework, and hierarchical
structure of the Church, which became the guardian of the faith
when the expected Day of Judgment did not come to pass.

The origins of Christianity, both as faith and institution,
were syncretistic in the extreme, but it was largely because of
this talent for borrowing ideas and forms and adapting them to
fresh uses that the nascent Christian movement was able to survive
a hostile environment and finally to triumph over its rivals. Un-
doubtedly Christianity absorbed "oriental" influences during the
two centuries flanking the ministry of Jesus.[7] The question for
this chapter is just what "oriental" can be taken to mean. Does
the term include only cultures as far east as Persia, or is there
evidence to warrant the inclusion of India?

The whole subject of Christian origins is a massive tangle,
involving complex factors whose interconnections are varied and
subtle. One confronts warring doctrines, bizarre eclecticism, and
all the manifold spiritual concerns of the Hellenistic age. If

Christianity were indebted to Indian religious ideas, one might expect other, less remotely based explanations of origins to be weak or unsatisfactory. In order to neutralize the Indian hypothesis of transmission, spiritual and intellectual, to Christianity, it is essential that we show in reasonable detail that nothing of substance in the outlook of Christianity is unaccounted for in its Greco-Roman environment. In this task, no attempt is made to exhaust available interpretations of Judaism and Christianity. The ones chosen enjoy a wide consensus of acceptance. Their function in this argument is to test the credibility of the Indian hypothesis, not to stand as interpretations beyond dispute.

As in the case of Greek philosophy and religion, we must take into account three classes of facts: historic contacts between India and the West, references to India in classical and patristic literature, and the existence of parallel ideas in the Judao-Christian and Indian traditions. The first two issues can be disposed of rapidly, for what has been said in earlier chapters of this study about contacts and sources remains in force.

In the three centuries before Christ, commerce with the Indian sub-continent was controlled by various middlemen, mostly Arabs, who monopolized the strategic southern sea route, a lucrative advantage which lasted into the second half of the first century B.C.[8] Thereafter, direct contact was established by Rome. Beyond the sources discussed previously in this essay, there is little to be added of possible relevance to Christianity. Pliny the Elder records a few embassies, among them an Indian embassy to the court of the emperor Claudius (10 B.C.-54 A.D.).[9] The Demetrius of Lucian's Toxaris sets out to study Indian thought, but there is no follow-up of his adventures.[10] Patristic writing, with the exception of Saint Hippolytus, is uniformly devoid of illuminating comment. Although Indians were supposed to have been a familiar sight in Alexandria, Clement of Alexandria (second century A.D.) reports nothing more than "some Indians who follow the precepts of Boutta, whom, by an excessive reverence, they have exalted into a god."[11] By the time of the fourth century, information about Buddhism has dwindled to a bare mention of his name and virgin birth.[12]

In an earlier chapter, Plotinus was mentioned as possibly encountering the mysticism of the Upanishads at Rome. Since Greek philosophical tradition passed into the mainstream of Christian theology chiefly through the Enneads of Plotinus, some importance attaches to the relations of his thought to Indian transcendentalism. Émile Bréhier has discussed "The Orientalism of Plotinus," and maintains that a crucial, jarring facet of his philosophy remains inexplicable without assuming the influence of the Upanishads.

There is a double perspective in Plotinus' notion of Intelligence. On the one hand, it is the intelligible

114

and eternal order, composed of fixed and definite relations, which serves as model of the senswble order. On the other hand, it is thought directed toward itself, in which all distinction of subject and object disappears, in which the self is merged in universal being. It seemed to me that the second perspective was foreign to the tradition of Greek thought. Intelligence becomes merely inward satisfaction (experienced in a vague and indefinite contemplation) of having escaped from all particular forms of being. It seeks no rational explanation. All ethical and intellectual relations which constitute a thought and a person are lost in contemplation. These are traits characteristic of the religious doctrine of the Hindus as expressed in the Upanishads. This is why it has seemed to me that the system of Plotinus must be linked to Indian thought ... This hypothesis is the only one which enables us to clear up difficulties in Plotinus' doctrine concerning the relations of Intelligence to the supreme principle and the very nature of this principle itself.[13]

Bréhier is convinced that where Plotinus dwells on the absorption of personality into the One, or on thought turning in upon itself, he has forsaken the philosophical mission of the Greek tradition, which sought to render the world and man's relationship to it intelligible. In effect, Plotinus poured alien waters into an otherwise native river of Hellenic speculation. "The fourth and fifth treatises of the sixth Ennead," he writes, "can easily be read without any reference to Greek philosophy."[14]

At first glance, the source of Plotinus' mystical inclination may have been the profusion of mystery religions in the Roman Empire. But Brehier argues that he could not have found in any mystery religion the concept of the One into which all is absorbed. The mysteries were innocent of a principle basically antagonistic to divine intermediaries, prayer, and formal worship. Moreover, Plotinus actively disliked salvationist religion, and placed himself above the intercession of a saviour. His was a philosophical and not a pious temperament. In Porphyry's Life of Plotinus, there is a revealing anecdote in which a long-time student of Plotinus invites him to pay his respects to the gods on a sacred holiday. The master's response is that "they ought to come to me, not I to them."[15] The point is that universal being is everywhere, even in the soul; thus it is needless to search for divinity.[16] An aversion for mediation, combined with an affirmation of omnipresent ultimate reality, sets Plotinus apart from all previous systems of Greek philosophy and religion. The puzzled student, says Bréhier, must look to India for an answer to the riddle.

Brehier supports these contentions rather thinly: a cursory

review of familiar data relating to historic contacts of east and
west; a reminder that Greek exoticism embraced India; fleeting mention of Megasthenes, Strabo, and Apollonius of Tyana; some comment
on Plotinus' ambition to study Persian and Indian thought, and his
dissatisfaction with Greek rationalism; and a firm analysis of the
parallel between Plotinus' first hypostasis and the Ātman-Brahman
formula.[17] Although Brehier seems unaware of the fact, his case is
all the stronger because of Filliozat's work on the gymnosophist
refutation of Saint Hippolytus, which creates at least a presump-
tion that Plotinus may have been acquainted with Indian mysticism
through a source unknown to us. Surely this is a fascinating and
difficult question, but one whose solution is elusive.

The demonstration of an exact parallel between the mysticism
of Plotinus and the Upanishads, which in this instance seems to
hold up, does not require an appeal to Indian thought by way of
explanation. Plotinus' notion of the One might just as well be a
hypostatization of Plato's Form of the Good, an abstraction of it
from all relational context in response to an experience of oceanic
consciousness. The outcome has been judged by some as a perversion
of Greek rationalism, a descent into irrationalism, a philosophical
"failure of nerve," the terminal gasp of Greek thought. However
that may be, Bréhier's arguments are not at all conclusive.[18] Re-
luctance to believe that Plotinus was a student of the Upanishads
does not signify, inevitably, a stubborn wish to defend the internal development of Greek thought at any cost. He could just as well
have been a philosophic mutation at the close of the Greek intellectual tradition. Either explanation for his mystical utterances
invites serious criticism, but one of them must be close to the
truth. Perhaps one's choice between them will have less to do with
the evidence (which invites suspension of judgment) than with one's
temperament.

Even if Plotinus were indebted to the Upanishads beyond a reasonable doubt, the fact would have minimal significance for Christian doctrine. His account of consciousness submerged in universal
reality seems to have lived on in the works of Dionysius the Areo-
pagite, Meister Eckhart, and a few others, but the ideal of oneness
void of all distinctions remained always peripheral to the main concerns of Christianity. Mystics of this type were always suspect and
often charged with heresy. A religion like Christianity, founded on
clear demarcations between God and man, saviour and saved, blessed
and damned, could not tolerate a theory of reality which dispensed
with all mediation. Theologians found his theory of emanations useful, but drew the line at the unqualified One.

The aspect of Plotinus most attractive to Christian thinkers
was thoroughly Greek: the three subsistent hypostases (oneness, intelligence, and soul), all exemplified in the realm of change, but
also standing apart from transience as eternal guarantors of other

levels of reality, a complex system of relations – the world in all its activity and interconnectedness – emanating from the supremely perfect and self-sufficient One. Plotinus' theory of generation, which Lovejoy has analyzed in a larger context as the principle of plenitude, attributes to the One a necessary tendency to overflow and create every conceivable species of existence.[19]

> How then should the most Perfect Being and the First
> Good remain shut up in itself, as though it were jea-
> lous or impotent – itself the potency of all things?
> ... Something must therefore be begotten of it.[20]

Each hypostasis generates lower forms of existence than itself, and out of infinite fecundity and generosity fill every gap imaginable, until the whole of reality consists of a majestic, exhaustive "chain of being," from the ineffable One to the lowest and simplest mode of existence.

It was this idea, derived from Plato and Aristotle by Plotinus, which caught the fancy of Christian theologians in search of materials to build an intellectually respectable home for the somewhat bare doctrine of redemption. From Plotinus came a philosophically ingenious representation of God the transcendent who was also God the creator, a self-sufficient Being which flows of necessity into a state of becoming.[21] One sees it, for example, in the fifth century transmitter of Plotinian ideas, Macrobius: "the attentive observer will discover a connection of parts, from the Supreme God down to the last dregs of things, mutually linked together and without a break. And this is Homer's golden chain, which God, he says, bade hang down from heaven to earth."[22] It should be said that even Plotinus' intelligible, eternal order of fixed and definite relations was more than some Christian thinkers could bear; it is understandable that they would be made nervous by the addition of a structure of pagan rationalism to the articles of faith.

But if the "Upanishadic" side of Plotinus' thought failed to influence Christianity, does not his system point to the same view of life as that found in the Upanishads? There is no simple answer to this question, for the presence of a unitary doctrine in Plotinus is less important than the main drift of his thought. It is undeniable that he possessed a religious consciousness attuned to non-duality, but his method and purpose in writing the Enneads were rational and didactic.[23] His analysis of the One is not intended to draw men into mystical annihilation of subject and object. His teaching is that ascent to the One and immersion in the final, silent ecstasy demands rational effort and insight. Without reason, the soul cannot journey to the Ens Entium.[24]

Even a casual reading of the Enneads can suggest the author's intense commitment to dialectic and to the task of holding the relational world in perspective against its background of immutable categories. Plotinus was drawn to the One, yet the context of the _Enneads_ is haunted also by a persistent dualism between nature and spirit.[25] There is an alternation of mood and emphasis, a shuttling back and forth, as it were, in what might might be called a tension between public and private worlds, the former concerned with sensible and abstract relations, the latter with subjective realization of unitary consciousness. Dualistic analysis characterizes matter, the lowliest form of being, as moving simultaneously in two directions, away from the One to non-being, and toward the One to the fullest manifestation of Being; "one finally arrives at a conception of matter which plays the double role, as primary evil, of attracting the forms, and, as the last hypostasis, of being the reality that is the limit from which no procession and, therefore, no conversion are any longer possible."[26] The implication is that Plotinus could not dispense with matter even if he had wished to do so. His is a worldview embodied in a continuum of being whose every gradation is _necessary_, for without them the perfection, creative power, and infinitude of the One would be impugned. The philosopher's vocation is equally dual. On one side, flight to the supremely real, on the other, rational explication of the chain of being. Here is a scheme of reality and human destiny whose affinities with the Upanishads can be maintained only if one violates the context.

Now we shall examine Radhakrishnan's belief that early Christian convictions are best understood by reference to the presence in or about Palestine of Hindu and Buddhist ideas.[27] The argument runs as follows:

(1) The uniqueness of Jesus' teaching, as set forth in the Gospels, lies in his emphasis on the Kingdom of God not of this world, rebirth through repentance and selfless living, immortality of the soul, non-violence, and renunciation of earthly goods and responsibilities.

(2) These ideas cannot be accounted for in their Jewish context.[28] Indeed, their otherworldly bent and radical inwardness are alien to traditional Judaism, which set its hopes on an earthly victory, led by Yahweh, over the foes of Israel. With the advent of God's Kingdom, all men, with the Jews as a chosen nation of priests, would acquiesce to the new order and witness a new era of peace and righteousness. In Hebrew eschatology, there was no mention of a more sublime spiritual goal - the immortality of the soul as mankind's true destiny.[29]

(3) What, then, was the origin of Jesus' unusual ideas? In the apocryphal _Book of Enoch_, a violent break occurs with traditional Hebrew expectations for the future. The older notion of an earthly kingdom is replaced by one of a transcendent, supernatural kingdom in heaven.[30] The Messiah, commonly thought of as an earthly king

anointed by God, is now described as a pre-existent being who des-
cends from heaven to exalt the righteous, stand at the head of the
"elect ones," and prepare the way for the inauguration of God's Kingdom. "Central features of Jesus' consciousness and teaching" may be
traced to this apocalyptic message of the heavenly kingdom, preached
by the transcendant Son of Man.[31] Also from the apocalyptic literature came the hope of resurrection on the Day of Judgment and eternal life for the righteous in God's Kingdom. The second condition-
ing factor in Jesus' background was the ascetic, monastic religious
sect known as the Essenes. In their isolated community in the vicinity of the Dead Sea, the Essenes practiced a form of one-pointed
religious devotion totally at odds with the family-centered, socially conscious Judaic tradition. They took rigorous vows, concealed
their doctrines from outsiders, and taught that salvation and immortality of the soul proceed from triumph over the pollution of the
body.[32] If Jesus were not affected by this particular sect, there
were others like it which held similar otherworldly views. Their
common denominator was to lift man's spiritual horizon above the
dust and transience of earthly bonds - the exact purport of Jesus'
message.

(4) Now, "most probably Indian religious ideas and legends were
well known in the circles in which the accounts of the Gospels originated," and it must be remembered that Buddhism was "closing in"
on Palestine at the time of Jesus' ministry and crucifixion.[33] Furthermore, "it is the ancient Hindu tradition which Enoch illustrates
and Jesus continues."[34] As for the Essenes and other monastic sects
of Palestine, their way of life and beliefs were suffused with the
spirit of Buddhism.[35] This spirit also pervades the lofty ethics of
the Sermon on the Mount, which is a paean to non-violence and purity
of soul, and one cannot but suspect more than coincidence at work in
the uncanny parallels between the lives of Buddha and Christ in the
traditional accounts.[36] For these reasons, there is justification
for contending that Jesus "breaks away from the Jewish tradition and
approximates to Hindu and Buddhist thought."[37]

Much of this argument is sustained by the assumption that Judaism was innocent of ascetic, mystical, otherworldly tendencies,
and therefore unable to provide raw material for the kind of religious upheaval initiated by Jesus and his followers. Such an interpretation of Hellenistic Judaism is too simplistic and contrary to
historical reality. The Jews of the Hellenistic age were hardly of
one mind about anything, except that, in one sense or another, wisdom consists in "fear of the Lord, unchangeable forever."[38] Variety
in Jewish thought and practice is not exhausted by the cleavage of
Pharisee and Sadducee, who fought mostly over the interpretation of
the law, the former defending modifications to fit altered circumstances of life, the latter insisting that nothing should be observed not explicitly enjoined by the law (they meant the entire
body of scripture, not just the Pentateuch). Apart from these two

great sects, whose teachers and scholars comprised the "rabbinical tradition," the spirit of Judaism was fed by many streams in the Hellenistic period; all Jews cannot be fitted into the same boat.[39]

Many of them succumbed to the omnipresence of Greek culture, even if superficially, by taking Greek names, speaking the Greek language, and adopting Greek customs. It might be imagined that religion, the sacred rock of Jewish thought and society, would escape gentile taint. Yet services in many synagogues were conducted in Greek, and "even in the third century /B.C./ the Hebrew Scriptures were useless to many Alexandrian Jews."[40] As early as the fourth century B.C., Yahweh was identified with Zeus, and in Asia Minor was given the Greek name Theos Hypsistos (God the Highest).[41]

Theos Hypsistos occurs in the writings of Philo, the prime speciman of a Hellenized Jewish intellectual.[42] He believed in the absolute, comprehensive authority of the Pentateuch, but also believed that Moses had instructed the Greeks in higher things. Careful study of the Pentateuch yielded to Philo all that he had learned from Greek philosophy. His magistral theological synthesis was written in Greek. It was indebted to Plato, Aristotle, and the Stoics; Pythagoreanism may have also contributed something. With one foot planted in Greek philosophy, Philo was at the same time the leader of the Jewish community in Alexandria. Like so many other Jews of his time, he felt a deep commitment to the Hebrew faith without belonging to the rabbinical camp. In Philo's thought, the existence of God is knowable to reason, but otherwise no quality can be imputed to Him. God is so far removed from the dross and impurity of material existence, so splendid in His eternality and incorporeality, that He used intermediary beings (angels) to create the world. For economy of expression, Philo often refers to God and His imtermediaries as though they are one, the Logos (meaning "reason" or "word") and, in De confusione Linguarum, "the first-begotten of God," the archangel who bears God's revelation to man. The concept of Logos is found in earlier Greek thought, but it also exists in the ancient Jewish distinction between the Wisdom of God and God himself, made, for example, in the twenty-eighth chapter of Job. The connection of this theological idea with Christian use of the "son of man" theme should be obvious. That innocuous phrase became a key to understanding the significance of Jesus when the predicted Son of Man did not appear to preside over a Day of Judgment.

India has no place in the fact that reincarnation is part of Philo's mystical otherworldly philosophy. Transmigration of souls is a necessary consequence of his premises, which are cut from Greek cloth. Souls existing closer to matter are drawn to it and take up residence in bodies. If purity of life is attained, the entrapped souls can fly back to God; if not, the price for clinging to the senses is rebirth in a prison of flesh. For the most part, Philo's theory of the soul is taken from the dialogues of Plato.[43]

120

Radhakrishnan's inadequate account of Judaism does not give a true estimate of the Jewish apocalyptic (from a Greek word cannoting "uncovering" or "unveiling") literature which grew up between the Old and New Testaments. A brief summary of what the apocalyptic writers stood for will clarify somewhat the background of the Jesus movement.[44] The most famous of the apocalyptic books is Daniel, the only one that became canonical. Other examples are Enoch, the Testament of the Twelve Patriarchs, Jubilees, and Esdras. The authors are anonymous, wrote in highly symbolic language, and conveyed esoteric doctrines purporting to reveal the course of future events, most dramatically the end of things, the Last Judgment, a secret knowledge reputedly acquired through visions and other supernatural means.

The apocalyptic message was inspired by troubled times for Israel. Invasions, oppression by foreign tyrants, persecution, a general deterioration Jewish hopes and fortunes - all combined to undermine traditional confidence in the earthly Kingdom of God and aroused expectations of a more violent, unearthly rectification of injustice. It began with the Book of Daniel, which emerged from the persecutions of Antiochus IV. Antiochus aimed to consolidate power by enforcing religious conformity throughout his realm, and ended by inciting the Maccabean revolt. At that time most Jews believed in the coming of a vague "golden age," an earthly theocratic state in which God would reveal Himself and be accepted by all men. This holy Messianic Age was not identified with one person; rather, the expectation was for the age itself, although for some the great event was to be a political restoration or the crowning of a Davidic king. Whatever the variations on this theme, the kingdom was to be an earthly one, which may be called the "pure" Jewish view.

In contrast to it, but not wholly out of keeping with its central direction of thought, is the new eschatology of the apocalyptic writers. In their vision the world is fraught with strange powers, divided into fixed ages moving implacably toward a final universal cataclysm, the Age to Come, when the world would be destroyed and the dead would rise to receive judgment from God. The kingdom of the righteous would not be in the wicked world, but in the bosom of God in heaven. The ancient Hebrew idea of Sheol, a shadowy realm of the dead reminiscent of Homer's underworld, was developed into a place of waiting for the souls of the dead, with one compartment for the wicked and another for the righteous. This dichotomy bred legions of angels and devils who fought and competed, in a cosmic struggle of light against darkness, for mastery of humanity. Evil came to be explained as the work of a malevolent power independent of God. These ideas are "not Jewish in essence but apparently Persian, yet which none the less came to be adopted by many Jews and regarded as genuinely as their own."[45]

Part and parcel with this shift from earth to heaven are the

notions of spiritual resurrection, immortality, and the divine Son
of Man who would herald a new age. A belief in personal immortality
was evident in some Jewish groups by the second century B.C., probably stemming from the persecutions of Antiochus IV; to keep faith
with God's justice, a way had to be found for martyrs to enjoy an
advantage over those who chose to conform with state policy.46 In
addition, there was mounting despair of ever seeing the Messianic
kingdom, which led many to a feeling of deeper communion with God,
thus engendering a more "spiritual" conception of man's nature and
destiny. The phrase "son of man" occurs first in Daniel, and means
there nothing more than man in the conventional sense.47 There is
no mystery in the fact that it came to be a tag for the divine being whom some associated with judgment day.

> Gradually this purely colorless phrase tended to be-
> come a technical title for the supernatural figure
> who was destined to come to judgment, and who accord-
> ingly was totally distinct from the anointed king of'
> the other cycle of ideas who would be of human origin
> and whose function was to rule over God's people.48

Like the promise of resurrection, which "became popular and came
to be regarded as an original part of God's revelation to Israel,"
the son of man found a wide and fervent audience ready to take him
to its heart on a new level.49

Apocalyptic Judaism was no more uniform in its ideas than orthodox Judaism. In general, however, all Jews believed God was to
look after them one way or another; the orthodox wing expected His
bounty in an earthly, temporal setting, while the apocalyptic wing
anticipated a heavenly, eternal setting. Beyond these rough distinctions, there was much disagreement about the exact nature of
the last day and its aftermath.

To complicate even further the picture of Judaism in the second and first centuries B.C., some of the more disaffected individuals organized themselves into close-knit, exclusive communities
which represented a radical departure from rabbinical orthodoxy.
The Essenes, the Therapeutae, the Covenanters of Demascus, and the
Qumran sect of the Dead Sea Scrolls - all represent a disillusioned
withdrawal from the mainstream. Much has been written about these
ascetic or otherwise highly specialized groups, but reliable information about them is both sparse and secondhand. We learn from
Josephus and Philo that the Essenes required stringent tests of
novices, exacted solemn vows of secrecy, and admitted newcomers to
full membership only after a three year period of probation. Violation of the rules or of one's vows could mean death by enforced
starvation. By their very nature, these clannish groups of alienated men (the Therapeutae accepted women) were hostile to the curiosity of outsiders.

It is not easy to surmise what Radhakrishnan has in mind when he attributes a Buddhistic spirit to the Essenes. The Saṅgha, the community of Buddhist monks, followed the Middle Way, composed of eight categories known as the Noble Eightfold Path (Ariya-Aṭṭangika-Magga), which repudiates asceticism and secret doctrines, has a missionary spirit, and would not condone the harming of a monk who fell away from the teaching.[50] In many ways the Essenes contradict the relative openness of Jesus, who disliked a minute attention to legalism, contrary to both the Essenes and orthodoxy, and offered his teaching to all Jews, whatever their quarrels with "pure" doctrine. Furthermore, there is no evidence, except loose speculation, for identifying Jesus with the mysterious Teacher of Righteousness of the Qumran sect.[51] All of these peripheral groups can be explained most sensibly, in the light of what is known about Hellenistic Judaism, as attempts to turn back the clock to a period when the law did not require troublesome intepretation, when God's word was clear to all and could be fitted to conditions of life without confusion and disagreement. Pharisees tried to bring the law into line with new social and economic circumstances; Sadducees merely ignored the changes and cleaved blindly to the letter of the law; the Essenes, and others like them, tried to recreate the kind of world in which the law applied with pristine simplicity. They looked backward, which is still another reason for denying their influence on Jesus, who broke with precedent, while claiming to retain the spirit of the law, and proclaimed the coming of an upheaval. If Jesus had been an Essene, it is likely that he would have ended his life on a starvation diet of grass.

How does this complex Jewish background relate to the origins of Christianity? What is most obvious is that Jesus, a Jew who was born and crucified in Palestine, had an incredibly rich heritage from which to select ideas and ideals. All the essential ingredients of primitive Christianity can be found in his immediate Jewish background: resurrection and immortality of the soul, angels and devils, the heavenly kingdom, the ethic of righteousness, the imminence of judgment, the supernatural Son of Man, and so on. Without digressing into the matter of whether or not Jesus considered himself to be the divine Son of Man,[52] there is no doubt that he believed the end of the world was due in his own generation, and that it was his mission, in the manner of the ancient Hebrew prophets, to be a guide and teacher on the eve of the cataclysm.[53] As Mark sums up his admonition to the world: "The time is fulfilled, and the kingdom of God is at hand; repent ye, and believe in the gospel."[54] In Mark it is said that "there be some of them that stand here, which shall not taste of death, till they have seen the kingdom of God come with power."[55] The air is charged with the threat of terrible events. A day of reckoning approaches, not the peaceful "golden age" of more orthodox vintage: "Think not that I am come to send peace on earth. I come not to send peace but a sword."[56] There is a pulse of urgency in Matthew, as one is told to abandon

123

material goods, turn the other cheek to evil and violence, allow oneself to be persecuted, have no regard for the morrow, renounce wife or husband, children, and parents, for "a man's foes <u>shall</u> <u>be</u> they of his own household."[57] In short, nothing in this world must interfere with preparing oneself for God's judgment. Those who fail to take heed will be in for it.

> The Son of Man shall send forth his angels, and they
> shall gather out of his kingdom all things that offend
> and them which do iniquity; and shall cast them into a
> furnace of fire: there shall be wailing and gnashing of
> teeth. Then shall the righteous shine forth as the sun
> in the kingdom of their Father.[58]

> So shall it be at the end of the world: the angels
> shall come forth, and sever the wicked from among the
> just, and shall cast them into a furnace of fire.[59]

One is expected to act as though the kingdom had already arrived, because it is that close to fulfillment, which accounts for the extraordinary demands of the Sermon on the Mount, an ethic designed to help one leave the world rather than live in it. It is an ethic that is a condition of individual salvation; it does not extoll the intrinsic value of a goodness that goes unrewarded. It is a prophetic call to righteousness, except that the call blazes with the fires of apocalyptic thought. Unlike the classic Hebrew prophets, Jesus doubts that man can be just, holy, peaceful, and charitable in the material world created by God, which for him becomes a staging area for the beyond.

Did Jesus break away from the Jewish tradition and approximate to Hindu and Buddhist thought? On the contrary, nothing about the origin of Christianity seems more patently evident than its utter Jewishness. Indeed, the word "Christian" is misleading even if convenient, because Christianity did not come into existence until the expected judgment day failed to materialize. It was roughly at that juncture that emphasis shifted from obeying and following Jesus to interpreting and reducing to dogma the meaning of his life and death. This unexpected turn of events fostered the growth of the Church (or of churches), whose function was to hold scattered believers together and enforce some uniformity of doctrine. Also, lest the teaching of the Master be forgotten or hopelessly distorted, a written literature was necessary. Even when Christians made these adjustments and gave up the immediate hope of witnessing the Son of Man coming in glory with his angel entourage, the otherworldly expectation of divine judgment had been shifted into a lower gear, for the other world still remained the goal. Now the faithful would enter it after death through the grace of Jesus Christ. The weeding out of repentant from unrepentant might take some time, but in God's own time the New Age would come when all souls faced the final drama of judgment.

This hope for personal salvation in another world is profoundly un-Buddhist. Suppose that Buddhists, as Radhakrishnan says, were active in the vicinity of Palestine around the first century B.C. Let us imagine that they were members of the Theravada School (followers of the Doctrine of the Elders), the conservative wing of Buddhism, whose scriptures, the Pali Canon, contain the most ancient tradtion. What is a Palestinian likely to have learned from a Bhikkhu (Theravadan monk) missionary about the nature and purpose of human life?

He would have learned that the Buddhist "hankereth neither for this world nor for any world," and that the object of seeking refuge in the Buddha, the Norm, and the Order (known as the Three Treasures) is to "pass away with that utter passing away which leaves no remnant for rebirth."[60] He would have learned that all conditioned existence is suffering (dukkha), impermanence (anicca), and no-soul, or self (anatta), that is, no soul exists as a permanent, unchanging entity through time.[61] He would have learned that "if one does not hold any self or anything of the nature of self in the five groups of grasping" (khandas) - material shape, sensation, perception, volitional activity, and consciousness - one is an Arahant (one who has attained Nirvāṇa, or Enlightenment), "the outflows extinguished" and release from the wheel of rebirth assured.[62] He would have learned that Buddhist spirituality is contingent on getting rid of craving (tanhā) for individual existence, and that the path to release from attachment to becoming or being must be walked entirely by onself, for the Buddha stressed self-reliance: "the mere sight of Me enables no one to conquer suffering; he will have to meditate for himself about the gnosis I have communicated. If self-controlled, a man may live away from Me as far as he can be."[63]

Had the missionaries been of the Mahāyāna School (the second great branch of Buddhism), the essential message would not have been different, only more metaphysical and therefore more difficult to comprehend.[64] Mahāyānists denied the historical importance of Gautama Buddha's life, saying there had been many Buddhas and that there would be many more. The ideal of the Bodhisattva was proclaimed, a compassionate being who has reached Nirvāṇa, or to its threshold, but refuses enlightenment until all sentient beings have been released from the toil of rebirth. The Bodhisattva ideal is centered on an ethic of universal compassion and toleration, while the abstruse metaphysics of Mahāyāna, dominated by the concept of "suchness" (tathātā), annihilates the notions of Being upon which all Jewish and Christian belief rest: "Suchness is neither brought about by duality nor by non-duality; Suchness is neither defiled nor purified ... Suchness is neither produced not stopped ... In this way the Tathāgata /a name for the Buddha/ is seen and honored."[65] Just what is this "suchness"? It is "a never-ceasing conflux of

125

life waves."[66] It is Emptiness, the Void, "when ideas of I and mine are extinct, both with regard to things within and without."[67] There is no comfortable place in this scheme of reality for Jesus the unique saviour, or for a physical incarnation of Being (the Word made Flesh), an unrepeatable act of redemption which invests the historical process with all its meaning and purpose.

Considered either as an apocaplytic vision or as a religion of exclusive revelation and salvation for the redeemed, Christianity has little in common with Buddhism. It is true, of course, that popular Buddhism had its saviours, demons, heavens and hells, virgin births, miraculous deeds, ideas of sin, purification, and redemption.[68] But these salvationist aspects of popular Mahāyāna sects were already known to the Near Eastern and Greek mystery religions, so even if they had been espoused by our hypothetical Buddhist missionaries, they would have been nothing new. There is no intrinsic affinity between Christianity and Buddhism, Theravada or Mahāyāna, in the area of ideas, if one deals with Buddhism in its mature, undebased forms. Perhaps Buddha and Jesus agreed on one strong point - the slim chances of human contentment in the midst of time and change.

But if Jesus was not influenced by Indian religious ideas, do not the moral precepts of Jesus and Buddha, like the mysticism of Plato and the Upanishads, express the "same view of life," as Radhakrishnan is wont to say? The Sermon on the Mount and the Buddhist Dhammapada ("Words of the Doctrine," from the Khuddaka Nikaya of the Sutta Pitaka) contain remarkably parallel exhortations; if this is not good evidence of a passage of ideas from the older to the younger source, does it not indicate a common sense of religious and moral values?

The Sermon on the Mount has been characterized as an "interim" or "kingdom" ethic, intended to guide the repentant soul on earth until the judgment announced by Jesus appeared almost immediately. The Buddhist ethic, although prudential in the sense of being geared to the task of achieving detachment from the world, and hence of escaping the burdens of karma, is set forth with no reference to deity, a divine saviour, or immortality of the individual soul. The spirit of Buddhist ethics is summed up in the opening verse of the Dhammapada: "All that we are is the result of what we have thought: it is founded on our thoughts, it is made up of our thoughts. If a man speaks or acts with an evil thought, pain follows him, as the wheel follows the foot of the ox that draws the carriage."[69] Man is wholly self-creating in the Buddhist context. He brings about his own suffering and controls his own prospects of enlightenment. It is not God in heaven who decides the outcome of his life, but his own grasping state of mind, or lack of it.

The Sermon on the Mount is rich with threats of appalling

126

severity. The "whole body" of the unrepentant shall "be cast into hell," or "cast into the fire."[70] There is no reason whatever to believe that such threats were not meant to be taken literally.[71] Without the rewards of heaven standing as a clear alternative to the punishments of hell, the Christian message of repentance and salvation would have seemed less compelling to the faithful and to potential converts. The point of the Sermon on the Mount might be summed up in three ideas: that God has called for repentance as the condition for entering his imminent kingdom; that repentance consists of breaking worldly ties and practicing righteousness; and that heaven awaits those who comply, while hell beckons those who do not, there being no third option.[72]

In chapter twenty-two of the Dhammapada there are five references to hell. However, in the context of the document, what is meant is the suffering that attends rebirth, not a place of torment for the spiritually unregenerate: "As a blade of grass, if badly grasped, cuts the arm, badly-practised asceticism leads to hell."[73] The imperative facing a Buddhist is not the commandment of God but the natural order of existence, the imperative of the flux. All sentient beings suffer attachment to the flux and consequent rebirth. There is no question of punishment being meted out, since each being punishes himself by craving for existence. What is called for is compassion among men, who have a common affliction: "All men tremble at punishment, all men fear death; remember that you are like unto them, and do not kill, nor cause slaughter."[74] Doing evil is the supreme manifestation of self, of clinging to the world and its discriminations. Self cannot be dissolved away without first conquering lust, greed, violence, and all their camp followers: "A fool does not know when he commits evil deeds; but the wicked man burns by his own deeds, as if burnt by fire."[75]

Words used in the two documents are often similar or even identical, but the meaning is not the same, or only so in rare instances. That Jesus and Buddha both preached non-violence is true, yet their cultural backgrounds and differing experiences of life must be taken into account. Thus Buddha enjoins compassion for all living things, animals and plants as well as men. Not only is Jesus concerned only with human life, many commentators argue that he was preaching only to the Jews. In each case, the ethic arose in different historical circumstances, rests on different premises, and leads to different consequences in action.

Historical Buddhism has proselytized without being militant, with the notable exception of some Japanese Buddhist sects like Nichirenism. It was rare in Buddhist countries to find loathing and fear of the unbeliever or heretic. The tolerance and forebearance of Buddhism is one its most endearing traits. One might argue, therefore, that the Dhammapada, an ethical treatise widely used in Buddhist education, has been a real force in mitigating violent human passion. Historical Christianity, on the other hand, with its dualisms of body and soul, sacred and profane, saved and damned, believers and heathens, faith and reason, heavenly and earthly cities, its concern with right belief, its insistence on being the exclusive agent of God's revelation for all time and all men, has contributed to a record of intolerance and institutionalized violence rivaled only by Islam. The kinder injunctions of the Sermon on the Mount have been subordinated often enough to cruel expediencies. Buddhist ethics have been regarded consistently by avowed Buddhists as indispensable to conduct and wisdom, the twin sails which take one to Enlightenment.[77]

In a controversial and intriguing line of argument, Joseph Campbell says:

> It is impossible to reconstruct the character, life, and actual teaching of the man who became the Buddha. He is supposed to have lived c. 563–483 B.C. However, his earliest biography, that of the Pali Canon, was set down in writing only c. 80 B.C. in Ceylon, five centuries and fifteen hundred miles removed from the actual historic scene. And the life, by then, had become mythology -- according to a pattern characteristic of World Saviours of the period from c. 500 B.C. to c. 500 A.D., whether in India, as in the legends of the Jains, or in the Near East, as in the Gospel view of Christ.[78]

The earliest biography of Jesus, that of Mark, composed at least a generation after the crucifixion, has more reliable historical material in it than documents relating to the Buddha. But even though written closer to events associated with Jesus, it has the form and substance of mythology. A birth attended by supernatural signs, a precocious youth, a spiritual crisis, a victorious battle against temptation, entrance into a holy calling after a period of trial - here are the preparatory stages marking the appearance of a World Saviour like Jesus or Gautama Buddha. In subsequent stages, the World Saviour performs miracles (healing the sick, walking on water, etc.), becomes a wandering teacher, preaches a doctrine of salvation to a group of disciples, one of whom, the slowest to learn (Peter with Jesus, Ananda with Buddha) becomes leader on the death of the Master, and another of whom (Judas with Jesus, Devadatta with Buddha) plots the Master's destruction.[79] Even if there were means of showing a definite connection between the two legends on historical grounds, the meaning of each one would still be profoundly different. As in the case of resemblances between the two ethics, so those between the two lives do not prove a common experience of life among the followers who shaped the legends.

In spite of its mythological flavor, the life of Jesus has no

128

significance for Christians unless it is credited with historicity. If the crucifixion and resurrection did not really happen, then no glad tidings exist to be spread through the world. Jesus is central to Christianity in a way that the Buddha is not, and never has been, central to Buddhism. Without Jeus and the fact of his immolation in an historic place and time, the breach created between God and man by the impertinence of Adam cannot be healed. The legend of the Buddha is valued largely for its heuristic qualities. The essence of Buddhism is not a redemptive sacrifice by the Buddha, but his awakened state (bodhi), his release from the conditioned state of existence in samsāra, the cycle of births. For the individual Buddhist, the historicity of the Buddha's life is relatively unimportant. What matters is that the legend provide a model and guide for the attainment of Enlightenment. The Dharma (the teaching) comes first, the Buddha himself is secondary.[80] Even the teaching was meant only for those ready to receive it, and was "never intended to interfere with either the life and habits of the multitude or the course of civilization."[81]

Any direct influence of Buddhist ideas on early or later Christian thought seems negligible. A more delicate question concerns the relation of Mahayana docetism (from the Greek dokein, "to appear") to Gnostic theology, and of the latter to nascent Christianity. Until recently, the chief sources for Gnostic (from the Greek gnosis, or "knowledge") belief were polemics from the hands of various Christian Fathers, the Egyptian literature of revelation attributed to Hermes Trismegistus (the Corpus Hermeticum, of Hellenistic vintage), a library of Coptic-Manichaean papyri discovered in 1930, and the sacred books of the Mandaeans, a Gnostic sect which survives in modern Iraq. The discovery in 1945 of a Coptic-Gnostic cache of some forty-eight documents in Upper Egypt has shed much light on the range of Gnostic convictions and practice. It is a mistake to identify Gnosticism solely as a Christian heresy or a Jewish aberration. Gnostic sects were scattered across the Near East, and there is even evidence for their presence in Chinese Turkestan.[82] As a movement of international scope, having its Iranian, Egyptian, Syrian, Jewish, and Christian branches, Gnosticism was a major religious phenomenon of the first and second centuries A.D. Hans Jonas identifies the "general religion of the period" as "a dualistic transcendent religion of salvation."[83] This description encompasses most of the salvationist sects which flourished at the peak of the Roman Empire, including Mithraism, Jewish Apocalyptic, Manichaeism, Palestinian Christianity, and the rites of Isis, all of which contained Gnostic elements.

All Gnostic sects shared a core of doctrine: emphasis on transmundane knowledge of God; assertion of God's complete transcendence and dissociation from the world; description of gnosis as fundamentally divergent from Greek rationalism; postulation of an intrinsically evil world, ruled over by malignant beings, into which the

129

soul has fallen and become imprisoned; denial of a uniform human nature in favor of a distinction of body, soul, and spirit. Campbell has seen instructive correspondences between some facets of Gnostic belief and certain Mahāyāna doctrines which were developed about the time of Gnostic ascendancy. These parallel ideas include an interpretation of Jesus and Buddha as mere appearance in their physical forms, delusory masks concealing a universal, inexplicable realm of divinity; a theory of perception which denies the objectivity of what is beheld by the senses, and reduces the beheld to a function of the beholder's mind; and a characterization of the phenomenal world as a snare, an illusory trap to be evaded in limitless consciousness. From this perspective, Gnosticism can be said to share with Mahāyāna Buddhism a view of salvation as a psychological problem rather than as a problem of historical incarnations or revelations. The way to salvation is non-historical, above all permutations of time and change. In Buddhist language:

> Stars, darkness, a lamp,
> A phantom, dew, a bubble;
> A dream, a flash of lightening, and a cloud;
> Thus should we look upon the world.[84]

In Gnostic language, from the Corpus Hermeticum: "If then you do not make yourself equal to God, you cannot apprehend God; for like is known by like. Leap clear of all that is corporeal, and make yourself grow to a like expanse with that greatness which is beyond all measure." And from a Coptic-Gnostic text:

> I am the Light that is above them all,
> I am the All.
> The All came forth from Me and All attained to Me.
> Cleave a piece of wood, I am there.
> Lift up the stone, you will find Me there.[85]

From the perspective of Mahāyāna metaphysics, these Gnostic passages place us in the Buddha Field where distinctions do not prevail, and where there can be no Illumined One because there is only Illumination: "If in a Bodhisattva the perception of a 'being' should take place, he would be called a 'Bodhi-being,' in whom the perception of a being should take place or the perception of a living soul, or the perception of a person."[86]

It has been long suspected that this "Buddhist Gnosticism" crept into the salvationist religions of the ancient world, or that it expresses much the same view of the world and the human condition.[87] Historical evidence supports the presence of Buddhist emissaries in the eastern Mediterranean during the Hellenistic period.[88] There is no textual evidence that Buddhist missionaries inspired or reinforced Gnostic tradition, but efforts have been made to explain this absence of written material.[89] The silence of Hellenistic literature about Buddhism could be attributable to the conservatism of literary transmission, to the habits of a backward-looking scholarly tradition immersed in the codification, copying, and writing of commentary on select manuscripts, a tradition disinclined to seek out and record fresh, unusual ideas. Also, Buddhism tended to shun theory and stressed practical forms of instruction aimed at the lower classes, a kind of religious populism which might have alienated the sort of people who wrote books. Written sources were not a necessary condition for communication. An easy exchange of mythic and philosophical symbols was potentiality of the age, and the "mixing of gods," or syncretism, was a standard modus operandi. From this point of view, may we not infer from expressions like "the kingdom of God is within you" that the Gospel writers were aware of Buddhist-Gnostic ideas?[90]

Unfortunately, this stimulating line of argument is weakly conjectural. Even if one could prove beyond a reasonable doubt that Gnosticism absorbed Mahayana Buddhist ideas, that fact would not alter our understanding of how Christian doctrine developed, for the growth of that doctrine was, in many instances, a hostile response to Gnosticism, attested by the apologetic writings of Origin, Hippolytus, and Clement.

Secondly, the origin of Gnosticism is problematic in the extreme, an opaque field of study obliged to cope with the presence of Gnostic ideas in Iranian, Egyptian, Babylonian, Greek, Jewish, and Christian sources.[91] Its genesis may have owed something to all of these traditions, the final synthesis being due to the creative vision and syncretic talents of some unknown religious genius. The hypothesis of Buddhist influence is welcome in an area of inquiry already juggling several alternative explanations, but its candidacy is by no means the best.

Thirdly, the Gnostic spirit lives in all salvationist religion; however, specifically Gnostic systems do not appear in the record before the close of the first century A.D., thus diminishing the probability of a cohesive Gnostic theology having some influence on Jesus. Since Mahāyāna is supposed to have entered the mainstream of Gnostic speculation about the same time, and assuming for the moment that this was the case, the late date removes Mahayana from the period of Jesus' ministry. Gnostic influence on the Gospel writers is entirely credible, but if something more than homologous phrases does not come out of future research to nail down such influence, there can be no warrant for asserting the intrusion of Buddhist ideas into the Gospels through the agency of Gnostic theology.

Fourthly, appeals to a general principle of symbolic excahnge, and to Hellenistic proclivities for the conservation of old knowledge rather than the discovery of new knowledge, are well taken, but do not substitute adequately for a visible medium of transmission

between Buddhist and Gnostic; it amounts to learned groping in the
dark. After all, virtually any plausible resemblance between ideas
might be explained as a causal relationship due to the activity of
amorphous, intangible oral traditions or informal exchanges of symbolic structures. There is too much arbitrariness in such procedures.

Fifthly, one can too easily forget, ignore, or minimize the
real differences between Mahāyāna metaphysics and Gnostic theology.
There is a self-conscious moral nihilism in the Gnostic antipathy
for the world's intrinsic wickedness. The absence of positive ethical values was accompanied by active indulgence of the flesh. The
debased realm of physical existence is no place for moral action,
only a gloomy prison from which the soul aspires to flee with the
help of gnosis, in hope of reunion with the God from whose estate
it has fallen. Irenaeus tells us that Gnostics "serve intemperately
the lusts of the flesh and say you must render the flesh to the
flesh and the spirit to the spirit."[93] In both Theravada and Mahāyāna Buddhism, active compassion for beings trapped in the web of
conditioned existence is a positive teaching; self-control and kindness must be practised as essential conditions for deliverance from
illusion, but they are also practiced in a spirit of empathy for
the plight of beings other than oneself.[94]

The highest level of gnosis is reunion with the "depth beyond
being," as the soul rises above the world to meet God: "thou hast
made us gods while still in our bodies through the vision of thee."[95]
Basilides invokes "Divinity beyond being" who "created universality beyond being."[96] These passages, and others like them, which
have an obvious likeness to some Mahāyāna texts, must be read in
the whole context of Gnostic thought. As a system trying to explain
the nature of the world, man, God, and salvation, Gnosticism is en-
demically and profoundly dualistic. The divine kingdom is sundered
from the degenerate world, the soul from the body, rational gnosis
from the gnosis which "sees" God, cosmic slavery of the soul from
its transcendent freedom, and so on.[97] The idea of the world as
illusion in the Mahāyāna sense can be found in Gnostic texts, but
its adumbration is clothed in dualistic language. The Hermetic hymn
of thanksgiving for mystical deification, quoted in part at the beginning of this paragraph, is dualistic in spirit and letter. Knowledge is opposed to to ignorance, light to darkness, life to death,
us to thee.[98] Mahāyāna scriptures of the New Wisdom School consistently attack duality and dualistic thinking. There is no equivoca-
tion about bodies and souls, debased worlds and transcendent deities,
this and that, mine and thine.[99]

Gnostic theology posits a world deliberately created by malevolent powers for the purpose of capturing fallen souls.[100] The
soul is held in thrall and maliciously prevented from returning to
the abode of God. These Gnostic metaphors convey a sense of the im-
prisoning world as objective reality, not an illusion. There is in

132

Mahāyāna texts an inflexible denial that good is divided from evil or the high from the low.

> Complexes have no inner might, are void in themselves;
> Rather like the stem of the plaintain tree, when
> One reflects on them,
> Like a mock show which deludes the mind
> Like an empty fist with which a child is teased.[101]

In Mahāyāna thought there is no self, no soul to be enchained, no sublime God from whom one can fall or to whom one can return, no world that one can despise or from which one can flee: "Indiscriminate, undifferentiated, those are the marks of true reality."[102]

Gnostic dualism is reinforced by its promulgation of an ascetic ideal, a logical consequence of the radical separation of soul and body and the belief that matter constrains the soul, an eschatology of flight from corporeality into the bosom of ineffable divinity. The combination of voluntary sensuality and self-mortification in the same religious context is remarkable, but both tendencies flow, oddly enough, from Gnostic premises.[103] In the Buddhist outlook, self-mortification is renounced as one of those futile activities not tending to edification. Assaulting the body merely distracts the novice from awareness of the real problem, which is rooted in grasping.

> Not nakedness, nor matted hair, nor filth,
> Nor fasting long, nor lying on the ground,
> Nor dust and dirt, nor squatting on the heels,
> Can cleanse the mortal that is full of doubt.[104]

With all these reservations, one cannot entirely discount a trace of Mahāyāna style in Gnostic theology. A confirmation of Buddhist influence will depend on more research into newly discovered documents, and perhaps on the excavation of more of them from the mountains and sands of the Near East. At present, however, there is no confirmation, only ingenious speculation.

Bringing this discussion back to Christianity, the movement of Christian thought was away from Gnostic dualism, which was uncompromising, and also away from the equally radical "suchness" of Mahāyāna metaphysics. In neither point of view was there a place for the divine intermediary of flesh and spirit whose death and resurrection was regarded as the sole instrument of salvation. In so far as Christianity was indebted to Gnosticism, the debt seems to have involved no more than misty metaphors of God's image being present in all persons, the fall of the soul from divine favor, and the its ultimate return to the source of goodness and perfection. It was the Christian style to borrow something from just about everybody, so long as the crucial mediation of Jesus was preserved.

So far in this chapter, no use has been made of Garbe's fami-liar _Indien_ und _Christentum_. The reason is that nothing in his book proves a connection between Indian thought and Christianity. The im-plications of various parallels are explored in light of relevant scholarship up to Garbe's time, but there is nothing conclusive to show, not even the influence of Buddhist _Jātaka_ tales (a large as-semblage of folk stories adapted to Buddhist ends) on the Apochry-phal Gospels. The general impact of Garbe's exposition and argument is only suggestive. It is well-documented speculation. Indeed, Garbe actually claims very little for his effort, nor does he argue that Buddhism, Hinduism, and Christianity converged on the same view of life. His main contentions can be summarized as follows:

(1) Each religion (Buddhist, Hindu, and Christian) arose inde-pendently, but the later origin of Christianity in the highly eclec-tic atmosphere of the Hellenistic world probably resulted in the borrowing, by Christians, of some Indian legends, ideas, and prac-tices.[105]

(2) While there is no convincing proof of direct Buddhist in-fluence on the New Testament,[106] there may be an indirect influence based on several striking parallels, although most parallels which have been claimed by scholarship must be rejected.[107]

(3) Only four parallels are acceptable as Buddhist-inspired: Saint Astia and child Buddha (parallel to Simeon in the Temple), the Temptation, Peter walking on water, and the miracle of the loaves.[108] There is no textual evidence of a link between parallels, but they are much too close for coincidence to explain them.

(4) Buddhist tales probably left an imprint on the Apochryphal Gospels (Proto-Gospel of James, Gospels of Thomas and Nicodemus, Gos-pel of Pseudo-Matthew, Gospel of Mary's Birth, etc., most of "Gnos-tic origin," which is not surprising since "Gnostic sects arose un-der strong Buddhistic influences."[109]

(5) Apart from items of legend lore and some parables, there appears to have been influence on Christian practices such as mo-nasticism, celibacy, confession, tonsure, veneration of relics, ro-sary, incense burning, as well as bells and steeples in Christian architecture, again because it is improbable that such a cluster of traits could exist without some borrowing from Buddhists, "in con-sideration of late evidence of Christian parallels throughout."[110]

Nearly all of these arguments can be accepted without forcing a serious revision of conclusions already reached in this chapter. The question of Jesus' teaching approximating to Hinduism is more of a problem, because Hinduism is a religious, intellectual, and social phenomenon of bewildering proportions. We shall leave Garbe's speculations at a respectful distance and turn to this issue.

Hinduism's main line of development lies between the fourth and the twelfth centuries A.D., well outside the time period of this essay. Nevertheless, many beliefs and practices, as well as religious and philosophical texts, associated with the "Hindu view of life" were in existence during the two centuries which saw the genesis of the Christian movement. Indians travelled in the eastern Mediterranean and contacts with southern India were more frequent.[111] Given the dynamic, cosmopolitan nature of the early Christian environment, and the fact that Christianity became the "most complete example of ancient religious syncretism," it is tempting to assume out of hand that some elements of Christian belief were taken from resident Indians.[112] It was a feature of the Hellenistic ethos that men thirsting for slavation or religious experience had "a confidence in the significance of sacred writings, especially those which were ancient and mysterious or cryptic, or in a foreign tongue."[113]

Once again it must be said that in the absence of hard evidence in the form of texts, we are in the dark about the details of any cross-fertilization of Christian and Indian thought; it is gratuitous merely to assume that a mechanism of diffusion was in operation. Whether in Alexandria or elsewhere, the resident Indians are very obscure figures. It is not known who they were, what views they held, how eager they were to communicate their views, or to whom, or how successful they were in explaining themselves if they were asked.[114]

A close look at the prominent features of Hinduism turns up few authentic parallels with the ideas expressed in the literature of the early Christian movement. Christian monotheism, both in its Palestinian and Hellenistic phases, implicitly rejected polytheism and henotheism. The Vedic pantheon and its later accretions would have been no less offensive than the pantheons of Greece and Rome. Both Hebrews and Christians invited persecution for refusing minor concessions to pagan deities honored by the Roman state. The essence of Vedic religion was ritual and sacrifice (yājña). In contrast, the traditionalism and ritualism of the Pharisees are criticized in the Gospels as impediments to the spiritual life, the emphasis being on purity of motive and inner submission to God.[115] When we turn to later Brahmanism and the ideal of renunciation (sannyāsa) set forth in the Upanishads, we need only remind ourselves that Christian faith, practice, and eschatology depended on firm distinctions between man, God the Father, and Jesus the Son.[116] The introspectiveness of the Upanishadic sages is not quite like the inwardness of Jesus; the former aimed at the abandonment of distinctions, the latter could not do without them. For Jesus, inwardness was referred to the will of God and implied a condition of readiness for divine judgment. Being "one with God" meant submission to the will of God and preparation for the advent of His kingdom.[117] The psychological concerns of the Upanishads do not have their counterpart in the teachings of Jesus.

The Hindu conception of God raises other problems, for many options were permitted in the matter of description and the mode of apprehension. Depending on the individual's level of spiritual development and cult or philosophical affiliation, God might be one or many, personal or impersonal, active in the world or aloof from it, subject to karma or free of it. The Hindu could select an ishtadevata (chosen deity) as his exclusive object of private worship without implying that other notions of deity were inadmissable.[118] In the larger conceptual framework of Hinduism, this personal god had an inferior ontological status, being one of numerous avatars which point beyond themselves to a higher plane of impersonal being, to Ishvara, or "Lord," beyond the world of gods, and finally to Brahman, the unqualified ground of all being.[119] Just as worship (pūjā) had a qualified value below the transcendental introspection of the renunciant (sannyāsan), so the gods endowed with qualities (saguṇa) were viewed as subordinate to the unconditioned Brahman. The generous idea of many avatars representing descending levels of truth and reality, an idea with which Hindus tried "to reconcile the urge toward monotheism with an irresistable fondness for a multiplicity of cults," was substantively incompatible with the early Christian insistence on a single, unique, historic incarnation.[120] Salvation for a Christian in the time of Jesus required faith in the imminent coming of the kingdom and God's judgment. After Paul the Apostle, who continued to expect the end of the world, the emphasis fell on a personal commitment to God the Father through the person of Christ the Redeemer, whose physical resurrection signified to followers the forgiveness of sins and immortal life.[121]

A Hindu, on the other hand, no matter how devotional his religious style, could rely entirely on himself for deliverance from samsāra, a point made quite early in the Bhagavad-Gītā.[122] The paths to salvation were various disciplines (sādhanās), of which devotion (bhakti yoga) to a deity or a guru was only one form.[123] Indeed, the yogic system based on love, faith, and a divinity whose grace is extended to humanity is a medieval development of Hinduism after about 712 A.D.[124] Hindu literature of the Hellenistic and and early Christian eras is silent on the point of an avatar who suffers, dies, and is resurrected to redeem the karma of individual beings. Everyone is responsible for the accumulation or diminution of his own karma.

At this time there is no true parallel bridging the Hindu and Christian notions of sin. An appeal to some common awareness of alienation from divine reality will not do. For the Hindu, sin might be construed variously as defiance of rita, violation of taboos, a state of personal immorality, or even in some vague sense "the finite superordinating itself to the infinite."[125] For the Christian, sin was a preference for the darkness of the world over the light of God, or, in Paul's formulation, the preference of the archetypal man (Adam) for his own will over God's, an act whose cosmic result was

136

the estrangement of mankind from God, which could be overcome only by the unilateral intervention of supernatural grace.[126]

A further difficulty for Christians would have been the elaborate cyclical cosmology and theory of time found in the Hindu scriptures.[127] A day of Brahma (the creator god) is a kalpa (4,320 earthly years), divided into fourteen smaller cycles, or manvantaras (each one lasting 306,720,000 years). Each of these, in turn, divide into seventy-one mahayugas, which individually contain four yugas: krita, treta, dvapara, and kali (lasting, respectively, 4,800, 3,600, 2,400, and 1,200 years). A night of Brahma is similarly constituted. Three hundred and sixty of these days and nights are one year of Brahma's life. He lives for a hundred years, after which the universe returns to the bosom of the world spirit to await the commencement of another cycle. These vast cycles – viewed as a total process – have no beginning or end. Thus samsāra is eternal and is governed in part by its own inner necessities. Moreover, this cosmological pattern is alleged to be uncreated and to exist without reference to human purposes or benefit. Transmigrating souls are subject to its rhythms indefinitely, so long as inflexible law of karmic retribution is at work. Confronted with "oceans of millions of years" through which the transmigratory effects of karma are felt, one can understand readily enough why Radhakrishnan describes Indian philosophy as a series of variations on the means of freeing the self from bondage to the world cycles.[128]

The Christian notion of time was finite, not only in the sense of distinguishing time from eternity, but in the more fundamental sense of imposing limits on all temporal existence as a condition for understanding the human condition. Historical time was linear in that it manifested a beginning (the Creation, Adam's sin), a middle (the Incarnation, Crucifixion, and Resurrection), and an end (the Day of Judgment). The motion of time was seen to lie between two pregnant events, the one signifying cosmic generation, the other cosmic fulfillment. This scheme can be described also as a one-cycle theory, a fall from paradise followed by a return to paradise.[129] Temporal succession was not, as in the Hindu frame of reference, eternal, for only God is eternal.

The early Christian gave time a positive function in God's ordained plan for human salavation. Time and the world had been created specifically for human welfare, except for which there would be no historical events. As an agent of God's will, mankind was understood as fulfilling itself, in part, with the aid of history. R.G. Collingwood comments aptly that Christian historiography was "a Copernican revolution."[130] It was universal, in that a complete history of man and the world was eventually sought for, so that God's will and purpose in the context of time might be grasped. It was providential, in that history was conceived as a preordained drama. It was apocalyptic, in that Christ's appearance was seen as a pivotal

event separating periods of darkness and light. And it was perio-
dized, in that all events were to be sorted out and assigned to
proper places in relation to the central event of Christ's incarnation.[131] This historical framework is implied in the Gospels and in
Paul, and is fully developed by Saint Augustine in The City of God.
An important consequence of this viewpoint on time and history is
that Christians came to reject the Gnostic doctrine of the pre-existence of souls.[132] Souls are created afresh by God. They are entities with an historical mission to perform before the advent of
eternal life. The divergence here from Hindu belief concerning the
pre-existence of souls is crucial. Time and the world not only had
value for Christians, they were essential conditions for true spirituality and salvation. The otherworldly tone of the Gospel writers
and Paul should not be allowed to obscure this point.

Between Christianity and HInduism there is a notable difference
in attitude toward rival systems of worship and thought. The Hindu
oulook was expansively tolerant of virtually every shade of doctrine
and practice, so long as the authority of the Vedas was acknowledged.
Even though Jainism and Buddhism were classified as heterodox sects
(nastika) because they rejected Vedic authority, many of their assumptions and beliefs were shared by Hindus, particularly the doctrines of karma and reincarnation and the cosmology of endless cycles. Hindu syncretism allowed for stages and degrees of spiritual
development. The class (varna) and caste (jāti) systems, the four
stages of life, or āshramas (student, householder, anchorite, and
renunciant), and the four ends of life (dharma, artha, kama, and
moksha), which reconciled worldly engagement with deliverance from
the world, were all linked to the ideas of karma and reincarnation,
which enabled Brahmanism to absorb and integrate a profusion of non-
Vedic cults, myths, deities, and beliefs.[133] The unifying thread
was a desire to disengage from the round of transmigrations, but the
paths to deliverance were "as many as the systems of thought in
which they are described." [134] The Bhagavad-Gītā recognizes several yogas, corresponding to the ways of knowledge, action, and devotion (which correspond, in turn, to three distinct temperaments),
which may lead equally to union with ultimate reality.[135] The Six
Classical Systems of philosophy were declared by their authors to
be darshanas (inward beholding, or "views"), each one valid as a
perspective on religious and philosophical truth.[136] In the Hindu
fold, it was very difficult to be a heretic.

Those who turned to Jesus as the focus of their religious as-
pirations were obliged to remain exclusive of rival sects.[137] At
first the Jewish apostles rejected the gentiles. When Paul made Jesus accessible to the gentiles, the true believer continued to be
him who gave one-pointed devotion to Christ, the one and authentic
saviour. The development of Christian doctrine was given substantially to a sorting out of the Christian from the non-Christian ideas
and practices, a struggle for identity that had to proceed against

138

uncomfortably similar sects (especially Gnosticism) which were not reluctant to recognize Christ as saviour: "struggle in this case meant definition, that is to say, drawing a sharp line of demarcation around what was Christian and declaring everything heathen that would not keep within it."[138] The forms and doctrines of the early Church originated in an effort to shake off the encroachments of Gnosticism and Hellenism, to define teaching and discipline, and to "exclude everyone who would not yield them /the priesthood/ obedience."[139]

Christianity and Hinduism both arose with a syncretistic style, something they have in common. With Christianity, however, all the diverse elements making up the Faith and the Church were compelled, more or less, to march in step to a single tune. With Hinduism, the elements were allowed to mill around in glorious confusion to dozens of tunes, unified tenuously, perhaps, by the ground bass of the Absolute.

1. Morton Enslin, Christian Beginnings (New York: Harper Torchbooks, 1956), p. 114.
2. This is Philo's "Bible Alchemy." Adolph Harnack, Outlines of the History of Dogma (Boston: Beacon Press, 1957), p. 31. Allegory was the method of Hellenistic philosophy, whether, Gnostic, Neo-Platonic, or Stoic: "it is applied to Homer, to the religious traditions, to the ancient rituals, to the whole world," which is "a thing whose value lies not in itself but in the spiritual meaning which it hides and reveals." Murray, Five Stages of Greek Religion, p. 158. Imagine the result of applying allegorical method to Hindu or Buddhist texts. A Christian reader, if sufficiently ingenious, no doubt could have discovered confirmation of his beliefs everywhere, without learning anything new. Also see Jean Danielou and Henri Marrou, The Christian Centuries: The First Six Hundred Years, trans. V. Cronin (New York: McGraw-Hill, 1964), pp. 128-130. The Catholic authors of this history are admirably balanced in their handling of the evidence.
3. See Edwin Hatch, The Influence of Greek Ideas on Christianity (New York: Harper Torchbooks, 1957), chapter 10. Also useful is S. Angus, The Mystery Religions and Christianity (3rd ed.; London, 1928), which stresses the indebtedness of Christian doctrine to its Near Eastern background. The historical ambiguity of Christian origins has stimulated much apologetic writing aimed at proving the originality of the Christian mystery. Hugo Rahner can be cited as an extreme example of this viewpoint: "Theories which postulate a genetic relationship or one of historical causality between the Hellenistic mystery cults and the essentials of Christian belief can no longer be taken seriously." Greek Myths and Christian Mystery (New York: Harper and Row, 1963), p. 9. It is fair to assume that Rahner would be even more adamant in denying substantive Buddhist or Brahmanical influence on early Christian belief. He quotes approvingly a denunciation by Harnack of comparative mythology and religion, "which endeavors to connect everything causally with everything else, which tears down solid fences, playfully bridges separating chasms and spins combinations out of superficial similarities." Ibid., p. 120. I believe that Harnack's criticism has merit in the case of Christianity's relations with Indian thought but not in the case of Christianity's relations with Near Eastern cults. I shall follow the perspectives of Angus, and of Charles Guignebert, who does not hesitate to say that Christianity was "profoundly syncretistic," but does not thereafter venture beyond Western Asia for "eastern" influences. The Early History of Christianity (New York: Twayne Publishers, n.d.), p. 123. One exception, however, can be noted immediately, for among the cults based on vegetation and seasonal cycles "the greatest of all the Oriental deities came from farther East - from Persia via Babylon and

originally from Vedic India - the sun god Mithras." Frederick Grant, ed., Hellenistic Religions: The Age of Syncretism (New York: The Bobbs-Merrill Company, 1953), p. xxxvii.

4. Tarn, Hellenistic Civilization, p. 3.

5. Ibid., pp. 333-335. The extent to which Christianity was indebted to Stoic ethics is seldom given enough credit. Hatch does not exaggerate when he says "the basis of Christian society is not Christian, but Roman and Stoical." The Influence of Greek Ideas on Christianity, p. 170. The Sermon on the Mount, popularly regarded as the basis of Chriatian moral life, could not, as an interim ethic, provide the practical guidelines for conduct to which Stoicism contributed so much.

6. The Gnostics, with their dualisms of light and dark, demons and angels, good and evil, clearly owe much to Persian Zoroastrianism. Harnack, pp. 67-70. Also see Rudolph Bultmann, Primitive Christianity in Its Contemporary Setting (New York: Meridean Books, 1956), pp. 162-171.

7. Franz Cumont, Oriental Religions in Roman Paganism (New York: Dover Publications, 1956), chapter 2, is admirable on the subject of Hellenistic orientalism.

8. Tarn, Hellenistic Civilization, pp. 244, 248.

9. Pliny Natural History vi. 21, 24.

10. Lucian Toxaris 34.

11. Clement Stromata i. 15. In a brief, undocumented article, Kishore Kumar Saxena tells us that "Indians formed part of the cosmopolitan city of Alexandria's population. The Buddhists had set up a flourishing monastery there." Furthermore, "Brahmanas also reached there and founded prosperous settlements." Indeed, "Indian sects had a stronghold in Ptolemic (sic) times ... the Brahmanas enjoyed high positions in the higher society and influenced the local sects. Their influence was a marked one on the Therapeutae." "Indus-Euphrates-Nile," The Indo-Asian Culture, 14 (July, 1965), 202-203. Tarn only goes so far as to say that "a gravestone with a wheel and trisula attests the presence of Buddhists in Alexandria." Hellenistic Civilization, p. 248. I have yet to see evidence which can support the strong claims made by Saxena.

12. Jerome Contra Jovinian i. 26.

13. The Philosophy of Plotinus, trans. Joseph Thomas (Chicago: Chicago University Press, 1958), pp. 132-133. The italics are mine. Also relevant to the "oriental" Plotinus is Olivier Lacombe's "Note sur Plotin et la pensée indienne," Annuaire de l'École Pratiques des Hautes Études, Section des Sciences Religieuses (1950-1951). Lacombe believes that Plotinus is linked definitely with the non-dualist (advaita) Vedanta system of Indian philosophy.

14. Bréhier, The Philosophy of Plotinus, p. 111.

15. Life of Plotinus 10.

16. Enneads vi. 5. 8, 12.

17. Ibid. v. 8. 6. Life of Plotinus 3.

141

18. Bréhier, pp. 107-108. For an extensive and persuasive critique of Bréhier's argument, see A.H. Armstrong, "Plotinus and India," _Classical Quarterly_, 30 (1936). He concludes that Greek philosophy was not incapable of producing a pantheistic notion of the infinite. Indeed, "there were elements even within the rationalist tradition of something that could easily develop into Plotinian pantheism." Ibid., p. 28.

19. _The Great Chain of Being_ (New York: Harper Torchbooks, 1960), p. 52.

20. Quoted in Ibid., p. 62.

21. Christian theologians were tolerant of the contradiction, while Plotinus was troubled by it, an illustration, perhaps, of one important difference between a theologian and a philosopher. See Lovejoy, pp. 66, 74-75, 79. Staal notes that mystics have no vested interest in defying the law of noncontradiction. However, "among the great religions of mankind, Christianity stresses faith and irrationalism to an extent that others (including Islam) never even considered." _Exploring Mysticism_, p. 23.

22. Quoted in Lovejoy, p. 63.

23. _Enneads_ i. 3. Joseph Katz points to Plotinus' "painstakingly rationalistic way of arguing." "Plotinus and the Gnostics," _Journal of the History of Ideas_, 15:2 (1954), 293. The larger issue addressed by Katz is Plotinus' essay against the Gnostics, which is an assault on all of those "who assert that the world of sense or its originating source are evil." Ibid., 289.

24. Joseph Katz, ed. and trans., _The Philosophy of Plotinus_ (New York: Appleton-Century-Crofts, 1950), pp. xxiv-xxv. _Enneads_ i. 3.

25. Katz, _The Philosophy of Plotinus_, p. xxviii.

26. Bréhier, _The Philosophy of Plotinus_, p. 181.

27. The relevant chapters in Radhakrishnan have been cited supra. An interesting but fantastic book along this line is A. Lillie's _India in Primitive Christianity_ (2nd ed.; London, 1909). For an attempt at detailed analysis of ethical parallels, see A.J. Edmunds, _Buddhist and Christian Gospels_ (Tokyo, 1905).

28. Radhakrishnan, _Eastern Religions and Western Thought_, p. 173.

29. Ibid., p. 174.

30. Ibid., pp. 160 ff.

31. Ibid., p. 160.

32. The Essenes are known through the writings of Josephus, who describes them as one of the four "philosophical" sects of Judaism (the others being the Pharisees, Sadducees, and "Fourth Philosophy"), and of Philo, who mentions them briefly. Enslin, p. 120. They have much in common with the Qumran sects of the Dead Sea Scrolls.

33. Radhakrishnan, _Eastern Religions and Western Thought_, pp. 157-158.

34. Ibid., p. 162.

35. Ibid., pp. 158 f.

36. Radhakrishnan calls on the authority of Rhys Davids with regard to the anticipation in Buddhist literature of Christian morality

142

as set forth in the Sermon on the Mount. Ibid., pp. 173 f. He has a lengthy biographical comparison of Buddha and Jesus, and draws a parallel between Christ and Krishna. Ibid., pp. 177 ff, 182 n.

37. Ibid., p. 176.
38. Danielou notes "the complexity of the Jewish world in which the Church was growing." The Christian Centuries, p. 17. A useful work on Jewish history, thought, and literature is Emil Schurer's History of the Jewish People in the Time of Jesus, 5 vols. (Edinburgh, 1885–1891).
39. Enslin, chapter 7.
40. Tarn Hellenistic Civilization, p. 224. Also see Salo W. Varon, A Social and Religious History of the Jews, 3 vols. (2nd ed. rev.; New York: Columbia University Press, 1952), II, 141 ff.
41. Tarn, Hellenistic Civilization, p. 225. These modifications were mostly surface reactions. For the Jews, wisdom remained, on the whole, fear and reverence before the majesty of the eternal Lord. See Moses Hadas, Hellenistic Culture, pp. 75 f, 94 f, 103 f, for a good discussion of Hebrew–Greek intellectual relations. Also see Werner Jaeger, "Greeks and Jews," Journal of Religion, 18 (1938), 127 ff.
42. Bultmann, pp. 94 ff. In a scholarly discussion of Jewish Gnosticism, W.F. Albright argues that the idea of the Logos, which Philo is alleged to have borrowed from Greek sources, was really of oriental origin, and that the idea of Sophia (Wisdom) "overshadowed that of the Logos in Jewish as well as in Gnostic thought." From the Stone Age to Christianity (New York: Doubleday and Co., 1957), p. 371. By "oriental" he means the Near East. His refined analysis of the origins of Logos and Sophia does not diminish Philo's reliance on Greek philosophy. On Philo's debt to Greece, see Erwin Goodenough, By Light, Light: The Mystic Gospel of Hellenistic Judaism (New Haven: Yale University Press, 1935), p. 72.
43. Helpful on Philo are J. Danielou, Philon d'Alexandrie (Paris, 1958) and Isaak Heinemann, Philons griechische und jüdische Bildung (Breslau, 1932).
44. Two useful works on apocalyptic thought and literature are H.H. Rowley, The Relevance of Apocalyptic (New York: Association Press, 1964), and D.S. Russell, Between the Testaments (Philadelphia: Mühlenberg Press, 1960).
45. Enslin, p. 141. We read in the Assumption of Moses, an apocalyptic document: "Then shall his kingdom appear throughout all his creation/ And then Satan shall be no more/ And sorrow shall depart with him." And in IV Ezra: "Then shall the heart of the inhabitants of the world be changed, and be converted to a different spirit/ For evil shall be blotted out, and deceit extinguished/ Faithfulness shall flourish, and corruption be vanquished/ And truth shall be made manifest." Again, IV Ezra: "Hades fled away/ Corruption forgotten, sorrows passed away; and in the end the treasures of immortality are made manifest."

Quoted in Bultmann, pp. 83-85. Compare with these passages one
in a late Avestan text, which describes what the world will be
like when the powers of darkness, led by Angra Mainyu, the De-
mon of the Lie, are defeated conclusively by Ahura Mazda, the
Lord of Life, Wisdom, and Light: "And it will thenceforth never
age and never die, never decay and never rot, ever living and
ever increasing, being master of its own wish: when the dead
will rise, life and immortality come, and the world be restored
to its wish." Quoted in Campbell, Occidental Mythology, p. 209.
46. Tarn, Hellenistic Civilization, p. 225.
47. Daniel 7:13. See Guignebert, p. 36.
48. Enslin, p. 142.
49. Ibid., p. 141.
50. Rahula, What the Buddha Taught, pp. 45-46. There is no example
in the Pali Canon, to my knowledge, of a Buddhist monk suffering abuse for disputing the Buddha's teaching or for behaving in
a manner contrary to the Sangha's high standards of conduct. In
the Vinaya Pitaka, monks are cautioned as follows: "A brother
... who is about to admonish another must realize within himself five qualities before doing so ... thus: 'In due season
will I speak, not out of season. In truth will I speak, not in
falsehood. Gently will I speak, not harshly. To his profit will
I speak, not in anger." Vinaya Pitaka ii. 9, in Some Sayings of
the Buddha According to the Pali Canon, trans. F.L. Woodward
(London: Oxford University Press, 1925), p. 113. On the Essene
policy regarding novices, see Edmund Wilson, The Dead Sea
Scrolls (New York: Oxford University Press, 1969), pp. 37-40.
51. According to Millar Burrows: "parallels have been seen ... between the careers and doctrines of Jesus and the Qumran Teacher
of Righteousness, but these have been grossly exaggerated. There
is no evidence that he waa crucified (through the machinations
of a 'Wicked Priest') or that his disciples expected him to
rise from the dead." "Dead Sea Scrolls," Encyclopedia Britannica, 1963 ed., 119. This negative view is disputed by A. Dupont-
Sommer in his The Dead Sea Scrolls: A Preliminary Survey, trans.
E. Margaret Rowley (Oxford: Blackwell, 1950), and The Jewish
Sect of Qumran and the Essenes, trans. R.D. Barnett (New York:
Macmillan Co., 1954). Controversy among scholars on the precise
relationship between Jesus and the Essenes does not include
speculation that the Essenes were influenced by Buddhism. The
Essenes can be accounted for satisfactorily within the context
Hellenistic Judaism. For a useful summary of the facts and relevant bibliography, see Jack Finegan, Light From the Ancient
Past: The Archeological Background of the Hebrew-Christian Religion (Princeton: Princeton University Press, 1959). Finegan's
discussion is also innocent of references to Buddhism in Palestine.
52. Bultmann denies that Jesus considered himself the Messiah, the
Coming One. Primitive Christianity, p. 90. Enslin says "that
the phrase 'son of man' was constantly upon Jesus' lips is

144

highly probable. That he meant himself by the phrase is far less
certain." Christian Beginnings, p. 162.
53. Ibid., p. 159. Also see Guignebert, p. 38.
54. Mark 1:15.
55. Ibid. 9:1. Cf. Matthew 16:28.
56. Ibid. 10:34.
57. Ibid. 10:36. In his discussion of "The Ethic of Jesus," in An
    Interpretation of Christian Ethics (New York: Harper and Bro-
    thers, 1935), Rheinhold Niebuhr argues that the ethic of Jesus
    is not prudential. See Walter Kaufmann's criticism of this posi-
    tion in Critique of Religion and Philosophy (New York: Double-
    day, 1961), pp. 296-302.
58. Matthew 13:41.
59. Matthew 13:49. Cf. Guignebert, p. 34.
60. Anguttara-Nikāya ii. 46. Digha Nikāya ii. 141. In Woodward, pp.
    34, 348.
61. See Conze, Buddhist Texts, pp. 74-76.
62. Samyutta-Nikāya iii. 127-128. In Conze, Buddhist Texts, p. 74.
    Cf. Conze's translation of an important passage from the Pali
    Canon in his Buddhist Thought in India (Ann Arbor: University
    of Michigan Press, 1967), p. 77. The passage deals with the
    meaning of Nirvāna, which has nothing to do with a place or
    state enjoyed by physical or spiritual beings.
63. Edward Conze, trans., Buddhist Scriptures (Baltimore: Penguin
    Books, 1959), p. 62. For an elaboration of these essentials of
    early Buddhist doctrine, and for comment on some differences be-
    tween the Theravada sects, see Conze's "map of the Path." Bud-
    dhist Thought in India, pp. 173-177.
64. A core of doctrine united a profusion of Mahayana sects. Conze,
    Buddhist Thought in India, pp. 195-237.
65. Saptasatika 195. In Conze, Buddhist Texts, pp. 144-145.
66. Takakusu, "Buddhism as a Philosophy of 'Thusness'," op. cit. 87.
67. Conze, Buddhist Texts, p. 167.
68. With nearly unparalleled luxuriance, Mahāyānists peopled the
    world with multitudes of Bodhisattvas, posited infinite Buddha
    realms, and tolerated the quest of weaker beings for salvation
    outside the context of rigorous thought and meditation. As Conze
    puts it, "the proto-Mahāyānists and the Mahāyānists themselves
    looked more kindly upon the religious needs of ordinary people."
    Buddhist Thought in India, p. 201. As might be expected, the sal-
    vationist cults which sprang from Mahāyāna stressed liturgy,
    ceremony, and accoutrements such as confession, veneration of
    relics, rosary and bells, the use of flowers, lights and sing-
    ing. The resemblances to Roman Catholicism are obvious. On the
    other hand, "the Mahāyāna writings ... are almost exclusively
    concerned with the problem of the Unconditioned, nothing but
    the absolute over and over again." Ibid., p. 202. In a now fa-
    mous book, William McNeill defines "three fundamental features"
    shared by Christianity, Mahāyāna Buddhism, and Hinduism which
    "distinguished them from anything that had gone before": the

goal of human life as salvation, equal access of men and women
to the rites necessary for salvation, and "the concept of a sav-
ior God who was both a person and at the same time universal in
his nature." The Rise of the West (Chicago: University of Chicago Press, 1963), pp. 338-339. There is no need to quibble
with these parallels on their very high level of generality, except perhaps the notion that Hindu ritual was egalitarian and
admitted women as the colleagues of men. McNeill is surely right
in pointing out that "Christian piety quickly plunged into a
thicket of saint worship, essentially similar to the adoration
of local deities which proliferated endlessly in both Hinduism
and Mahayana Buddhism." Ibid., p. 339.

69. The Dhammapada, trans. F. Max Muller, in Lin Yutang, ed., The
Wisdom of India and China (New York: Random House, 1942), p.
327.

70. Matthew 5:29; 7:19.

71. On this point, consult the greatest of the Church Fathers. In
The City of God (Book XXI), Saint Augustine attempts a factual
"proof that will convince unbelievers of the possibility of human bodies remaining not merely active, alive, and uncorrupted
after death, but also of continuing forever in the torments of
fire." The City of God, trans. G.G. Walsh et al. (New York:
Doubleday and Co., 1958), p. 495.

72. For references to hell, see Matthew 5:22, 29, 30.

73. The Dhammapada, in Lin Yutang, p. 348.

74. Ibid., p. 336.

75. Ibid. In a close analysis of the meaning of evil in Buddhist
texts of the Pali tradition, James W. Boyd says that "what the
Buddhist does regard as morally bad and injurious is not the
fact of samsara as such, but those karma-producing acts of de-
filement (kleśa) which bind one to an imperfect mode of samsaric
existence." Moreover, "the reality of an external māretā ('that
which kills') other than mundane intrusions is denied. The problem of 'evil' for the Buddhist is to bring about the cessation
of man's own internal māretā and thus break through the impermanence and suffering of samsara." "Symbols of Evil in Buddhism,"
The Journal of Asian Studies, 31 (November, 1971), 72, 75.

76. Saint Thomas Aquinas provides a vivid example of this expedien-
cy at work. In his comments on heresy, he writes that "in obedience to Our Lord's institution, the Church extends her charity
to all, not only to friends, but also to foes who prosecute her,
according to Matth. v. 44: "Love your enemies; do good to them
that hate you'." So far, so good. He then goes on to make a distinction between charity extended to the soul and charity extended to the body, assigns priority to the first and thereby
justifies an earlier statement that heretics "deserve not only
to be separated from the Church by excommunication, but also
to be severed from the world by death." The Summa Theologica of
St. Thomas Aquinas Translated by Fathers of the English Domini-
can Province (London, 1911-1935), part II, second part, pp. 153-

146

158. On Buddhist tolerance, see Conze, Buddhist Thought in India, p. 215.
77. Rahula, p. 46. On some of the "fruits" of historical Christianity, see Roland Bainton's account of the fate that overtook the Anabaptists in sixteenth century Europe. The Reformation of the Sixteenth Century (Boston: Beacon Press, 1952), pp. 96-106.
78. Campbell, Oriental Mythology, pp. 252-253.
79. Ibid., pp. 253-254. Cf. A. Foucher, The Life of the Buddha According to the Ancient Texts and Monuments of India, trans. S.B. Boas (Middletown, Conn.: Wesleyan University Press, 1963), passim.
80. "The Buddha has at all times been subordinated to the Dharma, and his significance lies in being a channel of its eternal truth." Conze, Buddhist Thought in India, pp. 171, 232-233.
81. Zimmer, Philosophies of India, p. 466.
82. Hans Jonas, The Gnostic Religion: The Message of the Alien God and the Beginnings of Christianity (2nd ed. rev.; Boston: Beacon Press, 1963), p. 41. Also see W.C. Van Unnik, Newly Discovered Gnostic Writings (1960).
83. Ibid., p. 32.
84. Quoted in Campbell, Occidental Mythology, p. 366. These are marks of the "conditioned." See the elaboration of the poem in Conze, Buddhist Texts, p. 161.
85. Both quotes are in Campbell, Occidental Mythology, pp. 366-367.
86. Vajracchedika 3. In Conze, Buddhist Texts, pp. 172-173.
87. See J. Kennedy, "Buddhist Gnosticism, the System of Basilides," Journal of the Royal Asiatic Society (1902), 377-415. Kennedy's views have not found disciples everywhere. Lubac believes "la thèse de J.M. Kennedy n'a-t-elle guère suscité d'adhesions." La rencontre du Buddhisme et de l'Occident, p. 23. Jonas cites a Coptic-Gnostic hymn whose via negativa is reminiscent of the method of negation used in the Upanishads. Jonas, pp. 288-289. Cf. Brihadāranyaka Upanishad 3.8.8.
88. The chief evidence is in the Ashokan rock edicts previously cited. The presence of emissaries and missionaries in Western Asia is, of course, one thing; their influence is quite another. Jesuits were installed in the Ming and Ch'ing courts of China from the time of Matteo Ricci (d. 1610) until the early nineteenth century. Although they won some converts (estimated at 300,000 by 1701), with the help of other Christian orders, the impact on Chinese ideas of morality and religion seems to have been minimal. John K. Fairbank et al., East Asia: The Modern Transformation (Boston: Houghton Mifflin Co., 1965), pp. 30-33, 36-43, 52-60.
89. Campbell, Occidental Mythology, p. 362.
90. Ibid., pp. 369-370.
91. G.R.S. Mead, The Gnostics: Fragments of a Faith Forgotten, A Contribution to the Study of the Origins of Christianity (New York: New Hyde Park, 1960), pp. xv, 35.
92. Robert M. Grant, A Historical Introduction to the New Testament

(New York: Harper and Row, 1963), p. 203.

93. Quoted in Jonas, p. 271.
94. Conze, Buddhist Texts, pp. 131, 136.
95. Quoted in Jonas, p. 287. Also see Mead, p. 312.
96. Ibid., p. 258.
97. Jonas, pp. 236-237. Mead, p. 496.
98. A bit more of the hymn: "Man's only thank-offering to thee is to know thry greatness. We came to three, O Light of human life, we came to thee, O Light of all gnosis, we have come to know thee, O womb impregnated by the seed of the Father." Jonas, p. 287.
99. Conze, Buddhist Texts, pp. 146 and passim.
100. Jonas, p. 281.
101. Lalitavistara xiii. 98. In Conze, Buddhist Texts, p. 158.
102. Conze, Buddhist Texts, p. 169.
103. Jonas, pp. 274 ff.
104. Quoted in Woodward, p. 26.
105. Garbe, p. 18 n.
106. Ibid., pp. 30, 78.
107. Ibid., pp. 31-48.
108. Ibid., pp. 48-61.
109. Ibid., p. 71.
110. Ibid., pp. 118-127.
111. Basham, The Wonder That Was India, pp. 228-229. Sastri Nilakanta, Foreign Notices of South India From Megasthenes to Ma Huan (Madras, 1939), has the relevant facts.
112. Grant, Hellenistic Religions, p. xv. A major account of Christian syncretism and its nature is in Hermann Gunkel, Zum religions-geschichtlichen Verständnis des Neuen Testaments (2nd ed.; n.p., 1910). One learns from Gunkel's study that Christian syncretism was seldom deliberate and self-conscious. The early Church Fathers frequently denied that Christian belief and practice were syncretic.
113. Grant, Hellenistic Religions, xviii.
114. A typically uninformative reference is to an ascetic (one Zarmanochegas, in Greek) who decided on a fiery self-immolation at Athens. Basham, pp. 228-229.
115. "Vedism is above all a religion of ritual." Louis Renou, The Nature of Hinduism, trans. Patrick Evans (New York: Walker and Co., 1962), p. 18. Bultmann, pp. 72, 202. Morton Enslin, The Literature of the Christian Movement (New York: Harper and Row, 1956), p. 251.
116. Romans 5:1.
117. Bultmann, pp. 180 ff.
118. Bhagavad-Gītā 9.4-14; 15.16-19. See Benjamin Walker, ed., The Hindu World: An Encyclopedic Survey of Hinduism (New York: Praeger, 1968), I, 396. For an advaitist expression of this point, see Moore, The Indian Mind, p. 232.
119. Renou, p. 55. Cf. Basham, p. 325.
120. Renou, p. 45. Harnack, p. 17.

121. I Corinthians 7. Paul is insistent on the fact of resurrection, without which faith is meaningless. I Corinthians 15.
122. Bhagavad-Gita 3.62. "A Hindu, even if he belongs to a group, considers himself alone to be responsible for his salvation." Renou, p. 20. Some qualification is needed for bhakti sects of the later Indian middle ages, but the statement is probably true of Hinduism in its early stages of development.
123. Das Gupta, A History of Indian Philosophy, I, 77.
124. In their most extreme form, these later devotional sects taught the total dependence of man on God, the power of God to bypass karma and save whomever he wishes, and the distinctness of the individual soul from God. Basham, pp. 332-333.
125. Zimmer, Philosophies of India, p. 175.
126. Romans 5.
127. A full but succinct discussion is in Walker, I, 6-10. Also see Grace Cairns, Philosophies of History: Meeting of East and West in Cycle-Pattern Theories of History (New York: Citadel Press, 1962), pp. 44-47.
128. Indian Philosophy, II, 26. Much earlier, Buddhism and Jainism developed cyclical cosmologies of a similar type. Cairns, pp. 62 f, 69 f. Cairns observes that "the true yogin ... loses his private space-time stream of consciousness and becomes one with Brahman's infinite Self, knower of the past, present, and future. The self, the microcosm, has become the macrocosm, Brahman, who is knower and evolver of time cycles." Idem., pp. 48-49. Cf. Samyutta-Nikāya xv. 5, and Visuddhi-Magga xiii.
129. Cairns, pp. 248 f. The resemblance with single world cycle theories of Hesiod and Zoroaster are obvious. Idem., pp. 196 f, 237 f.
130. The Idea of History (Oxford: Oxford University Press, 1946), p. 50.
131. Ibid., pp. 49 f.
132. Bultmann, pp. 190-191. Collingwood, The Idea of History, p. 47.
133. On class and caste, see Basham, pp. 137-151. On the āshramas, see the relevant texts in Radhakrishnan and Moore, Source Book, pp. 175-189.
134. Renou, p. 68. Also see Das Gupta, I, 77.
135. Radhakrishnan and Moore, Source Book, p. 102.
136. The six systems shared many ideas in common. Ibid., pp. 353 f.
137. Harnack, p. 12.
138. Adolf Harnack, What is Christianity? (New York: Harper Torch-books, 1957), p. 207.
139. Ibid. Also see Henry Chadwick, The Early Church (Baltimore: Penguin Books, 1967), pp. 68-69.

CHAPTER VII

EPILOGUE

India and the West jostled one another in the ancient world,
but lasting effects on either side seem to have been trivial and
historically unimportant. Darius and Alexander had their day with
the civilization of the Brahmans. It was an adventure replete with
color and romance, yet whatever feeble traces the western invaders
left were soon obliterated or neutralized. As Sarton has expressed
it, the impact of Persia and Greece on India is analogous to pour-
ing oil on the face of the waters; it spread over the surface without touching the depths.[1] A thousand years of fitful trade and conquest resulted in only a moderate exchange of material culture, not
to speak of ideas and myths, which transfer very reluctantly, diffuse at the slowest rate, and usually undergo extensive modification at the hand of the borrower.

The presence of Brahmanical and Buddhist ideas in Christian
thought cannot be dismissed summarily. The evidence available, however, cannot support more than intriguing speculations. There was,
for example, a Stoic school in Seleucia: "We may, if we will, let
fancy play round some meeting of Stoic and Buddhist, and seek to interprete for ourselves how far each would understand the other's
point of view. But it is only fancy; we <u>know</u> nothing - nothing but
a little Greek ivory pendant from Taxila, which bears on each of its
two faces the head of a philosopher."[2] Not one classical or Christian writer, at least in the works which survive, acknowledged an intellectual or spiritual debt to Indian sources. Aristotle probably
had the fullest knowledge of Greek intellectual history down to his
time, but there is no mention in his survey of earlier philosophical opinion of a thinker associated with Brahmanical, Buddhist, or
Jain ideas.[3] Christian sources are equally silent, with the exception of Hippolytus, whose exposition of Upanishadic doctrines is a
polemic rather than an appreciation. Where the mystical tradition
turns up in Greek or Christian theology, its presence can be explained within the general historical context of Greco-Roman civilization. A.J. Festugière has drawn attention to a literary tradition
of dialogues between Greek and Indian sages, but they are dialogues
which illustrate more differences than similarities between the dis-
putants.[4]

Tarn argues for definite information that five Greeks were
drawn to Indian religions; however, the degree of their assent and
what languages they learned, if any, is not known.[5] Not a particle
of evidence points unequivocally to a Persian, Greek, Roman, or
Christian mastering Sanskrit or Pali, the languages of the Vedas
and the Buddhist Canon, without a knowledge of which one could expect to make only uncertain progress toward the inner sanctum of

Indian religion and philosophy. When the anchorite Mandanis was asked by Onesicritus to discourse on his beliefs, he replied that working through interpreters, "who, except the language, understand nothing we say any more than the vulgar," would be like filtering pure water through mud.6 If this attitude were at all typical of priests and holy men, and most likely it was, the casual foreign traveller could not have hoped to learn much of value about the subtle thought patterns of a first-order civilization like that of India. At best, as in the case of Megasthenes, a few suggestive hints might have been gleaned from the popular level, and even that poor fare would have been vitiated by its removal from context, distortion by the informant, and flawed comprehension by a hearer up against all the limitations of oral transmission through an interpreter.7

Besides the obstacle posed by unfamiliar languages, a foreigner curious about Indian ideas would have encountered formidable restrictions designed to guard priestly and yogic prerogative. This point requires some elaboration despite the apparent openness of some Brāhmans of Southern India in the second and third centuries A.D. By dint of ancient class status, Brāhman keepers of the sacred Vedic scriptures were bound to exclusiveness and secrecy. Arcane doctrines could be imparted only with scrupulous discrimination. Students had to surmount an arduous screening process. Generally these requirements held for philosophical as well as religious study.

> The pupil had to be truly an adhikārin (the 'competent
> student') to receive such esoteric lore, truly mature
> and perfectly fit to bear the revealed wisdom. In the
> period when the books were first conceived the restric-
> tions imposed were even more severe than they came to
> be in later ages.8

Needless to say, the celebrity and commercial success of so many "gurus" in modern industrial states reflects at once the insecurity of values in the Occident and the fragmentation of India's great religious traditions, which were relatively fresh and vital in antiquity until the coming of the Muslims after the ninth century.

The Vedas were created by a people who accepted the efficacy of chants, spells, and incantations. Through the systematization of exhortation, propitiation, and yogic states of consciousness, their purpose was to achieve fruitful contact with the divine, whether this meant bountiful crops and safety from enemies or the discovery that Ātman and Brahman are one. Whatever the loftier spiritual implications of the Upanishads, one cannot evade the unmistakable aura of magic that pervades them, or escape the homely truth that "power, the supreme aim and instrument of magic, was in fact the great and determinative element in all Vedic priestcraft."9 The welfare and prosperity of the community rested with the priests, who were the touchstones for communion with the gods, conduits of the divine, solemn custodians of the verbal and ritual means of sustaining the activity of nature and insuring the very existence of the cosmos. The sacred scriptures were regarded as a source of magic power, to be approached with reverence, awe, and extreme caution. The potency stored in their words was not to be treated lightly. Hence the study of scripture fell to a special class, the Brāhmans, whose favorable karma through many reincarnations determined their status in the class system (varna). One had to be born of Brāhmans to share their advantages for study and esoteric learning, with some rare exceptions.

> Verily, a father may teach this Brahma to his eldest
> son, or to a worthy pupil (i.e., one already steeped
> in discipline and Vedic lore), but to no one else at
> all. Even if one should offer him this earth that is
> encompassed by water and filled with treasure, he
> should say: 'This, truly, is more than that!'[10]

Exposure to the deepest secrets of the Brāhmans demanded years of austerity, hard study, and unquestioning obedience to one's guru.

The doctrine of Ātman-Brahman was as hard to come by as for-mulas for curing illness and making rain.

> This profoundest mystery one should not mention
> to anyone who is not a son, or who is not a pu-
> pil, or who is not tranquil. However, to one who
> is devoted to none other than to his teacher or
> to one who is supplied with all the qualifications
> (guna), one may give it.[11]

The purity, and therefore the efficacy, of divine truth could be sustained only by keeping it within a tight circle of devotees pro-perly trained for its comprehension, application, and preservation. So as to keep the channels of power open, the Brāhmans shielded their lore with a wall of taboos and restrictions, the most impor-tant of which was a rigid class structure said to have originated with the creation of the universe.[12] Only the upper three classes – Brāhman, Kshatriya, Vaishya – whose membership was twice-born (referring to ritual investiture with a golden thread at a certain age) were fit to hear the Vedas. Should a lowly Shūdra willfully or inadvertently hear the Vedas chanted, his punishment, according to the code of Manu, was molten lead poured into his ears.[13]

This concern for purity was so serious a matter that Brāhmans were confined ritually to the interior of India to preclude contami-nation by foreigners.[14] Like the Greeks, who believed themselves culturally superior to other peoples (a trait shared with tradition-al Chinese), the Brāhmans clung to their distinctiveness with fierce pride and conviction, as many have in recent Indian history.[15] The chances were slim for a Greek, Roman, or Jew, each blinded by his own ethnocentrism, to cross the threshold into Brahmanical society, even if there had been a will to do so.[16]

With these considerations in view, there is good reason to set aside the hypothesis of a religious and philosophical transmission from India to the Mediterranean. The picture might change with new archeological discoveries, the unearthing of unknown texts, or some other fresh development. For the time being, caution seems a wiser policy than unsteady speculation raised on a foundation of mediocre historical evidence and deceptive parallels. On a stratospheric level of generalization, there does indeed appear to be a mystical tradition that runs like a thread through various historical traditions - Greek, Jewish, Christian, Islamic, Chinese, Indian - but the appearance is little more than an empty sack unable to stand up until filled with specific facts supplied by historical and philosophical analysis.

Where "mystical tradition" refers to familiar doctrines of the mystery religion - immortality of the soul, reincarnation, duality of the physical and the spiritual - the context of belief is all-important. It is moot that a close look at differences from one tradition to another can preserve similarities beyond the purview of verbal correspondence. It is necessary to ask: how does the idea of reincarnation fit into Plato's thought, Jain thought, Empedocles' thought, Hindu thought, Orphic thought, and so on? Religions, philosophies, and cultures are dynamic organisms of a sort. Their inner parts, including ideas and rituals, must be perceived in relation to the whole organism to be fully appreciated. Removal of a basic idea from context may be regarded as a form of amputation; one ends up with a dead member, anatomically correct but physiologically inactive.

The Indian hypothesis has been defended by writers inclined to accept some form of mystical idealism, which usually holds that reality transcends phenomena, sense experience, discursive reason, and history. Access to this reality is gained by intuitive experience, indubitable and "self-authenticating," which "does not look beyond itself for meaning or validity," and "is beyond the bounds of proof and so touches completeness."[17] The mystical idealist claims a reality that is certain, self-evident, and all-inclusive. He tends to disparage rational, empirical knowledge of phenomena as trivial at best, illusory at worst. Only the "true self" is real. Concealed behind the flux of ordinary phenomenal consciousness, it is the ultimate ground of becoming. Its nature defies "mere" understanding. Human purpose and destiny are outside of nature altogether. The key to that purpose and destiny is the Self, which has an ontological status immune to analysis, positive description, or rational comprehension.

154

Mystical metaphysics leads one into a philosophical tangle which cannot be undone by a claim of intuitive certainty. Quite apart from the arbitrariness hovering about such claims, the mystic who tries to interprete the ineffable is likely to become a dogmatist, for the "root metaphor" of his world-view is alleged to be exempt from rational examination or even doubt.[18] He will have no recourse but to present his "knowledge" for acceptance without argument. Radhakrishnan puts the issue baldly enough:

> Intuitive truths as simple acts of mental vision are
> free from doubt. They do not carry conviction on the
> ground of their logical validity. We cannot help assent-
> ting to them as soon as we intuit them. Doubts occur
> when reflection supervenes. Strictly speaking, logical
> knowledge is non-knowledge, avidyā, valid only till in-
> tuition arises. The latter is reached when we break
> down the shell of our private, egoistic existence,
> and we get back to the primeval spirit in us from
> which our intellect and our senses are derived.[19]

The problem with this theory of truth is that one has no reliable means of deciding between two self-authenticating experiences which contradict one another. Without such a criterion, one must accede that anything is possible, which amounts to a degree of cognitive tolerance that "would land us in a chaotic world of superstition unlike anything we call sanity."[20] The objection here is not to mystical experiences as such, but to the extravagant religious and philosophical claims which have been derived from them. The latter are "superstructures" which invite criticism.[21] The experiences themselves may be quite valuable. One cannot deny the value of an experience to an individual. The isolation of mystical experiences as significant manifestations of human consciousness will depend on two strategies: the abandonment of superstructures, and the willing-ness of more philosophers and psychologists to practice the kinds of disciplines which are said to be associated with mystical states.

Be that as it may, one superstructure invites comment, the one that sees the mystic's "pure experience" as the core or essence of the mystical tradition. Where the obliteration of ordinary cons-ciousness is identified as the heart of the mystical tradition, the historical contexts of such trans-dual experiences must be taken in-to account. It is pointless to deny that people across the world and through history have experienced oceanic consciousness of the sort described in the Upanishads and in the works of assorted Sufi, Taoist, Buddhist, and Christian mystics.[22] But an experience of un-differentiated unity does not and cannot mean anything in itself; interpretation must give the experience content, structure, and meaning, and once the process of interpretation begins, mystics di-verge in their formulations.[23] Christian mystics like Eckhart and Ruysbroeck emerge from the One convinced of the trinitarian Godhead;

Islamic mystics rhapsodize about the one God of Islam; Vedantists proclaim an impersonal, remote, aloof Absolute; Buddhists deny the existence of permanent being and speak of the Void, or "Thusness"; for the taoist Chuang-tzu, ultimate reality is the unimpeded, spontaneous operation of nature (Tao, or wu-wei, action without effort) when the distinction between subject and object is dropped.[24] The mystic's cultural background shapes the metaphysical, epistemological, and ethical content of his otherwise fathomless experience. The experience itself, being innocent of distinctions between this and that, right and wrong, true and false, is enveloped by the mystic's religious and philosophical milieu, psychological predispositions, general cultural background, especially language, educational level, and many other considerations. The mystic's view of life is embodied in concrete doctrines and practices, not in the impalpable memory of an experience to which feeling, thought, commitment, and even existence are irrelevant.

It may be that mystical experience of this sort has no importance for religion at all.

> Most writers on mysticism seem to take it for granted
> that mystical experience is a religious experience and
> that mysticism is necessarily a religious phenomenon.
> They seem to think that mysticism and religious mys-
> ticism are one and the same thing. But this is far from
> being correct. It is true that there is an important
> connection between mysticism and religion, but it is
> not nearly so direct and immediate as most writers
> have seemed to think, nor can it be simply taken for
> granted as an obvious fact.[25]

An experience of undifferentiated unity does not have much about it that seems religious in any specific sense. Interpretations after the fact of experience may result in beliefs or actions commonly acknowledged to be religious, such as belief in a Supreme Being or systematic mortification of the flesh. On the other hand, there is no reason why a mystical flight might not eventuate in no more than a gratifying memory of self-forgetting, a moment of non-engagement free of dualistic tensions.

If the meaning of pure consciousness is not yielded in the experience itself, which could not be done without the aid of distinctions, the mystic must supply meaning from the outside, which entails an even wider field of distinctions in the historical culture of which the mystic is a part. Description, explanation, and interpretation belong to the sphere of historical time and change. In that context the Hindu, Buddhist, or Greek philosopher, and the Gnostic, Zoroastrian, or Christian theologian do not share the "same view of life." Life is something they mold, direct, and relate to; conversely, it molds and directs them. So long as one is adrift in the ineffable and undifferentiated field of mystical experience, there is no view of life to be discussed, for there is no perspective from which a view of life can be recognized, described, or embraced. In the Bhagavad-Gita, Krishna argues with Arjuna on the field of battle that death and killing are of no consequence because there is an immutable "soul" in the mortal body.[26] In the unconditioned realm of Brahman, with whom the soul is one, no issues of moral decision ever arise, or can arise. On the battlefield, where Krishna exhorts Arjuna to execute selflessly the duties (dharma) of his class (he is a kshatriya), we participate in a social and historical drama which enables us to distinguish the behavior of a Hindu warrior in the Gita from that of a Greek warrior in the Iliad.

A distinctionless experience cannot be a source of specific ethical, philosophical, or religious doctrines; it can only serve to "validate" those already held or aspired to by the subject. It is not an illimitable state of consciousness which guides the mystic through the world of contingency, but rather a pattern of belief and action founded on innumerable distinctions, including the distinction between mystic and non-mystic. One wonders how mystical experience, in the sense of being awash in undifferentiated unity, could ever form the basis of a universal religion; all of those religions drawn together through the cultivation of oneness in the pure experience of their followers simply would retain their de facto historical doctrines and ceremonies.

Perhaps the nationalistic and ideological struggles of the twentieth century are at the root of misguided efforts to project onto the screen of history an ecumenical basis for spiritual values, one capable of mitigating cultural divisiveness in a physically interdependent world. Some Indian thinkers are drawn to the notion that India can furnish a spiritual complement to the West's scientific, technological, and managerial achievements.[27] But India and the West are separated by radically different historical traditions. A trek to common ground by means of mystical experience seems incredible and improbable. Even some westerners who affect Indian ways by joining cults, practicing yoga, and attaching themselves to gurus are merely skating on the surface of a very deep body of water.

It is instructive to consider the minor effect India had on European thought even when Hindu and Buddhist texts were mastered in the original languages by English, German, and French savants, and when Indian literature became something of a vogue with European authors.[28] Two traditions were brought together in the early decades of the nineteenth century: the Indian, steeped in subjectivity, love of universals, distrust of the physical, and longing to disengage from the empirical self; and the European, peering into objective relations, founding a host of new sciences, glorifying

157

the creative power of the individual imagination, at least among the romantics, and establishing the prototype of Faustian man in the careers of Napoleon, Beethoven, and Byron. It should come as no surprise that such a cleavage of values was papered over with a mythical image congenial to romantic exoticism, inquisitiveness, and cultural tolerance. Even when the languages of Indian texts had been thoroughly mastered, the response was to subordinate Indian ideas and mythic themes to European questions, and, in the end, to European answers, so that it remained a rare event for scholars and men of letters to contemplate and appreciate what was truly Indian.[29] The great advances of philology and oriental studies in the nineteenth century were not always accompanied by a spirit of empathy for the Indian view of life. The English were in the best position to appreciate Indian values and traditions, not only through the medium of a British empire on the subcontinent, but through the labors of the Asiatic Society of Bengal and its _Transactions_, which pioneered the systematic study of Indian languages, literature, religion, and history. It was the Englishmen Charles Wilkins, Sir William Jones, Henry Colebrooke, and Horace Wilson who first mastered Sanskrit and supplied Europe with its first examples of Indian literature in translation. Yet Thomas Babington Macaulay, surely no ignoramus, was able to say in his famous _Minute_ on _Education_:

> I have no knowledge of either Sanscrit or Arabic. But I have done what I could to form a correct estimate of their value. I have read translations of the most celebrated Arabic and Sanscrit works. I have conversed both here and at home with men distinguished by their proficiency in the Eastern tongues. I am quite ready to take the Oriental learning at the valuation of the Orientalists themselves. I have never found one among them who could deny that a single shelf of a good European library was worth the whole native literature of India and Arabia.[30]

This cultural chauvinism was hardened by the Sepoy Mutiny of 1857–1859, and persisted into the twentieth century.

Even with all the advantages of open and easy communication, East–West conferences, teacher exchanges, and global circulation of printed books, the ways and ideas of India are still poorly understood by the educated public of the contemporary West. Indeed, it was only in the nineteen twenties and thirties that Indian art was established as a great and coherent tradition ranking with that of Europe, mainly through the writings of Ananda K. Coomaraswamy, for many years curator of Indian art at the Boston Museum of Fine Arts, and much respected for his sophisticated knowledge of Western languages, history, philosophy, and art.[31] In the process of developing his views on Indian art and tradition, he became an impassioned critic of modern industrial societies, seeing in their obsession with economic values a flat denial of spiritual values, while the American cult of celebrity, fueled by movies and radio, struck him as a base capitulation to ephermeral selfhood of the lowest sort.[32] Few people from the West are capable of understanding Indian culture, for "a more loveless, and at the same time more sentimentally cynical, culture than that of modern Europe and America it would be impossible to imagine," a culture immersed in "a sort of frivolity, in which the real problem, that of knowing what should be believed, is evaded."[33]   India's advantage over Europe is in knowing what should be believed. Among a people who care a great deal about personal success and a high material standard of living, one wonders what would be made of Coomaraswamy's remark that "the task before us all is to 'become no one'."[34] He was so defensive of India's traditionalism, social and religious, and so distressed by the disintegrative intrusion of the West, that he regarded Radhakrishnan as a westernized Indian who had forgotten what it means to be a Hindu; in his willingness to effect compromises between Indian tradition and Western rationalism, he lost sight of the tradition altogether as the only means of achieving spiritual freedom.[35] Nevertheless, Coomaraswamy was a spokesman for the perennial philosophy at the same time that he saw little hope for the West. The closest the West ever came to an authentic tradition reflecting spiritual truth was in the middle ages. The salvation of the West, he believed, lies in reconstituting what India already has, a society built on religious and metaphysical principles.

The gap between Indian and Western views of life opens up from a different angle in Radhakamal Mukerjee's comment on types of "humanism": "Casteism, social segregation, oppression by the elite and degradation and disaster of man have not been the concerns of high Indian philosophy ... The dominant ontic interest and outlook of Indian humanism need to be enriched and deepened by the Western sense of the absolute worth of the individual."[36] Doubtless Coomaraswamy would have blanched to read this. That he and Mukerjee disagree about the value of Western individualism symptomizes the conflict of tradition with modernism in contemporary India, but the divergence also brings into focus a gulf between the East and the West which has barely narrowed in the past one hundred years.

It may be that no universal revelation is to be found beneath the flux of human experience, that no cosmic "soul" inhabits the mortal bodies of past and present historical cultures. It may be that various religious traditions have no option other than learning to tolerate, accommodate, and admire one another's differences. Perhaps it would be wise to put aside the notion that some peculiar feature of mind and spirit binds all Eastern peoples together in a majestic unity which sets them apart dramatically from Western peoples. Not only is the universal perennial philosophy elusive, so is this last type of spiritual brotherhood. Not only does it seem that East and West do not share the same view of life, it seems that all

major civilizations of the East have failed to develop an unequivocal consensus on the meaning and purpose of life. Not only are Greek
and Christian "ways of thinking" different when compared with the
transcendental philosophies of India, India has little in common
either spiritually or intellectually with China and Japan. Until
recently one heard a good deal about the "Orient" and the "Oriental mind," the implication being that all the important cultures,
languages, and religions of the vast region between Afghanistan
and Japan have displayed in the historical record a common spectrum
of underlying values and sensibilities.

In his _Lectures on the Philosophy of History_, Hegel dismis-
ses the Eastern individual as little more than a cipher, a being
without consciousness of himself as subject, an elusive non-person
absorbed ontologically in the Absolute and politically in Oriental
despotism.[37] Since Hegel's characterization was published, the
East has been interpreted variously as synthetic, intuitive, aesthetic, religious, metaphysical, irrational, passive, escapist,
while, conversely, the West has been interpreted as analytical, empirical, logical (or "postulational"), non-religious, rational, active, realistic. In _The Meeting of East and West_, F.S.C. Northrop
argues that "to specify the philosophical and religious differences
entering into the constitution of the cultures of the East is at
the same time to possess inescapable interconnections and identities. It is the unity provided by these essential relations and
identities which merges the cultures of the Oriental countries into one traditional culture of the Far East."[38] These lines of argument are, of course, shamelessly reductionist. Fortunately, they
have been decisively challenged.

The most effective refutation of uniformitarian approaches to
Eastern thought is Nakamura's _Ways of Thinking of Eastern Peoples_,
in which a multitude of differences with respect to assumptions,
specific content, style, and consequences for action are sifted
from the cultures of India, China, Japan, and Tibet; "after having
examined what has hitherto been designated as features peculiar to
Eastern thought, we find ourselves in reality incapable of isolat-
ing a definite trait which can be singled out for contrast with
the West."[39] Moreover, "we must acknowledge the fact that there
exists no single 'Eastern' feature but rather that there exist diverse ways of thinking in East Asia, characteristic of certain peoples but not of the whole of East Asia," a judgment whose context
includes India as well.[40] Finally, "there is no such thing as a
single fundamental principle which determines the characteristic
ways of thinking of a people. Various factors ... related in _mani-
fold_ ways, each exerting its influence, enter into the ways of
thinking of a people."[41]

The last quotation can be applied cogently enough to the
perennial philosophy. There is no coherent, persuasive evidence of

160

a spiritual bedrock upon which all human experience rests and from which universal spiritual ends for mankind can be traced. The claim that a mystical tradition threads its way through historical time, geographical space, and all the vicissitudes of human experience in varied cultural contexts is not itself the result of an indubitable, "self-authenticating" experience, but rather is an inference from historical and textual evidence. In Huxley's The Perennial Philosophy and in Das's The Essential Unity of All Religions, one is confronted with large-scale empirical generalizations developed from a plethora of religious, philosophical, and poetical texts associated with a half dozen major civilizations. Their insistence on an immutable "ground of being" as the foundation of phenomenal existence is an inference from a body of "mystical" literature. Like any such inference, it is more or less probable depending on the quantity and quality of the evidence and the soundness of the empirical analysis.[42] As this essay has tried to show, the evidence is too feeble to support the inference.

1. Sarton, Ancient Science Through the Golden Age, p. 491.
2. Tarn, The Greeks in Bactria and India, p. 387.
3. Aristotle Metaphysics i. 2-8.
4. "Trois rencontres entre la Grece et l'Inde," Revue de l'Histoire des Religions, 125 (1942-1943). The three encounters were between Alexander the Great and six holy men, Nagarjuna and Menander, and Apollonius and the sages of the "hills." An addition and emendation to this article is in Festugiere's "Grecs et sages orientaux," Revue de l'Histoire des Religions, 130 (1945), 29-41.
5. Tarn, The Greeks in Bactria and India, pp. 391-392.
6. Strabo Geography xv. 64.
7. Scriptures were communicated orally, making it doubly hard for a foreigner to learn the language. Texts remained unwritten in later Vedic times. Basham, The Wonder That Was India, p. 239.
8. Zimmer, Philosophies of India, p. 61. Das Gupta says that the study of Indian philosophy required a knowledge of technical terms, which would have been hard for a foreigner to come by even if had some grasp of Sanskrit: "These terms are seldom properly explained, and it is presupposed that the reader who wants to read the works should have a knowledge of them. Anyone in olden times who took to the study of any system of philosophy, had to do so with a teacher, who explained those terms to him. The teacher himself had got it from his teacher, and he from his. There was no tendency to popularize philosophy, for the idea then prevalent was that only the chosen few who had otherwise shown their fitness, deserved to become students." A History of Indian of Indian Philosophy, I, 2.
9. Ibid., p. 78.
10. Chāndogya Upanishad 3. 11. 5.
11. Maitri Upanishad 6. 29.
12. De Bary, Sources of Indian Tradition, p. 225.
13. Gautama, "Institutes of the Sacred Law," in Sacred Books of the East, ed. F. Max Müller (Oxford, 1891), I, part 1, 236.
14. Getting through to the Brahmans was tough even in the seventeenth century, when Hindu society had been softened up by over five hundred years of Moslem rule. Europeans in India discovered the the existence "d'une langue anterieure /Vedic Sanskrit/, langue morte, sacrée, liturgique et savante, reservée à une haute caste sacerdotale, illustré par une immense litterature mysterieuse, tracée en characteres dont le clé échappait." They discovered also that "redoutables prohibitions defendaient ce trésor contre l'impureté des Européens." Raymond Schwab, La Renaissance Orientale (Paris: Payot, 1950), p. 39. In the eighteenth century, a number of French savants spent time in India but were unable to procure the Vedas despite earnest attempts. The Vedas were not even described by a European until 1785, in the second anniversary Discourse of Sir William Jones, the great English linguist

and Orientalist. Ibid., p. 49.

15. A cause of discontent that led to the Indian Mutiny of 1857 was the General Service Enlistment Act, which required that Indian soldiers be prepared to serve abroad. "Previously only six battalions of the Bengal Army had been available for foreign service, it being considered impossible for a faithful Hindu to go to sea as he could not, in a wooden ship, have his own fire to cook his food which his faith obliged him to do himself; nor could he properly perform the prescribed rituals of daily ablution even if water butts, filled by men of the same caste and never approached by others, had been available. Hindu sepoys who had gone overseas or crossed the Indus were likely to be spurned by their comrades when they returned home." Christopher Hibbert, The Great Mutiny: India, 1857 (New York: Viking Press, 1978), pp. 53-54.

16. It would be silly to argue that under no circumstances could a foreigner acquire knowledge of the sacred lore, or that taboos were so rigorously enforced that no outsider could hope for contact with a teacher representative of the tradition. Jack Finegan notes a votive inscription on a column at Basnagar (dating from the second century B.C.), erected by a Greek ambassador living in Taxila, which shows that "an alien could at this time be accepted as a devoted worshipper within the fold of Hindu society." The Archeology of World Religions, I, 147. The inscription suggests admission to conventional worship, not intensive study with a guru. Nirad Chuadhuri observes that "knowledge was regarded as legitimate only when it was passed on from preceptor to disciple in a chain of privileged succession." The Intellectual in India (New York: Humanities Press, 1967), p. 49.

17. Sarvepalli Radhakrishnan, An Idealist View of Life (London: George Allen and Unwin, 1932), p. 92.

18. Stephen Pepper, World Hypotheses: A Study in Evidence (Berkeley: University of California Press, 1942), pp. 133-135. Pepper distinguishes two kinds of mysticism, with sub-divisions: first, Self, or phenomenological mysticism, and, second, cosmic mysticism, which breaks down into pantheistic, emanational, and theistic varieties.

19. An Idealist View of Life, p. 146.

20. Reason and Nature: An Essay on the Meaning of Scientific Method (Glencoe, Illinois: The Free Press, 1953), p. 34.

21. Staal, Exploring Mysticism, p. 173.

22. Mystical experience is not synonymous with unitive consciousness. R.M. Buck describes his experience, called "cosmic consciousness," as "consciousness ... of the life and order of the universe," as "intellectual enlightenment" and "moral exaltation." Quoted in William James, The Varieties of Religious Experience (New York: The Modern Library, n.d.), p. 389. A.C. Bouquet says there is agreement among mystics of the Upanishadic and Plotinian type that division is unreal, evil is illusory, and time is unreal, but concludes that "we are bound to recognize that on

163

almost everything else the mystics are much divided." Compara-tive Religion (6th ed.; Baltimore: Penguin Books, 1962), p. 288. After a shrewd analysis of mystical utterances from a num-ber of Oriental sources, Steadman concludes: "In their concep-tions of the mystical experience, the role of meditation and its object, and the nature of the Absolute, Oriental discussions of mysticism show significant divergences." The Myth of Asia, p. 162.

23. R.C. Zaehner has sorted out differences between Hindu and Sufi mysticism. He says "the respective roles of personal effort and and divine grace are as much the concern of Hindu as of Muslim mysticism, and the answers given in either case are largely con-ditioned by the theological background against which mystical experience is viewed and according to which it is explained." Hindu and Muslim Mysticism (London: Athlone Press, 1960), p. 12.

24. As Zaehner notes, "in the Hindu tradition the tendency is from monism to theism in the higher form of the religious life, where-as in Sufism the tendency is from theism, that is, a mysticism of love, towards what amounts to monism." Ibid., p. 11. On Chu-ang-tzu's concept of Tao, see Fung Yu-lan's commentary in his translation, Chuang Tzu: A New Selected Translation with an Ex-position of the Philosophy of Kuo Hsiang (Shanghai: Commercial Press, 1933), pp. 6-8.

25. W.T. Stace, The Teachings of the Mystics (New York: Mentor Books, 1960), p. 23. Also see Staal, pp. 196-197.

26. Bhagavad-Gita 2. 11-17.

27. This idea is implicit in Radhakrishnan's remark that "while the dominant feature of Eastern thought is its insistence on creative intuition, the Western systems are generally characterized by a greater adherence to critical intelligence." An Idealist View of Life, p. 129. For a devastating critique of this parti-cular dichotomy - the intuitive East versus the rational West - see Steadman, pp. 101-121.

28. See K.R. Stunkel, "English Orientalism and India, 1784-1830," Ohio University Review, 11 (1969), and A. Leslie Willson, A Mythical Image: The Ideal of India in German Romanticism (Durham, North Carolina, 1964).

29. For an example of how Indian materials were assimilated to Euro-pean religious interests, see K.R. Stunkel, "India and the Idea of a Primitive Revelation in French Neo-Catholic Thought," Jour-nal of Religious History (January, 1975).

30. De Bary, Sources of Indian Tradition, pp. 596-597.

31. See Singam, Ananda Coomaraswamy, pp. 24-26, 121-124, 213. Pio-neer works were The Aims of Indian Art (1908), Rajput Painting (1916), and The History of Indian and Indonesion Art (1926). Coomaraswamy believed the essence of Indian art to be its ico-nography, while style is no more than accident. The preoccupa-tion with individual style in Western art seemed to him the best evidence of its decadence and shallowness in the twenti-eth century.

32. No doubt Coomaraswamy's dichotomies are open to the charge of exaggeration, but his perception of India and the West, however questionable in objective fact, must be taken into account. See Steadman, pp. 26-30, for a lucid discussion of the East-West polarity and its merits.
33. Am I My Brother's Keeper?, p. 8.
34. Singam, 216.
35. For an analysis and "dialogue" touching on the differences in outlook of Radhakrishnan, the philosophical cosmopolitan, and Coomaraswamy, the philosophical traditionalist, see K.R. Stunkel, "The Meeting of East and West in Coomaraswamy and Radhakrishnan," Philosophy East and West, 23 (October, 1973). It is ironic that two men of such stature in comparative studies, both of whom affirmed the perennial philosophy, and both of whom came from the same Hindu culture, were at such odds on the means to authentic Selfhood.
36. The Way of Humanism: East and West (Bombay and New Delhi: Academic Books, 1968), p. 211. One must remember that India is two worlds since independence, one traditional and rural where most Indians live and follow ancient ways, the other modernized and urban where a relatively affluent minority is in pursuit of Western material success.
37. Lectures on the Philosophy of History, trans. J. Sibree (New York: Dover Publications, 1956), pp. 141, 143. This translation first appeared in 1857.
38. The Meeting of East and West: An Inquiry Concerning World Understanding (New York: The Macmillan Co., 1947), p. 313.
39. Nakamura, Ways of Thinking of Eastern Peoples, p. 21.
40. Ibid., pp. 21-22.
41. Ibid., p. 37.
42. See Ernest Nagle's harsh, but not unjust, review of Huxley's book in Logic Without Metaphysics (Glencoe, Illinois: The Free Press, 1956). "In his /Huxley's/ hands mystic doctrine becomes a sentimental yearning, a specious excuse for renouncing a world that wearies him, an undignified surrender of reason to obscurantism. He mistakes clever verbalism for competent argument, unctuous sermonizing for responsible moral and social theory, and hearsay testimony for warranted knowledge." Ibid., p. 390.

A

Ahura Mazda, 22
Ajita Kesakambalin, 60-61
Alexander the Great, 20, 23, 24, 26
Ananda, 128
Anaximander, 58
Angra Mainyu, 23
Angus, 140
Apollonius of Tyana, 36, 44-46, 49
Aquinas, 146
Aristobulus, 37, 39
Aristotle, 38
Arjuna, 157
Ashoka, 24-26

B

Banerjee, iii
Barthold, ii
Basilides, 132
Benz, ii
Bernier, 37
Bevan, 32
Boas, 11, 16
Bréhier, 114-116
Browne, 79
Buck, 164
Buddha, 2, 61, 125-126, 128-129
Burnet, 66, 68, 79, 85, 103

C

Campbell, 128
Chandragupta Maurya, 23
Childe, 8
Claudius Ptolemy, 36
Clement of Alexandria, 114
Collingwood, 65, 102
Conze, 145
Coomaraswamy, 6, 14, 86, 158-159
Cornford, 68, 79, 82, 85, 103
Cosmas Indicopleustes, 28
Cratylus, 88

Ctesias of Cnidus, 37-38
Cyrus the Great, 20

D

Dahlquist, 51
Darius, 20
Das, 14, 55-56, 161
Das Gupta, 31
Demetrius, 26
Democritus, 60-61
Devadatta, 128
Dicks, 66
Dijksterhuis, 67
Dio Chrysostomus, 27
Diogenes Laertius, 37, 86
Dill, 45
Dodds, 67, 107

E

Eckhart, 155
Edelstein, 107
Empedocles, 2, 60-61, 78-82, 96

F

Fa Hsien, 10
Festugière, 151
Filliozat, 4, 14, 36, 47-48, 50, 116
Finegan, 33
Foucher, 15
Frye, 30

G

Garbe, iii, 30, 134
Goldenweiser, 11
Gondopharnes, 27
Greene, 110
Guéneon, 6, 14, 134
Guthrie, 60, 64, 66, 79, 100